The &

SHERLOCK
HOLMES

The Daily
SHERLOCK HOLMES

EDITED BY LEVI STAHL AND STACEY SHINTANI

A YEAR OF QUOTES

FROM THE CASE-BOOK OF THE WORLD'S
GREATEST DETECTIVE

ARTHUR CONAN DOYLE

HarperCollins *Publishers* India

First published in India in 2020 by
HarperCollins *Publishers*
A-75, Sector 57, Noida, Uttar Pradesh 201301, India
www.harpercollins.co.in

Licensed by The University of Chicago Press,
Chicago, Illinois, USA

2 4 6 8 10 9 7 5 3 1

P-ISBN: 978-93-5357-592-2
E-ISBN: 978-93-5357-593-9

Printed and bound at
Thomson Press (India) Ltd.

Foreword
Michael Sims

A *Dun-Coloured Veil Hung over the House-Tops*

The tall bookcase just inside the door of my apartment holds books from my childhood and teen years: my earliest friends, still standing together as if posing for a class photo. Here are the primordial volumes I held while watching *Disney's Wonderful World of Color* in black and white in the 1960s. Here squat my halfling Big Little Books, with a picture facing every page of text in epics such as *Lassie: Adventure in Alaska*, wherein an earthquake coughs up a frozen mammoth.

Soon a detective-story theme appears. Encyclopedia Brown rakes in quarters by locating harmonicas and identifying vandals in Idaville. A much-loved Hardy Boys volume, *The Hooded Hawk Mystery*, is now ragged as an urchin but still upright. Between Scholastic paperbacks there stands, like a fat academic in the wrong ballroom, a single textbook, *Outlooks through Literature*, which opens "Unit One: The Short Story" with "The Adventure of the Speckled Band." A colorful painted montage portrays a woman in stages of collapse. Opposite, "'It is fear, Mr. Holmes. It is terror,'" reads the pull quote, promising that "these words were enough to challenge the

Master Detective, Sherlock Holmes, to an immediate investigation, some rapid deductions, and a brilliant solution."

Perhaps you could have read this teaser at thirteen and turned instead to watch *The Waltons*; since you hold this book in your hands, however, I doubt it. I could not. I think this was my first encounter with Sherlock Holmes as a character in a book. This story was my wardrobe that opened into Narnia, the tornado that whirled me to Oz. Recalling his own childhood, Arthur Conan Doyle once wrote, in an essay titled "Juvenilia," "I do not think that life has any joy to offer so complete, so soul-filling as that which comes upon the imaginative lad, whose spare time is limited, but who is able to snuggle down into a corner with his book, knowing that the next hour is all his own." He would be pleased to know how many people snuggle down with his own books almost a century after his death. When I met Holmes, I was in a wheelchair, thanks to juvenile rheumatic arthritis. Four decades later, I am a walking testament to the medicinal virtues of escapist fiction.

Within the lively pages of *The Daily Sherlock Holmes*, Stacey Shintani and Levi Stahl evoke what Sherlockians call the Canon. Their snapshots of atmosphere and clips of dialogue and action resurrect my teenage affair with Sherlock Holmes like a box full of love letters. They even cluster quotations into enlightening themes—Holmes's amusing rivalry with his older brother Mycroft, his fondness for the violin. They celebrate the chase, Holmes's sly technique of interrogating not only witnesses but also other detectives, his skepticism of authority. From January 1 on, Holmes's character is revealed—and, after all, it is this man's remarkable psyche that draws us into his cases.

I enjoy the musical rhythms of Victorian prose, but most of all I love the dialogue. The contrast between twenty-first-century American English and nineteenth-century British English wakes my own language for me. When asked what to do during a stakeout, Holmes replies, "Possess our souls in patience and make as little noise as possible." For a dangerous outing Holmes recommends a revolver and a toothbrush. "Depend upon it," he murmurs elsewhere, "there is nothing so unnatural as the commonplace." *The Daily Sherlock Holmes* includes many delicious mouthfuls of this dialect, such as Holmes's statement, "It is my belief, Watson, founded upon my experience, that the lowest and vilest alleys in London do not present a more dreadful record of sin than does the smiling and beautiful countryside."

Most charming of all is the ongoing conversation between Holmes and Watson. "I say, Watson," begins Holmes, and we perk up. The detective and the doctor are passionate talkers and great listeners. They don't just hold forth; they respond to each other. Doyle, a master of sketching character through dialogue, uses these conversations less to convey the details of his airy plots than to watch his team play together in a comedy of manners. After all but reading Watson's mind at Baker Street, Holmes remarks,

"The features are given to man as the means by which he shall express his emotions, and yours are faithful servants."

Elsewhere, "Have you the effrontery necessary to put it through?" Holmes asks Watson about a plan he has proposed.

"We can but try."

"Excellent, Watson! Compound of the Busy Bee and Excelsior. We can but try—the motto of the firm."

Despite Watson's marriage to Holmes's client Mary Morstan early in the series, this iconic team remains congenially yoked together over the years. Watson is always ready to assist our hero, and Holmes not only admits that he needs his Boswell but apologizes when he takes him for granted. People familiar only with cinematic impostures of Watson imagine that he is a loyal dunce, but the editors of this collection emphasize not only Watson's pluck but also his perceptive appraisal of Holmes's foibles and vanity.

This volume samples all of Doyle's narrative talents, which were not limited to dialogue. His chase scenes are legendary. He could also compose a nice cello overture of doom: "It was nine o'clock at night upon the second of August—the most terrible August in the history of the world. One might have thought already that God's curse hung heavy over a degenerate world, for there was an awesome hush and a feeling of vague expectancy in the sultry and stagnant air."

You will find your own favorites in *The Daily Sherlock Holmes*, but for me the *feel* of Sherlockian England is pressed like autumn leaves within its pages. Ever since I first began accompanying Holmes and Watson, I have loved the atmosphere, both literary and meteorological: "It was a foggy, cloudy morning, and a dun-coloured veil hung over the housetops, looking like the reflection of the mud-coloured streets beneath." I have felt a frisson of anticipation every time Watson or Holmes entered a hansom cab and "rattled through the crowded London streets." My own experiences of London streets have not dimmed this nostalgic romance, nor has my awareness of the dangers that Victorian smog created for lungs and purse. It doesn't matter that Holmes's original habitat has vanished from the real world. That's why we have literature, the great time machine.

Like Arthur Conan Doyle and Sherlock Holmes, Shintani and Stahl occasionally play games with their audience. The following pages include, for example, a spurious quotation solemnly attributed to a nonexistent Holmes story—but one that fans wish Doyle had written. This playfulness is in the spirit of the Baker Street Irregulars, the international organization that honors Holmes with banquets and toasts and lighthearted scholarship. I predict that you will dog-ear this volume, carry it in your pocket, read aloud from it.

———

Born among the wynds and closes of blustery Edinburgh in 1859, Doyle grew up reading writers such as Edgar Allan Poe. That outré American wrote a handful of detective stories, three of which featured a strutting French amateur named C. Auguste Dupin. Poe told readers that Dupin was a genius at observation, but he provided little evidence.

In 1886, after years of publishing minor stories anonymously, as was then the custom, the twenty-seven-year-old Arthur Conan Doyle, a fledgling MD, had an urge to write a detective story. He thought back a decade to his favorite professor in medical school at the University of Edinburgh, a renowned diagnostician named Joseph Bell. The good doctor inspired a brilliant detective because he was himself remarkably observant. Unlike Poe in his portrayal of Dupin, Doyle could provide countless examples of his hero's brilliance, because he had witnessed the method in medical school, day after day. Doyle was not the only student of Bell to record interactions such as the following (related in his article "The Truth about Sherlock Holmes"), in which his professor discerned a patient's history from a glance at his posture, clothing, and tan:

"Well, my man, you've served in the army?"

"Aye, sir."

"Not long discharged?"

"No, sir."

"A Highland regiment?"

"Aye, sir."

"A noncom officer?"

"Aye, sir."

Bell would explain his observations and inferences, and the devoted young Doyle would scribble copious notes.

Isn't literature a fine mystery? In the late 1880s and early 1890s, Doyle spends his off-hours dipping a pen in an ink bottle and writing his fine, neat hand across page after page. He rolls the stories up into mailing tubes and sends them out like messages in bottles. In a movie montage of rolling presses, publishers print the stories, and they shower down upon a public that does not yet know it suffers from a lack of heroes. Soon comes the day when Doyle casually writes to his mother, "Sherlock Holmes appears to have caught on."

In 1973, a couple of years after reading "The Speckled Band" in *Outlooks through Literature*, I received the two giant volumes of William S. Baring-Gould's *The Annotated Sherlock Holmes* from a mail-order book club called the Mystery Guild. They contained the species of footnotes and sidebars found in *Outlooks through Literature*, wherein I had learned about dogcarts and dark lanterns, but these glosses opened up to a tropical profusion of research and speculation: illustrations of hansom cabs, meditations on the supervillain snake of "The Speckled Band," biographies of illustrators. I stayed up all night.

Nowadays, when I prowl the bookshelves that hold my childhood and teenage treasures, I find myself reading Sherlock Holmes stories in the same mood in which I read natural history and science books. Holmes pays such close attention to the real world that he reminds us of cause and effect in this messy society, of the ripples that extend outward from our actions. I still admire Holmes's insights:

all those deductions from racing forms sticking out of coat pockets, inferences from a cabman's boots, cigar ash, and Watson's occasionally uneven shaving—Holmes following bicycle tire tracks in search of a kidnapped boy, or lying on the ground to peer with a scientist's eye at the grass we crush beneath our feet—

Often, on a cold, dark night, I wearily climb up the seventeen steps at 221B Baker Street and settle down with Holmes and Watson for the evening amid a cloud of pipe smoke. Mrs. Hudson has built a roaring fire. It glows like the light of reason to guard us from dangers that lurk out there in the fog.

Michael Sims is the author of seven books. He edits the Connoisseur's Collection series, and his Sherlockian pastiche appears in the anthology In the Company of Sherlock Holmes.

Preface

In making our selection of quotations for *The Daily Sherlock Holmes*, we aimed for a satisfying mix of variety, familiarity, comedy, action, dialogue, and description. We wanted longtime fans to feel welcomed back to cases and characters they love while also encountering forgotten gems from throughout the canon.

Attentive readers—and what other kind would Sherlock Holmes want?—will notice, however, that there are no selections from the final nine stories, as those are the only ones that now remain in copyright. While Holmes may not have scrupled at flouting the law to serve a larger purpose, we felt bound. We favored an uncluttered reading experience over textual exactitude, and so have silently altered capitalization and added closing punctuation where necessary.

As all but one of the stories we drew from were written from John Watson's point of view, readers can trust that any first-person narration not within quotation marks is his. An unidentified solo speaker within quotation marks can be assumed to be Holmes, barring a few instances where clear evidence indicates otherwise; in dialogue his voice is distinctive enough we trust you'll recognize him.

Now, to paraphrase the world's greatest detective: You know our methods. Enjoy them.

Stacey Shintani and Levi Stahl

THE DAILY SHERLOCK HOLMES

JANUARY

"I know, my dear Watson, that you share my love of all that is bizarre and outside the conventions and humdrum routine of everyday life. You have shown your relish for it by the enthusiasm which has prompted you to chronicle, and, if you will excuse my saying so, somewhat to embellish so many of my own little adventures."

"The Red-Headed League" (1891)

"Dr. Watson, Mr. Sherlock Holmes," said Stamford, introducing us.

"How are you?" he said cordially, gripping my hand with a strength for which I should hardly have given him credit. "You have been in Afghanistan, I perceive."

"How on earth did you know that?" I asked in astonishment.

"Never mind," said he, chuckling to himself.

JANUARY 2

"THE ADVENTURE OF THE ABBEY GRANGE" (1904)

It was on a bitterly cold night and frosty morning, towards the end of the winter of '97, that I was awakened by a tugging at my shoulder. It was Holmes. The candle in his hand shone upon his eager, stooping face, and told me at a glance that something was amiss.

"Come, Watson, come!" he cried. "The game is afoot. Not a word! Into your clothes and come!"

"My mind," he said, "rebels at stagnation. Give me problems, give me work, give me the most abstruse cryptogram, or the most intricate analysis, and I am in my own proper atmosphere. I can dispense then with artificial stimulants. But I abhor the dull routine of existence. I crave for mental exaltation. That is why I have chosen my own particular profession, or rather created it, for I am the only one in the world."

"The only unofficial detective?" I said, raising my eyebrows.

"The only unofficial consulting detective," he answered. "I am the last and highest court of appeal in detection."

JANUARY 4
"THE FIVE ORANGE PIPS" (1891)

"On the fourth day after the New Year I heard my father give a sharp cry of surprise as we sat together at the breakfast table. There he was, sitting with a newly opened envelope in one hand and five dried orange pips in the outstretched palm of the other one." (—John Openshaw)

When I look at the three massive manuscript volumes which contain our work for the year 1894, I confess that it is very difficult for me, out of such a wealth of material, to select the cases which are most interesting in themselves, and at the same time most conducive to a display of those peculiar powers for which my friend was famous. As I turn over the pages, I see my notes upon the repulsive story of the red leech and the terrible death of Crosby, the banker. Here also I find an account of the Addleton tragedy, and the singular contents of the ancient British barrow. The famous Smith-Mortimer succession case comes also within this period, and so does the tracking and arrest of Huret, the Boulevard assassin—an exploit which won for Holmes an autograph letter of thanks from the French President and the Order of the Legion of Honour.

JANUARY 6

A STUDY IN SCARLET (1887)

His very person and appearance were such as to strike the attention of the most casual observer. In height he was rather over six feet, and so excessively lean that he seemed to be considerably taller.

His eyes were sharp and piercing, save during those intervals of torpor to which I have alluded; and his thin, hawk-like nose gave his whole expression an air of alertness and decision. His chin, too, had the prominence and squareness which mark the man of determination. His hands were invariably blotted with ink and stained with chemicals, yet he was possessed of extraordinary delicacy of touch, as I frequently had occasion to observe when I watched him manipulating his fragile philosophical instruments.

JANUARY 7

"THE ADVENTURE OF THE BERYL CORONET" (1892)

"It is an old maxim of mine that when you have excluded the impossible, whatever remains, however improbable, must be the truth."

JANUARY 8

"THE ADVENTURE OF THE BLUE CARBUNCLE" (1892)

I seated myself in his armchair and warmed my hands before his crackling fire, for a sharp frost had set in, and the windows were thick with the ice crystals. "I suppose," I remarked, "that, homely as it looks, this [hat] has some deadly story linked on to it—that it is the clue which will guide you in the solution of some mystery, and the punishment of some crime."

"No, no. No crime," said Sherlock Holmes, laughing. "Only one of those whimsical little incidents which will happen when you have four million human beings all jostling each other within the space of a few square miles. Amid the action and reaction of so dense a swarm of humanity, every possible combination of events may be expected to take place, and many a little problem will be presented which may be striking and bizarre without being criminal."

JANUARY 9

"THE ADVENTURE OF THE DANCING MEN" (1903)

"Perhaps you can account also for the bullet which has so obviously struck the edge of the window?"

He had turned suddenly, and his long, thin finger was pointing to a hole which had been drilled right through the lower window-sash, about an inch above the bottom.

"By George!" cried the inspector. "How ever did you see that?"

"Because I looked for it."

"By the way, Holmes," I added, "I have no doubt the connection between my boots and a Turkish bath is a perfectly self-evident one to a logical mind, and yet I should be obliged to you if you would indicate it."

"The train of reasoning is not very obscure, Watson," said Holmes with a mischievous twinkle. "It belongs to the same elementary class of deduction which I should illustrate if I were to ask you who shared your cab in your drive this morning."

"An old soldier, I perceive," said Sherlock.

"And very recently discharged," remarked the brother.

"Served in India, I see."

"And a non-commissioned officer."

"Royal Artillery, I fancy," said Sherlock.

"And a widower."

"But with a child."

"Children, my dear boy, children."

"Come," said I, laughing, "this is a little too much."

"If I remember rightly, you on one occasion, in the early days of our friendship, defined my limits in a very precise fashion."

"Yes," I answered, laughing. "It was a singular document. Philosophy, astronomy, and politics were marked at zero, I remember. Botany variable, geology profound as regards the mud stains from any region within fifty miles of town, chemistry eccentric, anatomy unsystematic, sensational literature and crime records unique, violin player, boxer, swordsman, lawyer, and self-poisoner by cocaine and tobacco. Those, I think, were the main points of my analysis."

JANUARY 13

"THE NAVAL TREATY" (1893)

"Do you see any clue?"

"You have furnished me with seven, but of course I must test them before I can pronounce upon their value."

"You suspect someone?"

"I suspect myself."

"What!"

"Of coming to conclusions too rapidly."

In recording from time to time some of the curious experiences and interesting recollections which I associate with my long and intimate friendship with Mr. Sherlock Holmes, I have continually been faced by difficulties caused by his own aversion to publicity. To his sombre and cynical spirit all popular applause was always abhorrent, and nothing amused him more at the end of a successful case than to hand over the actual exposure to some orthodox official, and to listen with a mocking smile to the general chorus of misplaced congratulation.

JANUARY 15

"THE MAN WITH THE TWISTED LIP" (1891)

"Written in pencil upon the fly-leaf of a book, octavo size, no water-mark. Hum! Posted to-day at Gravesend by a man with a dirty thumb. Ha! And the flap has been gummed, if I am not very much in error, by a person who had been chewing tobacco."

A STUDY IN SCARLET (1887)

"They say that genius is an infinite capacity for taking pains," he remarked with a smile. "It's a very bad definition, but it does apply to detective work."

"THE RED-HEADED LEAGUE" (1891)

I took a good look at the man and endeavoured, after the fashion of my companion, to read the indications which might be presented by his dress or appearance.

I did not gain very much, however, by my inspection. Our visitor bore every mark of being an average commonplace British tradesman, obese, pompous, and slow. He wore rather baggy grey shepherd's check trousers, a not over-clean black frock-coat, unbuttoned in the front, and a drab waistcoat with a heavy brassy Albert chain, and a square pierced bit of metal dangling down as an ornament. A frayed top-hat and a faded brown overcoat with a wrinkled velvet collar lay upon a chair beside him. Altogether, look as I would, there was nothing remarkable about the man save his blazing red head, and the expression of extreme chagrin and discontent upon his features.

Sherlock Holmes's quick eye took in my occupation, and he shook his head with a smile as he noticed my questioning glances. "Beyond the obvious facts that he has at some time done manual labour, that he takes snuff, that he is a Freemason, that he has been in China, and that he has done a considerable amount of writing lately, I can deduce nothing else."

JANUARY 18
"SILVER BLAZE" (1892)

"Nothing clears up a case so much as stating it to another person."

JANUARY 19
THE HOUND OF THE BASKERVILLES (1902)

"Well, Watson, what do you make of it?"
Holmes was sitting with his back to me, and I had given him no sign of my occupation.
"How did you know what I was doing? I believe you have eyes in the back of your head."
"I have, at least, a well-polished, silver-plated coffee-pot in front of me."

JANUARY 20

THE SIGN OF FOUR (1890)

"There is nothing more unaesthetic than a policeman."

JANUARY 21

"THE ADVENTURE OF THE ABBEY GRANGE" (1904)

"I must admit, Watson, that you have some power of selection, which atones for much which I deplore in your narratives. Your fatal habit of looking at everything from the point of view of a story instead of as a scientific exercise has ruined what might have been an instructive and even classical series of demonstrations. You slur over work of the utmost finesse and delicacy, in order to dwell upon sensational details which may excite, but cannot possibly instruct, the reader."

"Why do you not write them yourself?" I said, with some bitterness.

"I will, my dear Watson, I will. At present I am, as you know, fairly busy, but I propose to devote my declining years to the composition of a text-book, which shall focus the whole art of detection into one volume."

JANUARY 22

"THE ADVENTURE OF CHARLES AUGUSTUS MILVERTON" (1904)

"I think there are certain crimes which the law cannot touch, and which therefore, to some extent, justify private revenge."

JANUARY 23

"THE RESIDENT PATIENT" (1893)

"Good-evening, Doctor [Trevelyan]," said Holmes cheerily. "I am glad to see that you have only been waiting a very few minutes."

"You spoke to my coachman, then?"

"No, it was the candle on the side-table that told me."

JANUARY 24

A STUDY IN SCARLET (1887)

"Ha!" cried Gregson, in a relieved voice; "you should never neglect a chance, however small it may seem."

"To a great mind, nothing is little," remarked Holmes, sententiously.

JANUARY 25

"I found the ash of a cigar, which my special knowledge of tobacco ashes enabled me to pronounce as an Indian cigar. I have, as you know, devoted some attention to this, and written a little monograph on the ashes of 140 different varieties of pipe, cigar, and cigarette tobacco."

JANUARY 26

"I think of writing another little monograph some of these days on the typewriter and its relation to crime. It is a subject to which I have devoted some little attention."

JANUARY 27

"I am fairly familiar with all forms of secret writings, and am myself the author of a trifling monograph upon the subject, in which I analyze one hundred and sixty separate ciphers."

JANUARY 28

"I have serious thoughts of writing a small monograph upon the uses of dogs in the work of the detective."

JANUARY 29

One of the most remarkable characteristics of Sherlock Holmes was his power of throwing his brain out of action and switching all thoughts on to lighter things whenever he had convinced himself that he could no longer work to advantage. I remember that during the whole of that memorable day he lost himself in a monograph which he had undertaken upon the Polyphonic Motets of Lassus.

JANUARY 30

"But your appearance, Holmes—your ghastly face?"

"Three days of absolute fast does not improve one's beauty, Watson. For the rest, there is nothing which a sponge may not cure. With vaseline upon one's forehead, belladonna in one's eyes, rouge over the cheek-bones, and crusts of beeswax round one's lips, a very satisfying effect can be produced. Malingering is a subject upon which I have sometimes thought of writing a monograph. A little occasional talk about half-crowns, oysters, or any other extraneous subject produces a pleasing effect of delirium."

JANUARY 31

"THE RED-HEADED LEAGUE" (1891)

"You reasoned it out beautifully," I exclaimed, in unfeigned admiration. "It is so long a chain, and yet every link rings true."

"It saved me from ennui," he answered, yawning. "Alas! I already feel it closing in upon me. My life is spent in one long effort to escape from the commonplaces of existence. These little problems help me to do so."

FEBRUARY

When we returned to Mrs. Warren's rooms, the gloom of a London winter evening had thickened into one grey curtain, a dead monotone of colour, broken only by the sharp yellow squares of the windows and the blurred haloes of the gas-lamps. As we peered from the darkened sitting-room of the lodging-house, one more dim light glimmered high up through the obscurity.

"Someone is moving in that room," said Holmes in a whisper, his gaunt and eager face thrust forward to the window-pane. "Yes, I can see his shadow. There he is again!"

"The Adventure of the Red Circle" (1911)

Looking over his shoulder, I saw that on the pavement opposite there stood a large woman with a heavy fur boa round her neck, and a large curling red feather in a broad-brimmed hat which was tilted in a coquettish Duchess-of-Devonshire fashion over her ear. From under this great panoply she peeped up in a nervous, hesitating fashion at our windows, while her body oscillated backwards and forwards, and her fingers fidgeted with her glove buttons. Suddenly, with a plunge, as of the swimmer who leaves the bank, she hurried across the road, and we heard the sharp clang of the bell.

"I have seen those symptoms before," said Holmes, throwing his cigarette into the fire. "Oscillation upon the pavement always means an *affaire de coeur*. She would like advice, but is not sure that the matter is not too delicate for communication. And yet even here we may discriminate. When a woman has been seriously wronged by a man she no longer oscillates, and the usual symptom is a broken bell wire. Here we may take it that there is a love matter, but that the maiden is not so much angry as perplexed, or grieved. But here she comes in person to relieve our doubts."

Soames hesitated.

"It is a very delicate question," said he. "One hardly likes to throw suspicion where there are no proofs."

"Let us hear the suspicions. I will look after the proofs."

FEBRUARY 3

"THE FIVE ORANGE PIPS" (1891)

Sherlock Holmes closed his eyes and placed his elbows upon the arms of his chair, with his fingertips together. "The ideal reasoner," he remarked, "would, when he has once been shown a single fact in all its bearings, deduce from it not only all the chain of events which led up to it but also all the results which would follow from it."

FEBRUARY 4

A STUDY IN SCARLET (1887)

"By Jove!" I cried; "if he really wants someone to share the rooms and the expense, I am the very man for him. I should prefer having a partner to being alone."

Young Stamford looked rather strangely at me over his wineglass. "You don't know Sherlock Holmes yet," he said; "perhaps you would not care for him as a constant companion."

"Why, what is there against him?"

"Oh, I didn't say there was anything against him. He is a little queer in his ideas—an enthusiast in some branches of science. As far as I know he is a decent fellow enough."

FEBRUARY 5

THE SIGN OF FOUR (1890)

Standing at the window, I watched her walking briskly down the street until the grey turban and white feather were but a speck in the sombre crowd.

"What a very attractive woman!" I exclaimed, turning to my companion.

He had lit his pipe again and was leaning back with drooping eyelids. "Is she?" he said languidly; "I did not observe."

"You really are an automaton—a calculating machine," I cried. "There is something positively inhuman in you at times."

FEBRUARY 6

"THE ADVENTURE OF THE BLUE CARBUNCLE" (1892)

"But pray tell me, before we go farther, who it is that I have the pleasure of assisting."

The man hesitated for an instant. "My name is John Robinson," he answered with a sidelong glance.

"No, no; the real name," said Holmes, sweetly. "It is always awkward doing business with an alias."

FEBRUARY 7

"THE ADVENTURE OF THE SIX NAPOLEONS" (1904)

As we drove up, we found the railings in front of the house lined by a curious crowd. Holmes whistled.

"By George! it's attempted murder at the least. Nothing less will hold the London message-boy. There's a deed of violence indicated in that fellow's round shoulders and outstretched neck."

FEBRUARY 8

"THE ADVENTURE OF THE EMPTY HOUSE" (1903)

Our route was certainly a singular one. Holmes's knowledge of the byways of London was extraordinary, and on this occasion he passed rapidly and with an assured step through a network of mews

and stables, the very existence of which I had never
known.

FEBRUARY 9

"THE DISAPPEARANCE OF
LADY FRANCES CARFAX" (1911)

"Where is your warrant?"

Holmes half drew a revolver from his pocket.
"This will have to serve till a better one comes."

"Why, you are a common burglar."

"So you might describe me," said Holmes cheerfully. "My companion is also a dangerous ruffian.
And together we are going through your house."

FEBRUARY 10

"THE BOSCOMBE VALLEY MYSTERY" (1891)

"And the murderer?"

"Is a tall man, left-handed, limps with the right
leg, wears thick-soled shooting boots and a grey
cloak, smokes Indian cigars, uses a cigar-holder, and
carries a blunt penknife in his pocket. There are several other indications, but these may be enough to
aid us in our search."

FEBRUARY 11

"THE FIVE ORANGE PIPS" (1891)

"A man should keep his little brain-attic stocked with all the furniture that he is likely to use, and the rest he can put away in the lumber room of his library, where he can get it if he wants it."

FEBRUARY 12

"THE ADVENTURE OF THE BLUE CARBUNCLE" (1892)

"My name is Sherlock Holmes. It is my business to know what other people don't know."

FEBRUARY 13

"SILVER BLAZE" (1892)

"Why didn't you go down yesterday?"

"Because I made a blunder, my dear Watson—which is, I am afraid, a more common occurrence than anyone would think who only knew me through your memoirs."

FEBRUARY 14

THE SIGN OF FOUR (1890)

Miss Morstan and I stood together, and her hand was in mine. A wondrous subtle thing is love, for here were we two, who had never seen each other before that day, between whom no word or even look of affection had ever passed, and yet now in an hour of trouble our hands instinctively sought for each other. I have marvelled at it since, but at the time it seemed the most natural thing that I should go out to her so, and, as she has often told me, there was in her also the instinct to turn to me for comfort and protection. So we stood hand in hand like two children, and there was peace in our hearts for all the dark things that surrounded us.

FEBRUARY 15

"A SCANDAL IN BOHEMIA" (1891)

To Sherlock Holmes she is always *the* woman. I have seldom heard him mention her under any other name. In his eyes she eclipses and predominates the whole of her sex. It was not that he felt any emotion akin to love for Irene Adler. All emotions, and that one particularly, were abhorrent to his cold, precise but admirably balanced mind. He was, I take it, the most perfect reasoning and observing machine that the world has seen; but, as a lover, he would have placed himself in a false position. He never spoke of the softer passions, save with a gibe and a sneer. They were admirable things for the observer—excellent for drawing the veil from men's motives and actions. But for the trained reasoner to admit such intrusions into his own delicate and finely adjusted temperament was to introduce a distracting factor which might throw a doubt upon all his mental results. Grit in a sensitive instrument, or a crack in one of his own high-power lenses, would not be more disturbing than a strong emotion in a nature such as his. And yet there was but one woman to him, and that woman was the late Irene Adler, of dubious and questionable memory.

FEBRUARY 16

"THE ADVENTURE OF THE COPPER BEECHES" (1892)

"I have devised seven separate explanations, each of which would cover the facts as far as we know them."

FEBRUARY 17

"THE ADVENTURE OF THE RED CIRCLE" (1911)

"It opens a pleasing field for intelligent speculation. The words are written with a broad-pointed, violet-tinted pencil of a not unusual pattern. You will observe that the paper is torn away at the side here after the printing was done, so that the 'S' of 'SOAP' is partly gone. Suggestive, Watson, is it not?"

"Of caution?"

"Exactly."

FEBRUARY 18

"THE ADVENTURE OF THE DEVIL'S FOOT" (1910)

"Well, then, I take our powder—or what remains of it—from the envelope, and I lay it above the burning lamp. So! Now, Watson, let us sit down and await developments."

They were not long in coming. I had hardly settled in my chair before I was conscious of a thick, musky odour, subtle and nauseous. At the very first whiff of it my brain and my imagination were beyond all control. A thick, black cloud swirled before my eyes, and my mind told me that in this cloud, unseen as yet, but about to spring out upon my appalled senses, lurked all that was vaguely horrible, all that was monstrous and inconceivably wicked in the universe.

FEBRUARY 19

"THE ADVENTURE OF THE
MISSING THREE-QUARTER" (1904)

He chuckled and rubbed his hands when we found ourselves in the street once more.

"Well?" I asked.

"We progress, my dear Watson, we progress. I had seven different schemes for getting a glimpse of that telegram, but I could hardly hope to succeed the very first time."

FEBRUARY 20

"THE ADVENTURE OF BLACK PETER" (1904)

Holmes was working somewhere under one of the numerous disguises and names with which he concealed his own formidable identity. He had at least five small refuges in different parts of London, in which he was able to change his personality.

FEBRUARY 21

"THE ADVENTURE OF THE
MISSING THREE-QUARTER" (1904)

Holmes rose. Taking the [telegraph] forms, he carried them over to the window and carefully examined that which was uppermost.

"It is a pity he did not write in pencil," said he, throwing them down again with a shrug of disappointment. "As you have no doubt frequently observed, Watson, the impression usually goes through—a fact which has dissolved many a happy marriage."

FEBRUARY 22

"THE ADVENTURE OF THE DEVIL'S FOOT" (1910)

"Upon my word, Watson!" said Holmes at last with an unsteady voice, "I owe you both my thanks and an apology. It was an unjustifiable experiment even for one's self, and doubly so for a friend. I am really very sorry."

"You know," I answered with some emotion, for I had never seen so much of Holmes's heart before, "that it is my greatest joy and privilege to help you."

He relapsed at once into the half-humorous, half-cynical vein which was his habitual attitude to those about him.

FEBRUARY 23

"THE NAVAL TREATY" (1893)

"The authorities are excellent at amassing facts, though they do not always use them to advantage."

FEBRUARY 24

"THE REIGATE SQUIRES" (1893)

"It is of the highest importance in the art of detection to be able to recognize, out of a number of facts, which are incidental and which vital. Otherwise your energy and attention must be dissipated instead of being concentrated."

FEBRUARY 25

"THE MUSGRAVE RITUAL" (1893)

An anomaly which often struck me in the character of my friend Sherlock Holmes was that, although in his methods of thought he was the neatest and most methodical of mankind, and although also he affected a certain quiet primness of dress, he was none the less in his personal habits one of the most untidy men that ever drove a fellow-lodger to distraction.

FEBRUARY 26

"THE ADVENTURE OF THE DYING DETECTIVE" (1913)

Mrs. Hudson, the landlady of Sherlock Holmes, was a long-suffering woman. Not only was her first-floor flat invaded at all hours by throngs of singular and often undesirable characters but her remarkable lodger showed an eccentricity and irregularity in his life which must have sorely tried her patience. His incredible untidiness, his addiction to music at strange hours, his occasional revolver practice within doors, his weird and often malodorous scientific experiments, and the atmosphere of violence and danger which hung around him made him the very worst tenant in London. On the other hand, his payments were princely. I have no doubt that the house might have been purchased at the price which Holmes paid for his rooms during the years that I was with him.

FEBRUARY 27

A STUDY IN SCARLET (1887)

"It was easier to know it than to explain why I knew it. If you were asked to prove that two and two made four, you might find some difficulty, and yet you are quite sure of the fact."

FEBRUARY 28

"THE ADVENTURE OF THE SIX NAPOLEONS" (1904)

Lestrade and I sat silent for a moment, and then, with a spontaneous impulse, we both broke out clapping, as at the well-wrought crisis of a play. A flush of colour sprang to Holmes's pale cheeks, and he bowed to us like the master dramatist who receives the homage of his audience. It was at such moments that for an instant he ceased to be a reasoning machine, and betrayed his human love for admiration and applause. The same singularly proud and reserved nature which turned away with disdain from popular notoriety was capable of being moved to its depths by spontaneous wonder and praise from a friend.

FEBRUARY 29

THE EXTRAORDINARY ADVENTURES OF
ARSÈNE LUPIN, GENTLEMAN-BURGLAR (1910)

By Maurice Leblanc

Holmes smiled and said: "Monsieur Devanne, everybody cannot solve riddles."

MARCH

It was a cold, dark March evening, with a sharp wind
and a fine rain beating upon our faces, a fit setting
for the wild common over which our road passed
and the tragic goal to which it led us.

"The Adventure of Wisteria Lodge" (1908)

MARCH 1

In glancing over my notes of the seventy odd cases in which I have during the last eight years studied the methods of my friend Sherlock Holmes, I find many tragic, some comic, a large number merely strange, but none commonplace; for, working as he did rather for the love of his art than for the acquirement of wealth, he refused to associate himself with any investigation which did not tend towards the unusual, and even the fantastic.

MARCH 2

"Was there any feature of interest?"

"I fancy not. The thieves ransacked the library and got very little for their pains. The whole place was turned upside down, drawers burst open, and presses ransacked, with the result that an odd volume of Pope's *Homer*, two plated candlesticks, an ivory letter-weight, a small oak barometer, and a ball of twine are all that have vanished."

"What an extraordinary assortment!" I exclaimed.

"Oh, the fellows evidently grabbed hold of everything they could get."

Holmes grunted from the sofa.

"The county police ought to make something of

that," said he; "why, it is surely obvious that—"

But I held up a warning finger.

"You are here for a rest, my dear fellow. For heaven's sake don't get started on a new problem when your nerves are all in shreds."

MARCH 3

"A CASE OF IDENTITY" (1891)

"You appeared to read a good deal upon her which was quite invisible to me," I remarked.

"Not invisible, but unnoticed, Watson. You did not know where to look, and so you missed all that was important. I can never bring you to realize the importance of sleeves, the suggestiveness of thumbnails, or the great issues that may hang from a bootlace."

MARCH 4

A STUDY IN SCARLET (1887)

"I never read such rubbish in my life."

"What is it?" asked Sherlock Holmes.

"Why, this article," I said, pointing at it with my egg spoon as I sat down to my breakfast. "I see that you have read it since you have marked it. I don't deny that it is smartly written. It irritates me though. It is evidently the theory of some armchair lounger who evolves all these neat little paradoxes in the seclusion of his own study. It is not practical. I should like to see him clapped down in a third class carriage on the Underground, and asked to give the trades of all his fellow-travellers. I would lay a thousand to one against him."

"You would lose your money," Sherlock Holmes remarked calmly. "As for the article, I wrote it myself."

MARCH 5

"THE ADVENTURE OF CHARLES AUGUSTUS MILVERTON" (1904)

"Well, I don't like it, but I suppose it must be," said I. "When do we start?"

"You are not coming."

"Then you are not going," said I. "I give you my word of honour—and I never broke it in my life—that I will take a cab straight to the police-station and give you away, unless you let me share this adventure with you."

"You can't help me."

"How do you know that? You can't tell what may happen. Anyway, my resolution is taken. Other people besides you have self-respect, and even reputations."

MARCH 6

"THE ADVENTURE OF THE COPPER BEECHES" (1892)

"Data! data! data!" he cried impatiently. "I can't make bricks without clay."

MARCH 7

"THE ADVENTURE OF THE SPECKLED BAND" (1892)

It was a perfect day, with a bright sun and a few fleecy clouds in the heavens. The trees and wayside hedges were just throwing out their first green shoots, and the air was full of the pleasant smell of the moist earth. To me at least there was a strange contrast between the sweet promise of the spring and this sinister quest upon which we were engaged.

MARCH 8

THE SIGN OF FOUR (1890)

"May I ask whether you have any professional inquiry on foot at present?"

"None. Hence the cocaine. I cannot live without brainwork. What else is there to live for? Stand at the window here. Was ever such a dreary, dismal, unprofitable world? See how the yellow fog swirls down the street and drifts across the dun-coloured houses. What could be more hopelessly prosaic and material? What is the use of having powers, Doctor, when one has no field upon which to exert them? Crime is commonplace, existence is commonplace, and no qualities save those which are commonplace have any function upon earth."

MARCH 9

A STUDY IN SCARLET (1887)

Desultory readers are seldom remarkable for the exactness of their learning. No man burdens his mind with small matters unless he has some very good reason for doing so.

MARCH 10

"A CASE OF IDENTITY" (1891)

"Do you not find," he said, "that with your short sight it is a little trying to do so much typewriting?"

"I did at first," she answered, "but now I know where the letters are without looking." Then, suddenly realizing the full purport of his words, she gave a violent start, and looked up with fear and astonishment upon her broad, good-humoured face. "You've heard about me, Mr. Holmes," she cried, "else how could you know all that?"

"Never mind," said Holmes, laughing; "it is my business to know things."

MARCH 11

"THE BOSCOMBE VALLEY MYSTERY" (1891)

"There is nothing more deceptive than an obvious fact."

MARCH 12

"THE GREEK INTERPRETER" (1893)

"There are many men in London, you know, who, some from shyness, some from misanthropy, have no wish for the company of their fellows. Yet they are not averse to comfortable chairs and the latest periodicals. It is for the convenience of these that the Diogenes Club was started, and it now contains the most unsociable and unclubbable men in town. No member is permitted to take the least notice of any other one. Save in the Stranger's Room, no talking is, under any circumstances, allowed, and three offenses, if brought to the notice of the committee, render the talker liable to expulsion. My brother was one of the founders, and I have myself found it a very soothing atmosphere."

MARCH 13

"And a singularly consistent investigation you have made, my dear Watson," said he. "I cannot at the moment recall any possible blunder which you have omitted. The total effect of your proceeding has been to give the alarm everywhere and yet to discover nothing."

MARCH 14

"THE ADVENTURE OF THE DEVIL'S FOOT" (1910)

We had arrived before the doctor or the police, so that everything was absolutely undisturbed. Let me describe exactly the scene as we saw it upon that misty March morning. It has left an impression which can never be effaced from my mind.

MARCH 15

"THE ADVENTURE OF THE RED CIRCLE" (1911)

Holmes was accessible upon the side of flattery, and also, to do him justice, upon the side of kindliness.

MARCH 16

"THE ADVENTURE OF THE DEVIL'S FOOT" (1910)

These were the two men who entered abruptly into our little sitting-room on Tuesday, March the 16th, shortly after our breakfast hour, as we were smoking together, preparatory to our daily excursion upon the moors.

"Mr. Holmes," said the vicar in an agitated voice, "the most extraordinary and tragic affair has occurred during the night. It is the most unheard-of business. We can only regard it as a special Providence that you should chance to be here at the time, for in all England you are the one man we need."

MARCH 17

"THE BOSCOMBE VALLEY MYSTERY" (1891)

"And this? Ha, ha! What have we here? Tip-toes! tip-toes! Square, too, quite unusual boots! They come, they go, they come again—of course that was for the cloak."

MARCH 18

"THE ADVENTURE OF THE RED CIRCLE" (1911)

He took down the great book in which, day by day, he filed the agony columns of the various London journals. "Dear me!" said he, turning over the pages, "what a chorus of groans, cries, and bleatings! What a rag-bag of singular happenings! But surely the most valuable hunting-ground that ever was given to a student of the unusual!"

MARCH 19

"THE ADVENTURE OF THE EMPTY HOUSE" (1903)

"Work is the best antidote to sorrow, my dear Watson."

MARCH 20

"A SCANDAL IN BOHEMIA" (1891)

One night—it was on the twentieth of March, 1888—I was returning from a journey to a patient (for I had now returned to civil practice), when my way led me through Baker Street. As I passed the well-remembered door, which must always be associated in my mind with my wooing, and with the dark incidents of the Study in Scarlet, I was seized with a keen desire to see Holmes again, and to know how he was employing his extraordinary powers. His rooms were brilliantly lit, and, even as I looked up, I saw his tall, spare figure pass twice in a dark silhouette against the blind. He was pacing the room swiftly, eagerly, with his head sunk upon his chest and his hands clasped behind him. To me, who knew his every mood and habit, his attitude and manner told their own story. He was at work again. He had risen out of his drug-created dreams and was hot upon the scent of some new problem.

MARCH 21
"THE ADVENTURE OF THE MISSING THREE-QUARTER" (1904)

"We have only to find to whom that telegram is addressed," I suggested.

"Exactly, my dear Watson. Your reflection, though profound, had already crossed my mind."

MARCH 22
"THE RED-HEADED LEAGUE" (1891)

My friend was an enthusiastic musician, being himself not only a very capable performer but a composer of no ordinary merit. All the afternoon he sat in the stalls wrapped in the most perfect happiness, gently waving his long, thin fingers in time to the music, while his gently smiling face and his languid, dreamy eyes were as unlike those of Holmes, the sleuth-hound, Holmes the relentless, keen-witted, ready-handed criminal agent, as it was possible to conceive. In his singular character the dual nature alternately asserted itself, and his extreme exactness and astuteness represented, as I have often thought, the reaction against the poetic and contemplative mood which occasionally predominated in him. The swing of his nature took him from extreme languor to devouring energy; and, as I knew well, he was never so truly formidable as when, for days on end, he had been lounging in his armchair amid his improvisations and his black-letter editions. Then it was that the lust of the chase would suddenly come upon him, and that his brilliant reasoning power would rise to the level of intuition, until those who were unacquainted with his methods would look askance at him as on a man whose knowledge was not that of other mortals.

MARCH 23

"THE PROBLEM OF THOR BRIDGE" (1922)

"You've done yourself no good this morning, Mr. Holmes, for I have broken stronger men than you. No man ever crossed me and was the better for it."

"So many have said so, and yet here I am," said Holmes, smiling.

MARCH 24

"THE BOSCOMBE VALLEY MYSTERY" (1891)

A lean, ferret-like man, furtive and sly-looking, was waiting for us upon the platform. In spite of the light brown dustcoat and leather leggings which he wore in deference to his rustic surroundings, I had no difficulty in recognizing Lestrade, of Scotland Yard.

MARCH 25

"THE ADVENTURE OF THE DANCING MEN" (1903)

"What one man can invent another can discover."

MARCH 26

"THE ADVENTURE OF THE PRIORY SCHOOL" (1904)

"Well, well," said he, at last. "It is, of course, possible that a cunning man might change the tyres of his bicycle in order to leave unfamiliar tracks. A criminal who was capable of such a thought is a man whom I should be proud to do business with."

MARCH 27

I find it recorded in my notebook that it was a bleak and windy day towards the end of March in the year 1892. Holmes had received a telegram while we sat at our lunch, and he had scribbled a reply. He made no remark, but the matter remained in his thoughts, for he stood in front of the fire afterwards with a thoughtful face, smoking his pipe, and casting an occasional glance at the message. Suddenly he turned upon me with a mischievous twinkle in his eyes.

MARCH 28

"THE ADVENTURE OF THE SECOND STAIN" (1904)

All that day and the next and the next Holmes was in a mood which his friends would call taciturn, and others morose. He ran out and ran in, smoked incessantly, played snatches on his violin, sank into reveries, devoured sandwiches at irregular hours, and hardly answered the casual questions which I put to him. It was evident to me that things were not going well with him or his quest.

MARCH 29

"THE ADVENTURE OF THE MAZARIN STONE" (1921)

"I'm a busy man and I can't waste time. I'm going into that bedroom. Pray make yourselves quite at home in my absence. You can explain to your friend how the matter lies without the restraint of my presence. I shall try over the Hoffmann 'Barcarole' upon my violin. In five minutes I shall return for your final answer. You quite grasp the alternative, do you not?"

MARCH 30

"THE FIVE ORANGE PIPS" (1891)

"There is nothing more to be said or to be done tonight, so hand me over my violin and let us try to forget for half an hour the miserable weather, and the still more miserable ways of our fellow men."

MARCH 31

"THE RED-HEADED LEAGUE" (1891)

"And now, Doctor, we've done our work, so it's time we had some play. A sandwich and a cup of coffee, and then off to violin-land, where all is sweetness and delicacy and harmony, and there are no red-headed clients to vex us with their conundrums."

APRIL

It was an ideal spring day, a light blue sky, flecked with little fleecy white clouds drifting across from west to east. The sun was shining very brightly, and yet there was an exhilarating nip in the air, which set an edge to a man's energy. All over the countryside, away to the rolling hills around Aldershot, the little red and grey roofs of the farm-steadings peeped out from amid the light green of the new foliage.

"Are they not fresh and beautiful?" I cried with all the enthusiasm of a man fresh from the fogs of Baker Street.

But Holmes shook his head gravely.

"Do you know, Watson," said he, "that it is one of the curses of a mind with a turn like mine that I must look at everything with reference to my own special subject. You look at these scattered houses, and you are impressed by their beauty. I look at them, and the only thought which comes to me is a feeling of their isolation, and of the impunity with which crime may be committed there."

"The Adventure of the Copper Beeches" (1892)

APRIL 1

"Elementary, my dear Watson."

APRIL 2

"THE FIVE ORANGE PIPS" (1891)

"Why did you come to me," he cried, "and, above all, why did you not come at once?"

APRIL 3

"THE ADVENTURE OF THE SPECKLED BAND" (1892)

It was early in April in the year '83 that I woke one morning to find Sherlock Holmes standing, fully dressed, by the side of my bed. He was a late riser as a rule, and as the clock on the mantelpiece showed me that it was only a quarter-past seven, I blinked up at him in some surprise, and perhaps just a little resentment, for I was myself regular in my habits.

"A SCANDAL IN BOHEMIA" (1891)

"By the way, Doctor, I shall want your co-operation."

"I shall be delighted."

"You don't mind breaking the law?"

"Not in the least."

"Nor running a chance of arrest?"

"Not in a good cause."

"Oh, the cause is excellent!"

"Then I am your man."

"I was sure that I might rely on you."

APRIL 5

"THE NAVAL TREATY" (1893)

"Do you think he expects to make a success of it?"

"He has said nothing."

"That is a bad sign."

"On the contrary. I have noticed that when he is off the trail he generally says so. It is when he is on a scent and is not quite absolutely sure yet that it is the right one that he is most taciturn."

APRIL 6

"THE STOCK-BROKER'S CLERK" (1893)

"I am afraid that I rather give myself away when I explain," said he. "Results without causes are much more impressive."

APRIL 7

"THE ADVENTURE OF THE MAZARIN STONE" (1921)

"I'm expecting something this evening."

"Expecting what?"

"To be murdered, Watson."

"No, no, you are joking, Holmes!"

"Even my limited sense of humour could evolve a better joke than that. But we may be comfortable in the meantime, may we not?"

APRIL 8

"THE ADVENTURE OF THE SPECKLED BAND" (1892)

"I am glad to see that Mrs. Hudson has had the good sense to light the fire. Pray draw up to it, and I shall order you a cup of hot coffee, for I observe that you are shivering."

"It is not cold which makes me shiver," said the woman in a low voice, changing her seat as requested.

"What, then?"

"It is fear, Mr. Holmes. It is terror."

APRIL 9

A STUDY IN SCARLET (1887)

"Have you read Gaboriau's works?" I asked. "Does Lecoq come up to your idea of a detective?"

Sherlock Holmes sniffed sardonically. "Lecoq was a miserable bungler," he said, in an angry voice; "he had only one thing to recommend him, and that was his energy. That book made me positively ill. The question was how to identify an unknown prisoner. I could have done it in twenty-four hours. Lecoq took six months or so. It might be made a text-book for detectives to teach them what to avoid."

APRIL 10

"THE REIGATE SQUIRES" (1893)

"But this is what we really wanted." He held up a little crumpled piece of paper.

"The remainder of the sheet!" cried the inspector.

"Precisely."

"And where was it?"

"Where I was sure it must be."

APRIL 11

Of all ruins, that of a noble mind is the most deplorable.

APRIL 12

"The London criminal is certainly a dull fellow," said he in the querulous voice of the sportsman whose game has failed him. "Look out of this window, Watson. See how the figures loom up, are dimly seen, and then blend once more into the cloud-bank. The thief or the murderer could roam London on such a day as the tiger does the jungle, unseen until he pounces, and then evident only to his victim."

"There have," said I, "been numerous petty thefts."

Holmes snorted his contempt.

"This great and sombre stage is set for something more worthy than that," said he. "It is fortunate for this community that I am not a criminal."

THE VALLEY OF FEAR (1915)

"Well, Holmes," I murmured, "have you found anything out?"

He stood beside me in silence, his candle in his hand. Then the tall, lean figure inclined towards me. "I say, Watson," he whispered, "would you be afraid to sleep in the same room with a lunatic, a man with softening of the brain, an idiot whose mind has lost its grip?"

"Not in the least," I answered in astonishment.

"Ah, that's lucky," he said, and not another word would he utter that night.

APRIL 14

"THE REIGATE SQUIRES" (1893)

On referring to my notes I see that it was upon the fourteenth of April that I received a telegram from Lyons which informed me that Holmes was lying ill in the Hotel Dulong. Within twenty-four hours I was in his sick-room and was relieved to find that there was nothing formidable in his symptoms. Even his iron constitution, however, had broken down under the strain of an investigation which had extended over two months, during which period he had never worked less than fifteen hours a day and had more than once, as he assured me, kept to his task for five days at a stretch. Even the triumphant issue of his labours could not save him from reaction after so terrible an exertion, and at a time when Europe was ringing with his name and when his room was literally ankle-deep with congratulatory telegrams I found him a prey to the blackest depression. Even the knowledge that he had succeeded where the police of three countries had failed, and that he had out-manoeuvred at every point the most accomplished swindler in Europe, was insufficient to rouse him from his nervous prostration.

APRIL 15

THE HOUND OF THE BASKERVILLES (1902)

"One last question, Holmes," I said as I rose. "Surely there is no need of secrecy between you and me. What is the meaning of it all? What is he after?"

Holmes's voice sank as he answered:

"It is murder, Watson—refined, cold-blooded, deliberate murder."

APRIL 16

THE SIGN OF FOUR (1890)

At Greenwich we were about three hundred paces behind them. At Blackwall we could not have been more than two hundred and fifty. I have coursed many creatures in many countries during my checkered career, but never did sport give me such a wild thrill as this mad, flying man-hunt down the Thames.

APRIL 17

"THE ADVENTURE OF
THE NORWOOD BUILDER" (1903)

"You mentioned your name, as if I should recognise it, but I assure you that, beyond the obvious facts that you are a bachelor, a solicitor, a Freemason, and an asthmatic, I know nothing whatever about you."

Familiar as I was with my friend's methods, it was not difficult for me to follow his deductions, and to observe the untidiness of attire, the sheaf of legal papers, the watch-charm, and the breathing which had prompted them. Our client, however, stared in amazement.

APRIL 18

THE VALLEY OF FEAR (1915)

Mediocrity knows nothing higher than itself; but talent instantly recognizes genius.

APRIL 19

"There are only those three capable of playing so bold a game—there are Oberstein, La Rothière, and Eduardo Lucas. I will see each of them."

I glanced at my morning paper.

"Is that Eduardo Lucas of Godolphin Street?"

"Yes."

"You will not see him."

"Why not?"

"He was murdered in his house last night."

My friend has so often astonished me in the course of our adventures that it was with a sense of exultation that I realized how completely I had astonished him.

APRIL 20

"What do you make of it, Watson?"

"A cipher message, Holmes."

My companion gave a sudden chuckle of comprehension. "And not a very obscure cipher, Watson," said he. "Why, of course, it is Italian!"

APRIL 21

THE HOUND OF THE BASKERVILLES (1902)

"The more *outré* and grotesque an incident is the more carefully it deserves to be examined, and the very point which appears to complicate a case is, when duly considered and scientifically handled, the one which is most likely to elucidate it."

APRIL 22

"THE ADVENTURE OF THE CREEPING MAN" (1923)

"Have you the effrontery necessary to put it through?"

"We can but try."

"Excellent, Watson! Compound of the Busy Bee and Excelsior. We can but try—the motto of the firm."

APRIL 23

THE HOUND OF THE BASKERVILLES (1902)

I am certainly developing the wisdom of the serpent, for when Mortimer pressed his questions to an inconvenient extent I asked him casually to what type Frankland's skull belonged, and so heard nothing but craniology for the rest of our drive. I have not lived for years with Sherlock Holmes for nothing.

APRIL 24

"I think that you know me well enough, Watson, to understand that I am by no means a nervous man. At the same time, it is stupidity rather than courage to refuse to recognize danger when it is close upon you."

APRIL 25

"The features are given to man as the means by which he shall express his emotions, and yours are faithful servants."

APRIL 26

"You have a grand gift of silence, Watson," said he. "It makes you quite invaluable as a companion."

APRIL 27

I have so deep a respect for the extraordinary qualities of Holmes that I have always deferred to his wishes, even when I least understood them. But now all my professional instincts were aroused. Let him be my master elsewhere, I at least was his in a sick room.

APRIL 28

"THE CARDBOARD BOX" (1893)

"You remember," said he, "that some little time ago when I read you the passage in one of Poe's sketches in which a close reasoner follows the unspoken thoughts of his companion, you were inclined to treat the matter as a mere *tour-de-force* of the author. On my remarking that I was constantly in the habit of doing the same thing you expressed incredulity."

"Oh, no!"

"Perhaps not with your tongue, my dear Watson, but certainly with your eyebrows."

APRIL 29

"THE ADVENTURE OF THE EMPTY HOUSE" (1903)

"There are some trees, Watson, which grow to a certain height, and then suddenly develop some unsightly eccentricity. You will see it often in humans. I have a theory that the individual represents in his development the whole procession of his ancestors, and that such a sudden turn to good or evil stands for some strong influence which came into the line of his pedigree. The person becomes, as it were, the epitome of the history of his own family."

"It is surely rather fanciful."

"Well, I don't insist upon it."

APRIL 30

"THE MAN WITH THE TWISTED LIP" (1891)

"I am sure, Mr. Holmes, that we are very much indebted to you for having cleared the matter up. I wish I knew how you reach your results."

"I reached this one," said my friend, "by sitting upon five pillows and consuming an ounce of shag. I think, Watson, that if we drive to Baker Street we shall just be in time for breakfast."

MAY

A rainy night had been followed by a glorious morning, and the heath-covered countryside, with the glowing clumps of flowering gorse, seemed all the more beautiful to eyes which were weary of the duns and drabs and slate greys of London. Holmes and I walked along the broad, sandy road inhaling the fresh morning air and rejoicing in the music of the birds and the fresh breath of the spring.

"The Adventure of the Solitary Cyclist" (1903)

MAY 1

"A CASE OF IDENTITY" (1891)

"I shall glance into the case for you," said Holmes, rising, "and I have no doubt that we shall reach some definite result. Let the weight of the matter rest upon me now, and do not let your mind dwell upon it further."

MAY 2

"THE ADVENTURE OF THE SPECKLED BAND" (1892)

"But I have heard, Mr. Holmes, that you can see deeply into the manifold wickedness of the human heart. You may advise me how to walk amid the dangers which encompass me."

MAY 3

"THE FINAL PROBLEM" (1893)

It was on the third of May that we reached the little village of Meiringen, where we put up at the Englischer Hof, then kept by Peter Steiler the elder. Our landlord was an intelligent man and spoke excellent English, having served for three years as waiter at the Grosvenor Hotel in London. At his advice, on the afternoon of the fourth we set off together, with the intention of crossing the hills and spending the night at the hamlet of Rosenlaui. We had strict injunctions, however, on no account to pass the falls of Reichenbach, which are about halfway up the hills, without making a small detour to see them.

MAY 4

"THE FINAL PROBLEM" (1893)

As I turned away, I saw Holmes, with his back against a rock and his arms folded, gazing down at the rush of the waters. It was the last that I was ever destined to see of him in this world.

MAY 5

"THE ADVENTURE OF THE EMPTY HOUSE" (1903)

"The instant that the Professor had disappeared, it struck me what a really extraordinarily lucky chance Fate had placed in my way. I knew that Moriarty was not the only man who had sworn my death. There were at least three others whose desire for vengeance upon me would only be increased by the death of their leader. They were all most dangerous men. One or other would certainly get me. On the other hand, if all the world was convinced that I was dead they would take liberties, these men, they would soon lay themselves open, and sooner or later I could destroy them. Then it would be time for me to announce that I was still in the land of the living. So rapidly does the brain act that I believe I had thought this all out before Professor Moriarty had reached the bottom of the Reichenbach Fall."

MAY 6
"THE YELLOW FACE" (1893)

"Pipes are occasionally of extraordinary interest," said he. "Nothing has more individuality, save perhaps watches and bootlaces."

MAY 7
"THE ADVENTURE OF CHARLES AUGUSTUS MILVERTON" (1904)

"We have shared this same room for some years, and it would be amusing if we ended by sharing the same cell."

MAY 8
"THE ADVENTURE OF THE RED CIRCLE" (1911)

Our official detectives may blunder in the matter of intelligence, but never in that of courage. Gregson climbed the stair to arrest this desperate murderer with the same absolutely quiet and businesslike bearing with which he would have ascended the official staircase of Scotland Yard. The Pinkerton man had tried to push past him, but Gregson had firmly elbowed him back. London dangers were the privilege of the London force.

MAY 9

"THE ADVENTURE OF THE COPPER BEECHES" (1892)

"It is my belief, Watson, founded upon my experience, that the lowest and vilest alleys in London do not present a more dreadful record of sin than does the smiling and beautiful countryside."

MAY 10

"THE ADVENTURE OF THE BLUE CARBUNCLE" (1892)

"Then, what clue could you have as to his identity?"

"Only as much as we can deduce."

"From his hat?"

"Precisely."

"A CASE OF IDENTITY" (1891)

"Depend upon it, there is nothing so unnatural as the commonplace."

"THE YELLOW FACE" (1893)

Sherlock Holmes was a man who seldom took exercise for exercise's sake. Few men were capable of greater muscular effort, and he was undoubtedly one of the finest boxers of his weight that I have ever seen; but he looked upon aimless bodily exertion as a waste of energy, and he seldom bestirred himself save where there was some professional object to be served. Then he was absolutely untiring and indefatigable. That he should have kept himself in training under such circumstances is remarkable, but his diet was usually of the sparest, and his habits were simple to the verge of austerity. Save for the occasional use of cocaine, he had no vices, and he only turned to the drug as a protest against the monotony of existence when cases were scanty and the papers uninteresting.

MAY 13

"A SCANDAL IN BOHEMIA" (1891)

Indeed, apart from the nature of the investigation which my friend had on hand, there was something in his masterly grasp of a situation, and his keen, incisive reasoning, which made it a pleasure to me to study his system of work, and to follow the quick, subtle methods by which he disentangled the most inextricable mysteries. So accustomed was I to his invariable success that the very possibility of his failing had ceased to enter into my head.

MAY 14

"THE DISAPPEARANCE OF
LADY FRANCES CARFAX" (1911)

"Besides, on general principles it is best that I should not leave the country. Scotland Yard feels lonely without me, and it causes an unhealthy excitement among the criminal classes."

MAY 15

"Remarkable!" he said, when the story was unfolded, "most remarkable! I can hardly recall any case where the features have been more peculiar."

"I thought you would say so, Mr. Holmes," said White Mason in great delight. "We're well up with the times in Sussex."

MAY 16

"I trust that there is nothing of consequence which I have overlooked?"

"I am afraid, my dear Watson, that most of your conclusions were erroneous. When I said that you stimulated me I meant, to be frank, that in noting your fallacies I was occasionally guided towards the truth."

MAY 17

"Then, pray tell me what it is that you can infer from this hat?"

He picked it up and gazed at it in the peculiar introspective fashion which was characteristic of him. "It is perhaps less suggestive than it might have been," he remarked, "and yet there are a few inferences which are very distinct, and a few others which represent at least a strong balance of probability. That the man was highly intellectual is of course obvious upon the face of it, and also that he was fairly well-to-do within the last three years, although he has now fallen upon evil days. He had foresight, but has less now than formerly, pointing to a moral retrogression, which, when taken with the decline of his fortunes, seems to indicate some evil influence, probably drink, at work upon him. This may account also for the obvious fact that his wife has ceased to love him."

"My dear Holmes!"

MAY 18

"THE ADVENTURE OF THE SPECKLED BAND" (1892)

"Indeed," said Holmes. "Was it your custom always to lock yourselves in at night?"

"Always."

"And why?"

"I think that I mentioned to you that the doctor kept a cheetah and a baboon. We had no feeling of security unless our doors were locked."

"Quite so."

MAY 19

"A dog reflects the family life. Whoever saw a frisky dog in a gloomy family, or a sad dog in a happy one? Snarling people have snarling dogs, dangerous people have dangerous ones."

MAY 20

THE HOUND OF THE BASKERVILLES (1902)

"And the dog?"

"Has been in the habit of carrying this stick behind his master. Being a heavy stick the dog has held it tightly by the middle, and the marks of his teeth are very plainly visible. The dog's jaw, as shown in the space between these marks, is too broad in my opinion for a terrier and not broad enough for a mastiff. It may have been—yes, by Jove, it *is* a curly-haired spaniel."

He had risen and paced the room as he spoke. Now he halted in the recess of the window. There was such a ring of conviction in his voice that I glanced up in surprise.

"My dear fellow, how can you possibly be so sure of that?"

"For the very simple reason that I see the dog himself on our very door-step."

MAY 21

THE SIGN OF FOUR (1890)

"You will bring Toby back in the cab with you."

"A dog, I suppose."

"Yes, a queer mongrel with a most amazing power of scent. I would rather have Toby's help than that of the whole detective force of London."

MAY 22

"SILVER BLAZE" (1892)

"Is there any point to which you would wish to draw my attention?"

"To the curious incident of the dog in the night-time."

"The dog did nothing in the night-time."

"That was the curious incident," remarked Sherlock Holmes.

MAY 23

"THE ADVENTURE OF THE MISSING THREE-QUARTER" (1904)

"I do not know whether it came from his own innate depravity or from the promptings of his master, but he was rude enough to set a dog at me. Neither dog nor man liked the look of my stick, however, and the matter fell through. Relations were strained after that, and further inquiries out of the question."

"THE ADVENTURE OF CHARLES AUGUSTUS
MILVERTON" (1904)

I knew that the opening of safes was a particular hobby with him, and I understood the joy which it gave him to be confronted with this green and gold monster, the dragon which held in its maw the reputations of many fair ladies.

A STUDY IN SCARLET (1887)

"I have already explained to you that what is out of the common is usually a guide rather than a hindrance. In solving a problem of this sort, the grand thing is to be able to reason backward. That is a very useful accomplishment, and a very easy one, but people do not practise it much. In the everyday affairs of life it is more useful to reason forward, and so the other comes to be neglected. There are fifty who can reason synthetically for one who can reason analytically."

MAY 26

"As I bent over her she suddenly shrieked out in a voice which I shall never forget, 'Oh, my God! Helen! It was the band! The speckled band!'"

MAY 27

THE SIGN OF FOUR (1890)

"He speaks as a pupil to his master," said I.

"Oh, he rates my assistance too highly," said Sherlock Holmes lightly. "He has considerable gifts himself. He possesses two out of the three qualities necessary for the ideal detective. He has the power of observation and that of deduction. He is only wanting in knowledge, and that may come in time."

MAY 28

THE HOUND OF THE BASKERVILLES (1902)

"My eyes have been trained to examine faces and not their trimmings. It is the first quality of a criminal investigator that he should see through a disguise."

MAY 29
"THE PROBLEM OF THOR BRIDGE" (1922)

A problem without a solution may interest the student, but can hardly fail to annoy the casual reader.

MAY 30
A STUDY IN SCARLET (1887)

"You see, the whole thing is a chain of logical sequences without a break or flaw."

"It is wonderful!" I cried. "Your merits should be publicly recognized. You should publish an account of the case. If you won't, I will for you."

"You may do what you like, Doctor," he answered.

MAY 31
"THE ADVENTURE OF THE SECOND STAIN" (1904)

"Mr. Holmes, you are a wizard, a sorcerer! How did you know it was there?"

"Because I knew it was nowhere else."

JUNE

"How sweet the morning air is! See how that one little cloud floats like a pink feather from some gigantic flamingo. Now the red rim of the sun pushes itself over the London cloud-bank. It shines on a good many folk, but on none, I dare bet, who are on a stranger errand than you and I. How small we feel with our petty ambitions and strivings in the presence of the great elemental forces of Nature!"

The Sign of Four (1890)

JUNE 1

"You then went to the vicarage, waited outside it for some time, and finally returned to your cottage."

"How do you know that?"

"I followed you."

"I saw no one."

"That is what you may expect to see when I follow you."

JUNE 2

"I have had to move into the chamber in which my sister died, and to sleep in the very bed in which she slept. Imagine, then, my thrill of terror when last night, as I lay awake, thinking over her terrible fate, I suddenly heard in the silence of the night the low whistle which had been the herald of her own death."

JUNE 3

"On June 3, that is, on Monday last, McCarthy left his house at Hatherley about three in the afternoon and walked down to the Boscombe Pool, which is a small lake formed by the spreading out of the stream which runs down the Boscombe Valley. He had been out with his serving-man in the morning at Ross, and he had told the man that he must hurry, as he had an appointment of importance to keep at three. From that appointment he never came back alive."

JUNE 4
"A CASE OF IDENTITY" (1891)

"'Pon my word, Watson, you are coming along wonderfully. You have really done very well indeed. It is true that you have missed everything of importance, but you have hit upon the method, and you have a quick eye for colour. Never trust to general impressions, my boy, but concentrate yourself upon details."

JUNE 5
"THE ADVENTURE OF THE EMPTY HOUSE" (1903)

"That you, Lestrade?" said Holmes.

"Yes, Mr. Holmes. I took the job myself. It's good to see you back in London, sir."

"I think you want a little unofficial help. Three undetected murders in one year won't do, Lestrade. But you handled the Molesey Mystery with less than your usual—that's to say, you handled it fairly well."

JUNE 6

"Here is a very fashionable epistle," I remarked as he entered. "Your morning letters, if I remember right, were from a fishmonger and a tide waiter."

"Yes, my correspondence has certainly the charm of variety."

JUNE 7

Holmes took up the stone and held it against the light. "It's a bonny thing," said he. "Just see how it glints and sparkles. Of course it is a nucleus and focus of crime. Every good stone is. They are the devil's pet baits. In the larger and older jewels every facet may stand for a bloody deed."

JUNE 8

"When you combine the ideas of whistles at night, the presence of a band of gipsies who are on intimate terms with this old Doctor, the fact that we have every reason to believe that the Doctor has an interest in preventing his stepdaughter's marriage, the dying allusion to a band, and, finally, the fact that Miss Helen Stoner heard a metallic clang, which might have been caused by one of those metal bars which secured the shutters falling back into its place, I think that there is good ground to think that the mystery may be cleared along those lines."

JUNE 9

THE VALLEY OF FEAR (1915)

Three centuries had flowed past the old Manor House, centuries of births and of homecomings, of country dances and of the meetings of fox hunters. Strange that now in its old age this dark business should have cast its shadow upon the venerable walls! And yet those strange, peaked roofs and quaint, overhung gables were a fitting covering to grim and terrible intrigue. As I looked at the deep-set windows and the long sweep of the dull-coloured, water-lapped front, I felt that no more fitting scene could be set for such a tragedy.

JUNE 10

"THE ADVENTURE OF THE RED CIRCLE" (1911)

"The matches have, of course, been used to light cigarettes. That is obvious from the shortness of the burnt end. Half the match is consumed in lighting a pipe or cigar. But, dear me! this cigarette stub is certainly remarkable. The gentleman was bearded and moustached, you say?"

"Yes, sir."

"I don't understand that. I should say that only a clean-shaven man could have smoked this. Why, Watson, even your modest moustache would have been singed."

"A holder?" I suggested.

"No, no; the end is matted."

JUNE 11

"THE MAN WITH THE TWISTED LIP" (1891)

"I perceive also that whoever addressed the envelope had to go and inquire as to the address."

"How can you tell that?"

"The name, you see, is in perfectly black ink, which has dried itself. The rest is of the greyish colour, which shows that the blotting-paper has been used. If it had been written straight off, and then blotted, none would be of a deep black shade. This man has written the name, and there has then been a pause before he wrote the address, which can only mean that he was not familiar with it. It is, of course, a trifle, but there is nothing so important as trifles."

"But I assure you you are mistaken about my alleged agents."

Count Sylvius laughed contemptuously.

"Other people can observe as well as you. Yesterday there was an old sporting man. To-day it was an elderly woman. They held me in view all day."

"Really, sir, you compliment me. Old Baron Dowson said the night before he was hanged that in my case what the law had gained the stage had lost. And now you give my little impersonations your kindly praise?"

"It was you—you yourself?"

Holmes shrugged his shoulders. "You can see in the corner the parasol which you so politely handed to me in the Minories before you began to suspect."

"You are proud of your brains, Holmes, are you not? Think yourself smart, don't you? You came across someone who was smarter this time."

JUNE 14

A STUDY IN SCARLET (1887)

"This fellow may be very clever," I said to myself, "but he is certainly very conceited."

JUNE 15

"THE MAN WITH THE TWISTED LIP" (1891)

One night—it was in June, '89—there came a ring to my bell, about the hour when a man gives his first yawn and glances at the clock.

JUNE 16

"THE ADVENTURE OF THE CREEPING MAN" (1923)

"Always look at the hands first, Watson. Then cuffs, trouser-knees, and boots."

JUNE 17

A STUDY IN SCARLET (1887)

"You remind me of Edgar Allan Poe's Dupin. I had no idea that such individuals did exist outside of stories."

Sherlock Holmes rose and lit his pipe. "No doubt you think that you are complimenting me in comparing me to Dupin," he observed. "Now, in my opinion, Dupin was a very inferior fellow. That trick of his of breaking in on his friends' thoughts with an apropos remark after a quarter of an hour's silence is really very showy and superficial. He had some analytical genius, no doubt; but he was by no means such a phenomenon as Poe appeared to imagine."

JUNE 18

"THE ADVENTURE OF THE SECOND STAIN" (1904)

"Only one important thing has happened in the last three days, and that is that nothing has happened."

JUNE 19

"THE ADVENTURE OF BLACK PETER" (1904)

Holmes, however, like all great artists, lived for his art's sake, and, save in the case of the Duke of Holdernesse, I have seldom known him claim any large reward for his inestimable services. So unworldly was he—or so capricious—that he frequently refused his help to the powerful and wealthy where the problem made no appeal to his sympathies, while he would devote weeks of most intense application to the affairs of some humble client whose case presented those strange and dramatic qualities which appealed to his imagination and challenged his ingenuity.

JUNE 20

THE SIGN OF FOUR (1890)

"Yes, I have been guilty of several monographs. They are all upon technical subjects. Here, for example, is one 'Upon the Distinction between the Ashes of the Various Tobaccos.' In it I enumerate a hundred and forty forms of cigar, cigarette, and pipe tobacco, with coloured plates illustrating the difference in the ash. It is a point which is continually turning up in criminal trials, and which is sometimes of supreme importance as a clue. If you can say definitely, for example, that some murder had been done by a man who was smoking an Indian lunkah, it obviously narrows your field of search. To the trained eye there is as much difference between the black ash of a Trichinopoly and the white fluff of bird's-eye as there is between a cabbage and a potato."

"You have an extraordinary genius for minutiae," I remarked.

"I appreciate their importance."

JUNE 21

His ignorance was as remarkable as his knowledge. Of contemporary literature, philosophy and politics he appeared to know next to nothing. Upon my quoting Thomas Carlyle, he inquired in the naivest way who he might be and what he had done. My surprise reached a climax, however, when I found incidentally that he was ignorant of the Copernican Theory and of the composition of the Solar System. That any civilized human being in this nineteenth century should not be aware that the earth travelled round the sun appeared to be to me such an extraordinary fact that I could hardly realize it.

JUNE 22

"THE ADVENTURE OF
THE ENGINEER'S THUMB" (1892)

The story has, I believe, been told more than once in the newspapers, but, like all such narratives, its effect is much less striking when set forth *en bloc* in a single half-column of print than when the facts slowly evolve before your own eyes, and the mystery clears gradually away as each new discovery furnishes a step which leads on to the complete truth.

During the first week or so we had no callers, and I had begun to think that my companion was as friendless a man as I was myself. Presently, however, I found that he had many acquaintances, and those in the most different classes of society. There was one little sallow rat-faced, dark-eyed fellow, who was introduced to me as Mr. Lestrade, and who came three or four times in a single week.

Gregson and Lestrade had watched the manoeuvres of their amateur companion with considerable curiosity and some contempt. They evidently failed to appreciate the fact, which I had begun to realize, that Sherlock Holmes's smallest actions were all directed towards some definite and practical end.

"What do you think of it, sir?" they both asked.

"It should be robbing you of the credit of the case if I was to presume to help you," remarked my friend. "You are doing so well now that it would be a pity for anyone to interfere." There was a world of sarcasm in his voice as he spoke.

JUNE 25

"THE BOSCOMBE VALLEY MYSTERY" (1891)

"We have got to the deductions and the inferences," said Lestrade, winking at me. "I find it hard enough to tackle facts, Holmes, without flying away after theories and fancies."

"You are right," said Holmes demurely; "you do find it very hard to tackle the facts."

JUNE 26

THE HOUND OF THE BASKERVILLES (1902)

The London express came roaring into the station, and a small, wiry bulldog of a man had sprung from a first-class carriage. We all three shook hands, and I saw at once from the reverential way in which Lestrade gazed at my companion that he had learned a good deal since the days when they had first worked together. I could well remember the scorn which the theories of the reasoner used then to excite in the practical man.

JUNE 27

"THE ADVENTURE OF THE SIX NAPOLEONS" (1904)

It was no very unusual thing for Mr. Lestrade, of Scotland Yard, to look in upon us of an evening, and his visits were welcome to Sherlock Holmes, for they enabled him to keep in touch with all that was going on at the police headquarters. In return for the news which Lestrade would bring, Holmes was always ready to listen with attention to the details of any case upon which the detective was engaged, and was able occasionally, without any active interference, to give some hint or suggestion drawn from his own vast knowledge and experience.

JUNE 28

THE HOUND OF THE BASKERVILLES (1902)

"Are you armed, Lestrade?"

The little detective smiled.

"As long as I have my trousers I have a hip-pocket, and as long as I have my hip-pocket I have something in it."

JUNE 29

"THE ADVENTURE OF
THE NORWOOD BUILDER" (1903)

At one end of the corridor we were all marshalled by Sherlock Holmes, the constables grinning and Lestrade staring at my friend with amazement, expectation, and derision chasing each other across his features. Holmes stood before us with the air of a conjurer who is performing a trick.

JUNE 30

"THE ADVENTURE OF THE SIX NAPOLEONS" (1904)

"Well," said Lestrade, "I've seen you handle a good many cases, Mr. Holmes, but I don't know that I ever knew a more workmanlike one than that. We're not jealous of you at Scotland Yard. No, sir, we are very proud of you, and if you come down to-morrow, there's not a man, from the oldest inspector to the youngest constable, who wouldn't be glad to shake you by the hand."

"Thank you!" said Holmes. "Thank you!" and as he turned away, it seemed to me that he was more nearly moved by the softer human emotions than I had ever seen him. A moment later he was the cold and practical thinker once more.

JULY

During the first week of July, my friend had been absent so often and so long from our lodgings that I knew he had something on hand. The fact that several rough-looking men called during that time and inquired for Captain Basil made me understand that Holmes was working somewhere under one of the numerous disguises and names with which he concealed his own formidable identity.

"The Adventure of Black Peter" (1904)

JULY 1

"If this young person should produce her letters for blackmailing or other purposes, how is she to prove their authenticity?"

"There is the writing."

"Pooh, pooh! Forgery."

"My private note-paper."

"Stolen."

"My own seal."

"Imitated."

"My photograph."

"Bought."

"We were both in the photograph."

"Oh, dear! That is very bad! Your Majesty has indeed committed an indiscretion."

JULY 2

"Between ourselves, I think Mr. Holmes has not quite got over his illness yet. He's been behaving very queerly, and he is very much excited."

"I don't think you need alarm yourself," said I. "I have usually found that there was method in his madness."

"Some folk might say there was madness in his method."

JULY 3

"Really, Watson, you excel yourself," said Holmes, pushing back his chair and lighting a cigarette. "I am bound to say that in all the accounts which you have been so good as to give of my own small achievements you have habitually underrated your own abilities. It may be that you are not yourself luminous, but you are a conductor of light. Some people without possessing genius have a remarkable power of stimulating it. I confess, my dear fellow, that I am very much in your debt."

JULY 4

"There was no complete maker's name; but the printed letters 'P-E-N' were on the fluting between the barrels, and the rest of the name had been cut off by the saw."

"A big 'P' with a flourish above it, 'E' and 'N' smaller?" asked Holmes.

"Exactly."

"Pennsylvania Small Arms Company—well-known American firm," said Holmes.

White Mason gazed at my friend as the little village practitioner looks at the Harley Street specialist who by a word can solve the difficulties that perplex him.

JULY 5

To Holmes, as I could see by his eager face and peering eyes, very many other things were to be read upon the trampled grass. He ran round, like a dog who is picking up a scent.

JULY 6

"Any truth is better than indefinite doubt."

JULY 7

"This morning I received this letter, which you will perhaps read for yourself."

"Thank you," said Holmes. "The envelope, too, please. Post-mark, London, S. W. Date, July 7. Hum! Man's thumb-mark on corner—probably postman. Best quality paper. Envelopes at sixpence a packet. Particular man in his stationery. No address. 'Be at the third pillar from the left outside the Lyceum Theatre to-night at seven o'clock. If you are distrustful bring two friends. You are a wronged woman and shall have justice. Do not bring police. If you do, all will be in vain. Your unknown friend.' Well, really, this is a very pretty mystery! What do you intend to do, Miss Morstan?"

JULY 8

A STUDY IN SCARLET (1887)

"There is a mystery about this which stimulates the imagination; where there is no imagination there is no horror."

JULY 9

"SILVER BLAZE" (1892)

"It is one of those cases where the art of the reasoner should be used rather for the sifting of details than for the acquiring of fresh evidence. The tragedy has been so uncommon, so complete, and of such personal importance to so many people that we are suffering from a plethora of surmise, conjecture, and hypothesis. The difficulty is to detach the framework of fact—of absolute undeniable fact—from the embellishments of theorists and reporters. Then, having established ourselves upon this sound basis, it is our duty to see what inferences may be drawn and what are the special points upon which the whole mystery turns."

JULY 10

"My dear Watson," said he, "I cannot agree with those who rank modesty among the virtues. To the logician all things should be seen exactly as they are, and to underestimate one's self is as much a departure from truth as to exaggerate one's own powers. When I say, therefore, that Mycroft has better powers of observation than I, you may take it that I am speaking the exact and literal truth."

JULY 11
A STUDY IN SCARLET (1887)

"I should have more faith," he said; "I ought to know by this time that when a fact appears to be opposed to a long train of deductions, it invariably proves to be capable of bearing some other interpretation."

JULY 12
"THE BOSCOMBE VALLEY MYSTERY" (1891)

Sherlock Holmes was transformed when he was hot upon such a scent as this. Men who had only known the quiet thinker and logician of Baker Street would have failed to recognize him. His face flushed and darkened. His brows were drawn into two hard black lines, while his eyes shone out from beneath them with a steely glitter. His face was bent downward, his shoulders bowed, his lips compressed, and the veins stood out like whipcord in his long, sinewy neck. His nostrils seemed to dilate with a purely animal lust for the chase, and his mind was so absolutely concentrated upon the matter before him that a question or remark fell unheeded upon his ears, or, at the most, only provoked a quick, impatient snarl in reply.

JULY 13

"THE ADVENTURE OF
THE MISSING THREE-QUARTER" (1904)

A cold supper was ready upon the table, and when his needs were satisfied and his pipe alight he was ready to take that half comic and wholly philosophic view which was natural to him when his affairs were going awry.

JULY 14

"THE ADVENTURE OF THE ABBEY GRANGE" (1904)

"Be frank with me and we may do some good. Play tricks with me, and I'll crush you."

JULY 15

THE SIGN OF FOUR (1890)

He whipped out his lens and a tape measure and hurried about the room on his knees, measuring, comparing, examining, with his long thin nose only a few inches from the planks and his beady eyes gleaming and deep-set like those of a bird. So swift, silent, and furtive were his movements, like those of a trained bloodhound picking out a scent, that I could not but think what a terrible criminal he would have made had he turned his energy and sagacity against the law instead of exerting them in its defence.

JULY 16

"THE ADVENTURE OF THE SPECKLED BAND" (1892)

"Ha! You put me off, do you?" said our new visitor, taking a step forward and shaking his hunting-crop. "I know you, you scoundrel! I have heard of you before. You are Holmes the meddler."

My friend smiled.

"Holmes the busybody!"

His smile broadened.

"Holmes the Scotland Yard Jack-in-office!"

Holmes chuckled heartily. "Your conversation is most entertaining," said he. "When you go out close the door, for there is a decided draught."

JULY 17

THE VALLEY OF FEAR (1915)

It was one of those dramatic moments for which my friend existed. It would be an overstatement to say that he was shocked or even excited by the amazing announcement. Without having a tinge of cruelty in his singular composition, he was undoubtedly callous from long overstimulation. Yet, if his emotions were dulled, his intellectual perceptions were exceedingly active. There was no trace then of the horror which I had myself felt at this curt declaration; but his face showed rather the quiet and interested composure of the chemist who sees the crystals falling into position from his oversaturated solution.

JULY 18

"THE DISAPPEARANCE OF
LADY FRANCES CARFAX" (1911)

My companion started. "Well?" he asked, in that vibrant voice which told of the fiery soul behind the cold grey face.

JULY 19

THE VALLEY OF FEAR (1915)

"All knowledge comes useful to the detective."

JULY 20

"THE ADVENTURE OF THE SPECKLED BAND" (1892)

"I am a dangerous man to fall foul of! See here." He stepped swiftly forward, seized the poker, and bent it into a curve with his huge brown hands.

"See that you keep yourself out of my grip," he snarled, and hurling the twisted poker into the fireplace, he strode out of the room.

"He seems a very amiable person," said Holmes, laughing. "I am not quite so bulky, but if he had remained I might have shown him that my grip was not much more feeble than his own." As he spoke he picked up the steel poker and, with a sudden effort, straightened it out again.

JULY 21

"THE ADVENTURE OF THE EMPTY HOUSE" (1903)

"Just give me down my index of biographies from the shelf."

He turned over the pages lazily, leaning back in

his chair and blowing great clouds from his cigar.

"My collection of M's is a fine one," said he. "Moriarty himself is enough to make any letter illustrious, and here is Morgan the poisoner, and Merridew of abominable memory, and Mathews, who knocked out my left canine in the waiting-room at Charing Cross."

JULY 22

THE SIGN OF FOUR (1890)

"He had doubtless planned beforehand that, should he slay the major, he would leave some such record upon the body as a sign that it was not a common murder but, from the point of view of the four associates, something in the nature of an act of justice. Whimsical and bizarre conceits of this kind are common enough in the annals of crime and usually afford valuable indications as to the criminal."

JULY 23

THE HOUND OF THE BASKERVILLES (1902)

"The world is full of obvious things which nobody by any chance ever observes."

JULY 24

"I should be very much obliged if you would slip your revolver into your pocket. An Eley's No. 2 is an excellent argument with gentlemen who can twist steel pokers into knots. That and a tooth-brush are, I think, all that we need."

JULY 25

THE HOUND OF THE BASKERVILLES (1902)

"The past and the present are within the field of my inquiry, but what a man may do in the future is a hard question to answer."

JULY 26

"THE RED-HEADED LEAGUE" (1891)

I trust that I am not more dense than my neighbours, but I was always oppressed with a sense of my own stupidity in my dealings with Sherlock Holmes.

JULY 27

"You see, but you do not observe. The distinction is clear. For example, you have frequently seen the steps which lead up from the hall to this room."

"Frequently."

"How often?"

"Well, some hundreds of times."

"Then how many are there?"

"How many? I don't know."

"Quite so! You have not observed. And yet you have seen. That is just my point."

JULY 28

"The detection of types is one of the most elementary branches of knowledge to the special expert in crime, though I confess that once when I was very young I confused the *Leeds Mercury* with the *Western Morning News*."

JULY 29

I spent a few minutes in assisting a venerable Italian priest, who was endeavouring to make a porter understand, in his broken English, that his luggage was to be booked through to Paris. Then, having taken another look round, I returned to my carriage, where I found that the porter, in spite of the ticket, had given me my decrepit Italian friend as a travelling companion. It was useless for me to explain to him that his presence was an intrusion, for my Italian was even more limited than his English, so I shrugged my shoulders resignedly, and continued to look out anxiously for my friend. A chill of fear had come over me, as I thought that his absence might mean that some blow had fallen during the night. Already the doors had all been shut and the whistle blown, when—

"My dear Watson," said a voice, "you have not even condescended to say good-morning."

I turned in uncontrollable astonishment. The aged ecclesiastic had turned his face towards me. For an instant the wrinkles were smoothed away, the nose drew away from the chin, the lower lip ceased to protrude and the mouth to mumble, the dull eyes regained their fire, the drooping figure expanded. The next the whole frame collapsed again, and Holmes had gone as quickly as he had come.

"All this seems strange to you," continued Holmes, "because you failed at the beginning of the inquiry to grasp the importance of the single real clue which was presented to you. I had the good fortune to seize upon that, and everything which has occurred since then has served to confirm my original supposition, and, indeed, was the logical sequence of it."

JULY 31

"THE FIVE ORANGE PIPS" (1891)

Sherlock Holmes was able, by winding up the dead man's watch, to prove that it had been wound up two hours before, and that therefore the deceased had gone to bed within that time—a deduction which was of the greatest importance in clearing up the case.

AUGUST

It was a blazing hot day in August. Baker Street was like an oven, and the glare of the sunlight upon the yellow brickwork of the house across the road was painful to the eye. It was hard to believe that these were the same walls which loomed so gloomily through the fogs of winter. Our blinds were half-drawn, and Holmes lay curled upon the sofa, reading and re-reading a letter which he had received by the morning post. For myself, my term of service in India had trained me to stand heat better than cold, and a thermometer at ninety was no hardship.

"The Cardboard Box" (1893)

AUGUST 1

"My dear Watson, you know how bored I have been since we locked up Colonel Carruthers. My mind is like a racing engine, tearing itself to pieces because it is not connected up with the work for which it was built. Life is commonplace; the papers are sterile; audacity and romance seem to have passed forever from the criminal world. Can you ask me, then, whether I am ready to look into any new problem, however trivial it may prove?"

AUGUST 2

"HIS LAST BOW" (1917)

It was nine o'clock at night upon the second of August—the most terrible August in the history of the world. One might have thought already that God's curse hung heavy over a degenerate world, for there was an awesome hush and a feeling of vague expectancy in the sultry and stagnant air.

AUGUST 3

THE HOUND OF THE BASKERVILLES (1902)

"A cast of your skull, sir, until the original is available, would be an ornament to any anthropological museum. It is not my intention to be fulsome, but I confess that I covet your skull."

Sherlock Holmes waved our strange visitor into a chair. "You are an enthusiast in your line of thought, I perceive, sir, as I am in mine."

AUGUST 4

"THE ADVENTURE OF THE SPECKLED BAND" (1892)

"Ah, me! it's a wicked world, and when a clever man turns his brains to crime it is the worst of all."

AUGUST 5

"THE RED-HEADED LEAGUE" (1891)

"My dear doctor, this is a time for observation, not for talk. We are spies in an enemy's country."

AUGUST 6

"THE BOSCOMBE VALLEY MYSTERY" (1891)

"I very clearly perceive that in your bedroom the window is upon the right-hand side, and yet I question whether Mr. Lestrade would have noted even so self-evident a thing as that."

"How on earth—!"

"My dear fellow, I know you well. I know the military neatness which characterizes you. You shave every morning, and in this season you shave by the sunlight, but since your shaving is less and less complete as we get farther back on the left side, until it becomes positively slovenly as we get round the angle of the jaw, it is surely very clear that that side is less illuminated than the other. I could not imagine a man of your habits looking at himself in an equal light and being satisfied with such a result. I only quote this as a trivial example of observation and inference."

AUGUST 7

THE VALLEY OF FEAR (1915)

"I am inclined to think—" said I.

"I should do so," Sherlock Holmes remarked impatiently.

I believe that I am one of the most long-suffering of mortals; but I'll admit that I was annoyed at the sardonic interruption. "Really, Holmes," said I severely, "you are a little trying at times."

"It is a mistake to confound strangeness with mystery. The most commonplace crime is often the most mysterious, because it presents no new or special features from which deductions may be drawn. This murder would have been infinitely more difficult to unravel had the body of the victim been simply found lying in the roadway without any of those *outré* and sensational accompaniments which have rendered it remarkable. These strange details, far from making the case more difficult, have really had the effect of making it less so."

AUGUST 9

"THE ADVENTURE OF THE MAZARIN STONE" (1921)

Holmes looked at him thoughtfully like a master chess-player who meditates his crowning move. Then he threw open the table drawer and drew out a squat notebook.

"Do you know what I keep in this book?"

"No, sir, I do not!"

"You!"

"Me!"

"Yes, sir, *you*! You are all here—every action of your vile and dangerous life."

AUGUST 10

"You will not apply my precept," he said, shaking his head. "How often have I said to you that when you have eliminated the impossible, whatever remains, *however improbable*, must be the truth?"

AUGUST 11

"THE RED-HEADED LEAGUE" (1891)

"None the less you must come round to my view, for otherwise I shall keep piling fact upon fact on you, until your reason breaks down under them and acknowledges me to be right."

AUGUST 12

"A SCANDAL IN BOHEMIA" (1891)

"The facts are briefly these: Some five years ago, during a lengthy visit to Warsaw, I made the acquaintance of the well-known adventuress, Irene Adler. The name is no doubt familiar to you."

"Kindly look her up in my index, Doctor," murmured Holmes without opening his eyes. For many years he had adopted a system of docketing all paragraphs concerning men and things, so that it was difficult to name a subject or a person on which he could not at once furnish information. In this case I found her biography sandwiched in between that of a Hebrew Rabbi and that of a staff-commander who had written a monograph upon the deep-sea fishes.

AUGUST 13
THE SIGN OF FOUR (1890)

"I think you must recollect me, Mr. Athelney Jones," said Holmes quietly.

"Why, of course I do!" he wheezed. "It's Mr. Sherlock Holmes, the theorist. Remember you! I'll never forget how you lectured us all on causes and inferences and effects in the Bishopgate jewel case. It's true you set us on the right track; but you'll own now that it was more by good luck than good guidance."

"It was a piece of very simple reasoning."

"Oh, come, now, come! Never be ashamed to own up."

AUGUST 14
THE HOUND OF THE BASKERVILLES (1902)

"Footprints?"

"Footprints."

"A man's or a woman's?"

Dr. Mortimer looked strangely at us for an

instant, and his voice sank almost to a whisper as he answered:

"Mr. Holmes, they were the footprints of a gigantic hound!"

AUGUST 15

"THE FIVE ORANGE PIPS" (1891)

Sherlock Holmes sat for some time in silence, with his head sunk forward and his eyes bent upon the red glow of the fire. Then he lit his pipe, and leaning back in his chair he watched the blue smoke rings as they chased each other up to the ceiling.

"I think, Watson," he remarked at last, "that of all our cases we have had none more fantastic than this."

AUGUST 16

A STUDY IN SCARLET (1887)

"You have brought detection as near an exact science as it ever will be brought in this world."

My companion flushed up with pleasure at my words, and the earnest way in which I uttered them. I had already observed that he was as sensitive to flattery on the score of his art as any girl could be of her beauty.

AUGUST 17

"Indeed, I have found that it is usually in unimportant matters that there is a field for the observation, and for the quick analysis of cause and effect which gives the charm to an investigation. The larger crimes are apt to be the simpler, for the bigger the crime, the more obvious, as a rule, is the motive."

AUGUST 18

THE SIGN OF FOUR (1890)

"Very sorry, Mr. Thaddeus," said the porter inexorably. "Folk may be friends o' yours, and yet no friend o' the master's. He pays me well to do my duty, and my duty I'll do. I don't know none o' your friends."

"Oh, yes you do, McMurdo," cried Sherlock Holmes genially. "I don't think you can have forgotten me. Don't you remember that amateur who fought three rounds with you at Alison's rooms on the night of your benefit four years back?"

"Not Mr. Sherlock Holmes!" roared the prizefighter. "God's truth! how could I have mistook you? If instead o' standin' there so quiet you had just stepped up and given me that cross-hit of yours under the jaw, I'd ha' known you without a question. Ah, you're one that has wasted your gifts, you have! You might have aimed high, if you had joined the fancy."

"You see, Watson, if all else fails me, I have still one of the scientific professions open to me."

AUGUST 19

THE VALLEY OF FEAR (1915)

"The temptation to form premature theories upon insufficient data is the bane of our profession."

AUGUST 20

"THE RED-HEADED LEAGUE" (1891)

"As a rule," said Holmes, "the more bizarre a thing is the less mysterious it proves to be. It is your commonplace, featureless crimes which are really puzzling, just as a commonplace face is the most difficult to identify."

AUGUST 21

THE SIGN OF FOUR (1890)

"See here," said Holmes, pointing to the wooden hatchway. "We were hardly quick enough with our pistols." There, sure enough, just behind where we had been standing, stuck one of those murderous darts which we knew so well. It must have whizzed between us at the instant we fired. Holmes smiled at it and shrugged his shoulders in his easy fashion, but I confess that it turned me sick to think of the horrible death which had passed so close to us that night.

AUGUST 22

"THE DISAPPEARANCE OF
LADY FRANCES CARFAX" (1911)

"One of the most dangerous classes in the world," said he, "is the drifting and friendless woman. She is the most harmless and often the most useful of mortals, but she is the inevitable inciter of crime in others."

AUGUST 23

"THE GREEK INTERPRETER" (1893)

During my long and intimate acquaintance with Mr. Sherlock Holmes I had never heard him refer to his relations, and hardly ever to his own early life. This reticence upon his part had increased the somewhat inhuman effect which he produced upon me, until sometimes I found myself regarding him as an isolated phenomenon, a brain without a heart, as deficient in human sympathy as he was preeminent in intelligence. His aversion to women and his disinclination to form new friendships were both typical of his unemotional character, but not more so than his complete suppression of every reference to his own people. I had come to believe that he was an orphan with no relatives living; but one day, to my very great surprise, he began to talk to me about his brother.

AUGUST 24

"THE ADVENTURE OF THE
BRUCE-PARTINGTON PLANS" (1908)

"By the way, do you know what Mycroft is?"

I had some vague recollection of an explanation at the time of the Adventure of the Greek Interpreter.

"You told me that he had some small office under the British government."

Holmes chuckled.

"I did not know you quite so well in those days. One has to be discreet when one talks of high matters of state. You are right in thinking that he is under the British government. You would also be right in a sense if you said that occasionally he *is* the British government."

AUGUST 25

"THE GREEK INTERPRETER" (1893)

"If the art of the detective began and ended in reasoning from an armchair, my brother would be the greatest criminal agent that ever lived. But he has no ambition and no energy. He will not even go out of his way to verify his own solutions, and would rather be considered wrong than take the trouble to prove himself right."

AUGUST 26

"THE ADVENTURE OF THE
BRUCE-PARTINGTON PLANS" (1908)

"[Mycroft] has the tidiest and most orderly brain, with the greatest capacity for storing facts, of any man living. . . . All other men are specialists, but his specialism is omniscience."

AUGUST 27

"THE GREEK INTERPRETER" (1893)

Mycroft Holmes was a much larger and stouter man than Sherlock. His body was absolutely corpulent, but his face, though massive, had preserved something of the sharpness of expression which was so remarkable in that of his brother. His eyes, which were of a peculiarly light, watery grey, seemed to always retain that far-away, introspective look which I had only observed in Sherlock's when he was exerting his full powers.

"I am glad to meet you, sir," said he, putting out a broad, fat hand like the flipper of a seal. "I hear of Sherlock everywhere since you became his chronicler. By the way, Sherlock, I expected to see you round last week to consult me over that Manor House case. I thought you might be a little out of your depth."

"No, I solved it," said my friend, smiling.

"It was Adams, of course."

"Yes, it was Adams."

"I was sure of it from the first."

AUGUST 28

"THE ADVENTURE OF THE
BRUCE-PARTINGTON PLANS" (1908)

"It is as if you met a tram-car coming down a country lane. Mycroft has his rails and he runs on them. His Pall Mall lodgings, the Diogenes Club, Whitehall —that is his cycle. Once, and only once, he has been here. What upheaval can possibly have derailed him?"

AUGUST 29

"THE ADVENTURE OF THE
BRUCE-PARTINGTON PLANS" (1908)

"What is there for us to do?"

"To act, Sherlock—to act!" cried Mycroft, springing to his feet. "All my instincts are against this explanation. Use your powers! Go to the scene of the crime! See the people concerned! Leave no stone unturned! In all your career you have never had so great a chance of serving your country."

"Well, well!" said Holmes, shrugging his shoulders.

AUGUST 30

THE HOUND OF THE BASKERVILLES (1902)

"We have him, Watson, we have him, and I dare swear that before to-morrow night he will be fluttering in our net as helpless as one of his own butterflies. A pin, a cork, and a card, and we add him to the Baker Street collection!" He burst into one of his rare fits of laughter as he turned away from the picture. I have not heard him laugh often, and it has always boded ill to somebody.

AUGUST 31

"THE BOSCOMBE VALLEY MYSTERY" (1891)

"Holmes," I said, "you have drawn a net round this man from which he cannot escape, and you have saved an innocent human life as truly as if you had cut the cord which was hanging him. I see the direction in which all this points. The culprit is—"

"Mr. John Turner," cried the hotel waiter, opening the door of our sitting-room, and ushering in a visitor.

SEPTEMBER

It was a September evening, and not yet seven o'clock, but the day had been a dreary one, and a dense drizzly fog lay low upon the great city. Mud-coloured clouds drooped sadly over the muddy streets. Down the Strand the lamps were but misty splotches of diffused light which threw a feeble circular glimmer upon the slimy pavement. The yellow glare from the shop-windows streamed out into the steamy, vaporous air and threw a murky, shifting radiance across the crowded thoroughfare. There was, to my mind, something eerie and ghost-like in the endless procession of faces which flitted across these narrow bars of light—sad faces and glad, haggard and merry. Like all humankind, they flitted from the gloom into the light, and so back into the gloom once more.

The Sign of Four (1890)

SEPTEMBER 1

"A very commonplace little murder," said he. "You've got something better, I fancy. You are the stormy petrel of crime, Watson."

SEPTEMBER 2

"You never heard me talk of Victor Trevor?" he asked. "He was the only friend I made during the two years I was at college. I was never a very sociable fellow, Watson, always rather fond of moping in my rooms and working out my own little methods of thought, so that I never mixed much with the men of my year. Bar fencing and boxing I had few athletic tastes, and then my line of study was quite distinct from that of the other fellows, so that we had no points of contact at all. Trevor was the only man I knew, and that only through the accident of his bull terrier freezing on to my ankle one morning as I went down to chapel.

"It was a prosaic way of forming a friendship, but it was effective."

SEPTEMBER 3

THE SIGN OF FOUR (1890)

"Strange," said I, "how terms of what in another man I should call laziness alternate with your fits of splendid energy and vigour."

"Yes," he answered, "there are in me the makings of a very fine loafer, and also of a pretty spry sort of a fellow."

SEPTEMBER 4

"THE FINAL PROBLEM" (1893)

"I think that you had better return to England, Watson."

"Why?"

"Because you will find me a dangerous companion now. This man's occupation is gone. He is lost if he returns to London. If I read his character right he will devote his whole energies to revenging himself upon me. He said as much in our short interview, and I fancy that he meant it. I should certainly recommend you to return to your practice."

It was hardly an appeal to be successful with one who was an old campaigner as well as an old friend.

SEPTEMBER 5

"THE ADVENTURE OF WISTERIA LODGE" (1908)

"Come, come, sir," said Holmes, laughing. "You are like my friend, Dr. Watson, who has a bad habit of telling his stories wrong end foremost."

SEPTEMBER 6

"THE ADVENTURE OF THE CREEPING MAN" (1923)

It was one Sunday evening early in September of the year 1903 that I received one of Holmes's laconic messages:

Come at once if convenient—if inconvenient come all the same.

SEPTEMBER 7

"THE ADVENTURE OF THE SPECKLED BAND" (1892)

"Do you know, Watson," said Holmes, as we sat together in the gathering darkness, "I really have some scruples as to taking you to-night. There is a distinct element of danger."

"Can I be of assistance?"

"Your presence might be invaluable."

"Then I shall certainly come."

"It is very kind of you."

"Look here, Watson; you look regularly done. Lie down there on the sofa and see if I can put you to sleep."

He took up his violin from the corner, and as I stretched myself out he began to play some low, dreamy, melodious air—his own, no doubt, for he had a remarkable gift for improvisation. I have a vague remembrance of his gaunt limbs, his earnest face and the rise and fall of his bow. Then I seemed to be floated peacefully away upon a soft sea of sound until I found myself in dreamland, with the sweet face of Mary Morstan looking down upon me.

"You really have done remarkably badly. He returns to the house, and you want to find out who he is. You come to a London house agent!"

"What should I have done?" I cried, with some heat.

"Gone to the nearest public-house. That is the centre of country gossip. They would have told you every name, from the master to the scullery-maid."

SEPTEMBER 10

"THE ADVENTURE OF THE COPPER BEECHES" (1892)

"To the man who loves art for its own sake," remarked Sherlock Holmes, tossing aside the advertisement sheet of the *Daily Telegraph*, "it is frequently in its least important and lowliest manifestations that the keenest pleasure is to be derived. It is pleasant to me to observe, Watson, that you have so far grasped this truth that in these little records of our cases which you have been good enough to draw up, and, I am bound to say, occasionally to embellish, you have given prominence not so much to the many *causes célèbres* and sensational trials in which I have figured but rather to those incidents which may have been trivial in themselves, but which have given room for those faculties of deduction and of logical synthesis which I have made my special province."

SEPTEMBER 11

THE SIGN OF FOUR (1890)

"I never guess. It is a shocking habit—destructive to the logical faculty."

SEPTEMBER 12

"THE ADVENTURE OF BLACK PETER" (1904)

He had gone out before breakfast, and I had sat down to mine when he strode into the room, his hat upon his head and a huge barbed-headed spear tucked like an umbrella under his arm.

"Good gracious, Holmes!" I cried. "You don't mean to say that you have been walking about London with that thing?"

"I drove to the butcher's and back."

"The butcher's?"

"And I return with an excellent appetite. There can be no question, my dear Watson, of the value of exercise before breakfast."

SEPTEMBER 13

"THE DISAPPEARANCE OF LADY FRANCES CARFAX" (1911)

Sherlock Holmes was too irritable for conversation and too restless for sleep. I left him smoking hard, with his heavy, dark brows knotted together, and his long, nervous fingers tapping upon the arms of his chair, as he turned over in his mind every possible solution of the mystery.

"It has been a duel between you and me, Mr. Holmes. You hope to place me in the dock. I tell you that I will never stand in the dock. You hope to beat me. I tell that you will never beat me. If you are clever enough to bring destruction upon me, rest assured that I shall do as much to you."

"You have paid me several compliments, Mr. Moriarty," said [Holmes]. "Let me pay you one in return when I say that if I were assured of the former eventuality I would, in the interests of the public, cheerfully accept the latter."

"You have a theory then, [Inspector Baynes]?"

"And I'll work it myself, Mr. Holmes. It's only due to my own credit to do so. Your name is made, but I still have to make mine. I should be glad to be able to say afterwards that I had solved it without your help."

"Well, and there is the end of our little drama," I remarked, after we had sat some time smoking in silence. "I fear that it may be the last investigation in which I shall have the chance of studying your methods. Miss Morstan has done me the honour to accept me as a husband in prospective."

He gave a most dismal groan.

"I feared as much," said he. "I really cannot congratulate you."

I was a little hurt.

"Have you any reason to be dissatisfied with my choice?" I asked.

"Not at all. I think she is one of the most charming young ladies I ever met and might have been most useful in such work as we have been doing. She had a decided genius that way; witness the way in which she preserved that Agra plan from all the other papers of her father. But love is an emotional thing, and whatever is emotional is opposed to that true cold reason which I place above all things. I should never marry myself, lest I bias my judgment."

"I trust," said I, laughing, "that my judgment may survive the ordeal."

SEPTEMBER 17

"THE ADVENTURE OF WISTERIA LODGE" (1908)

"Now, my dear Watson, is it beyond the limits of human ingenuity to furnish an explanation which would cover both these big facts? If it were one which would also admit of the mysterious note with its very curious phraseology, why, then it would be worth accepting as a temporary hypothesis. If the fresh facts which come to our knowledge all fit themselves into the scheme, then our hypothesis may gradually become a solution."

"But what is our hypothesis?"

Holmes leaned back in his chair with half-closed eyes.

SEPTEMBER 18

THE VALLEY OF FEAR (1915)

"Well, what are we to do now?" asked MacDonald with some gruffness.

"Possess our souls in patience and make as little noise as possible," Holmes answered.

SEPTEMBER 19

"I have frequently gained my first real insight into the character of parents by studying their children."

SEPTEMBER 20

"It was in January, '85, that my poor father met his end, and two years and eight months have elapsed since then. During that time I have lived happily at Horsham, and I had begun to hope that this curse had passed away from the family, and that it had ended with the last generation. I had begun to take comfort too soon, however; yesterday morning the blow fell in the very shape in which it had come upon my father."

SEPTEMBER 21

The Count had risen from his chair, and his hand was behind his back. Holmes held something half protruding from the pocket of his dressing-gown.

"You won't die in your bed, Holmes."

"I have often had the same idea. Does it matter

very much? After all, Count, your own exit is more likely to be perpendicular than horizontal."

SEPTEMBER 22

"THE ADVENTURE OF CHARLES AUGUSTUS MILVERTON" (1904)

"You would not call me a marrying man, Watson?"

"No, indeed!"

"You'll be interested to hear that I'm engaged."

"My dear fellow! I congrat—"

"To Milverton's housemaid."

"Good heavens, Holmes!"

"I wanted information, Watson."

"Surely you have gone too far?"

"It was a most necessary step."

SEPTEMBER 23

THE SIGN OF FOUR (1890)

"It is of the first importance," he said, "not to allow your judgment to be biased by personal qualities. A client is to me a mere unit, a factor in a problem. The emotional qualities are antagonistic to clear reasoning. I assure you that the most winning woman I ever knew was hanged for poisoning three little children for their insurance-money, and the most repellent man of my acquaintance is a philanthropist who has spent nearly a quarter of a million upon the London poor."

SEPTEMBER 24
"THE RED-HEADED LEAGUE" (1891)

"What are you going to do, then?" I asked.

"To smoke," he answered. "It is quite a three pipe problem, and I beg that you won't speak to me for fifty minutes."

SEPTEMBER 25
"THE MAN WITH THE TWISTED LIP" (1891)

He took off his coat and waistcoat, put on a large blue dressing-gown, and then wandered about the room collecting pillows from his bed and cushions from the sofa and armchairs. With these he constructed a sort of Eastern divan, upon which he perched himself cross-legged, with an ounce of shag tobacco and a box of matches laid out in front of him.

SEPTEMBER 26

"THE ADVENTURE OF THE DEVIL'S FOOT" (1910)

He sat coiled in his armchair, his haggard and ascetic face hardly visible amid the blue swirl of his tobacco smoke, his black brows drawn down, his forehead contracted, his eyes vacant and far away. Finally he laid down his pipe and sprang to his feet.

"It won't do, Watson!" said he with a laugh. "Let us walk along the cliffs together and search for flint arrows. We are more likely to find them than clues to this problem. To let the brain work without sufficient material is like racing an engine. It racks itself to pieces. The sea air, sunshine, and patience, Watson—all else will come."

SEPTEMBER 27

"SILVER BLAZE" (1892)

For a whole day my companion had rambled about the room with his chin upon his chest and his brows knitted, charging and recharging his pipe with the strongest black tobacco, and absolutely deaf to any of my questions or remarks. Fresh editions of every paper had been sent up by our news agent, only to be glanced over and tossed down into a corner. Yet, silent as he was, I knew perfectly well what it was over which he was brooding. There was but one problem before the public which could challenge his powers of analysis, and that was the singular disappearance of the favourite for the Wessex Cup, and the tragic murder of its trainer. When, therefore, he suddenly announced his intention of setting out for the scene of the drama, it was only what I had both expected and hoped for.

SEPTEMBER 28

"THE FIVE ORANGE PIPS" (1891)

It was in the latter days of September, and the equinoctial gales had set in with exceptional violence. All day the wind had screamed and the rain had beaten against the windows, so that even here in the heart of great, hand-made London we were forced to raise our minds for the instant from the routine of life, and to recognize the presence of those great elemental forces which shriek at mankind through the bars of his civilization, like untamed beasts in a cage. As evening drew in, the storm grew higher and louder, and the wind cried and sobbed like a child in the chimney. Sherlock Holmes sat moodily at one side of the fireplace cross-indexing his records of crime, whilst I at the other was deep in one of Clark Russell's fine sea-stories, until the howl of the gale from without seemed to blend with the text, and the splash of the rain to lengthen out into the long swash of the sea waves.

SEPTEMBER 29

Suddenly there broke from the silence of the night the most horrible cry to which I have ever listened. It swelled up louder and louder, a hoarse yell of pain and fear and anger all mingled in one dreadful shriek. They say that away down in the village, and even in the distant parsonage, that cry raised the sleepers from their beds. It struck cold to our hearts, and I stood gazing at Holmes, and he at me, until the last echoes of it had died away into the silence from which it rose.

"What can it mean?" I gasped.

"It means that it is all over," Holmes answered. "And perhaps, after all, it is for the best."

SEPTEMBER 30

I could not help laughing at the ease with which he explained his process of deduction. "When I hear you give your reasons," I remarked, "the thing always appears to me to be so ridiculously simple that I could easily do it myself, though at each successive instance of your reasoning I am baffled, until you explain your process,"

OCTOBER

It was a wild morning in October, and I observed as I was dressing how the last remaining leaves were being whirled from the solitary plane tree which graces the yard behind our house. I descended to breakfast prepared to find my companion in depressed spirits, for, like all great artists, he was easily impressed by his surroundings. On the contrary, I found that he had nearly finished his meal, and that his mood was particularly bright and joyous, with that somewhat sinister cheerfulness which was characteristic of his lighter moments.

"You have a case, Holmes?" I remarked.

"The faculty of deduction is certainly contagious."

"The Problem of Thor Bridge" (1922)

OCTOBER 1

THE SIGN OF FOUR (1890)

"You see," he said with a significant raising of the eyebrows.

In the light of the lantern I read with a thrill of horror, "The sign of the four."

"In God's name, what does it all mean?" I asked.

"It means murder."

OCTOBER 2

THE HOUND OF THE BASKERVILLES (1902)

"And you, a trained man of science, believe it to be supernatural?"

"I do not know what to believe."

Holmes shrugged his shoulders.

"I have hitherto confined my investigations to this world," said he. "In a modest way I have combated evil, but to take on the Father of Evil himself would, perhaps, be too ambitious a task."

OCTOBER 3

"SILVER BLAZE" (1892)

"We are going well," said he, looking out of the window and glancing at his watch. "Our rate at present is fifty-three and a half miles an hour."

"I have not observed the quarter-mile posts," said I.

"Nor have I. But the telegraph posts upon this line are sixty yards apart, and the calculation is a simple one."

OCTOBER 4

THE HOUND OF THE BASKERVILLES (1902)

"You will see how impossible it is for me to go to Dartmoor."

"Whom would you recommend, then?"

Holmes laid his hand upon my arm.

"If my friend would undertake it there is no man who is better worth having at your side when you are in a tight place. No one can say so more confidently than I."

OCTOBER 5

"THE ADVENTURE OF CHARLES AUGUSTUS MILVERTON" (1904)

Holmes had remarkable powers, carefully cultivated, of seeing in the dark.

OCTOBER 6

"You come at a crisis, Watson," said he. "If this paper remains blue, all is well. If it turns red, it means a man's life." He dipped it into the test-tube and it flushed at once into a dull, dirty crimson. "Hum! I thought as much!" he cried.

OCTOBER 7
"THE ADVENTURE OF THE SPECKLED BAND" (1892)

"Holmes," I cried, "I seem to see dimly what you are hinting at. We are only just in time to prevent some subtle and horrible crime."

"Subtle enough, and horrible enough. When a doctor does go wrong, he is the first of criminals. He has nerve and he has knowledge."

OCTOBER 8
"THE FINAL PROBLEM" (1893)

"It has been an intellectual treat to me to see the way in which you have grappled with this affair, and I say, unaffectedly, that it would be a grief to me to be forced to take any extreme measure. You smile, sir, but I assure you that it really would."

"Danger is part of my trade," [Holmes] remarked.

"This is not danger," said [Moriarty]. "It is inevitable destruction."

OCTOBER 9
"THE RED-HEADED LEAGUE" (1891)

"The door was shut and locked, with a little square of card-board hammered on to the middle of the panel with a tack. Here it is, and you can read for yourself."

He held up a piece of white card-board about the size of a sheet of note-paper. It read in this fashion—

THE RED-HEADED LEAGUE

IS

DISSOLVED.

October 9, 1890

OCTOBER 10
THE SIGN OF FOUR (1890)

My mind ran upon our late visitor—her smiles, the deep rich tones of her voice, the strange mystery which overhung her life. If she were seventeen at the time of her father's disappearance she must be seven-and-twenty now—a sweet age, when youth has lost its self-consciousness and become a little sobered by experience.

OCTOBER 11

"It has long been an axiom of mine that the little things are infinitely the most important."

OCTOBER 12

I had seen little of Holmes lately. My marriage had drifted us away from each other. My own complete happiness, and the home-centred interests which rise up around the man who first finds himself master of his own establishment, were sufficient to absorb all my attention; while Holmes, who loathed every form of society with his whole Bohemian soul, remained in our lodgings in Baker Street, buried among his old books, and alternating from week to week between cocaine and ambition, the drowsiness of the drug, and the fierce energy of his own keen nature. He was still, as ever, deeply attracted by the study of crime, and occupied his immense faculties and extraordinary powers of observation in following out those clues, and clearing up those mysteries which had been abandoned as hopeless by the official police.

OCTOBER 13

"THE CROOKED MAN" (1893)

"That one word, my dear Watson, should have told me the whole story had I been the ideal reasoner which you are so fond of depicting."

OCTOBER 14

"THE MAN WITH THE TWISTED LIP" (1891)

Sherlock Holmes was a man, however, who, when he had an unsolved problem upon his mind, would go for days, and even for a week, without rest, turning it over, rearranging his facts, looking at it from every point of view, until he had either fathomed it, or convinced himself that his data were insufficient.

OCTOBER 15

"THE ADVENTURE OF THE CREEPING MAN" (1923)

It was a fine night, but chilly, and we were glad of our warm overcoats. There was a breeze, and clouds were scudding across the sky, obscuring from time to time the half-moon. It would have been a dismal vigil were it not for the expectation and excitement which carried us along, and the assurance of my comrade that we had probably reached the end of the strange sequence of events which had engaged our attention.

OCTOBER 16

"THE GREEK INTERPRETER" (1893)

"It will not be an easy door to force, but we will try if we cannot make someone hear us."

He hammered loudly at the knocker and pulled at the bell, but without any success. Holmes had slipped away, but he came back in a few minutes.

"I have a window open," said he.

"It is a mercy that you are on the side of the force, and not against it, Mr. Holmes," remarked the inspector as he noted the clever way in which my friend had forced back the catch.

OCTOBER 17

THE SIGN OF FOUR (1890)

"I never make exceptions. An exception disproves the rule."

OCTOBER 18

"But why not eat?"

"Because the faculties become refined when you starve them. Why, surely, as a doctor, my dear Watson, you must admit that what your digestion gains in the way of blood supply is so much lost to the brain. I am a brain, Watson. The rest of me is a mere appendix. Therefore, it is the brain I must consider."

OCTOBER 19

"That hurts my pride, Watson," he said at last. "It is a petty feeling, no doubt, but it hurts my pride. It becomes a personal matter with me now, and, if God sends me health, I shall set my hand upon this gang. That he should come to me for help, and that I should send him away to his death—!"

OCTOBER 20

Making our way among the trees, we reached the lawn, crossed it, and were about to enter through the window, when out from a clump of laurel bushes there darted what seemed to be a hideous and distorted child, who threw itself upon the grass with writhing limbs and then ran swiftly across the lawn into the darkness.

"My God!" I whispered; "did you see it?"

Holmes was for the moment as startled as I. His hand closed like a vise upon my wrist in his agitation. Then he broke into a low laugh and put his lips to my ear.

"It is a nice household," he murmured. "That is the baboon."

OCTOBER 21

"THE ADVENTURE OF THE COPPER BEECHES" (1892)

"But in avoiding the sensational, I fear that you may have bordered on the trivial."

"The end may have been so," I answered, "but the methods I hold to have been novel and of interest."

"Pshaw, my dear fellow, what do the public, the great unobservant public, who could hardly tell a weaver by his tooth or a compositor by his left thumb, care about the finer shades of analysis and deduction!"

OCTOBER 22

"THE ADVENTURE OF BLACK PETER" (1904)

"One should always look for a possible alternative, and provide against it. It is the first rule of criminal investigation."

OCTOBER 23

THE SIGN OF FOUR (1890)

As we drove away I stole a glance back, and I still seem to see that little group on the step—the two graceful, clinging figures, the half-opened door, the hall-light shining through stained glass, the barometer, and the bright stair-rods. It was soothing to catch even that passing glimpse of a tranquil English home in the midst of the wild, dark business which had absorbed us.

OCTOBER 24

"A SCANDAL IN BOHEMIA" (1891)

He disappeared into his bedroom, and returned in a few minutes in the character of an amiable and simple-minded Nonconformist clergyman. His broad black hat, his baggy trousers, his white tie, his sympathetic smile, and general look of peering and benevolent curiosity were such as Mr. John Hare alone could have equalled. It was not merely that

Holmes changed his costume. His expression, his manner, his very soul seemed to vary with every fresh part that he assumed. The stage lost a fine actor, even as science lost an acute reasoner, when he became a specialist in crime.

OCTOBER 25

"THE MAN WITH THE TWISTED LIP" (1891)

As I passed the tall man who sat by the brazier I felt a sudden pluck at my skirt, and a low voice whispered, "Walk past me, and then look back at me." The words fell quite distinctly upon my ear. I glanced down. They could only have come from the old man at my side, and yet he sat now as absorbed as ever, very thin, very wrinkled, bent with age, an opium pipe dangling down from between his knees, as though it had dropped in sheer lassitude from his fingers. I took two steps forward and looked back. It took all my self-control to prevent me from breaking out into a cry of astonishment. He had turned his back so that none could see him but I. His form had filled out, his wrinkles were gone, the dull eyes had regained their fire, and there, sitting by the fire and grinning at my surprise, was none other than Sherlock Holmes.

OCTOBER 26

"I left the house a little after eight o'clock this morning in the character of a groom out of work. There is a wonderful sympathy and freemasonry among horsy men. Be one of them, and you will know all that there is to know."

OCTOBER 27

"THE ADVENTURE OF CHARLES AUGUSTUS MILVERTON" (1904)

Holmes sat motionless by the fire, his hands buried deep in his trouser pockets, his chin sunk upon his breast, his eyes fixed upon the glowing embers. For half an hour he was silent and still. Then, with the gesture of a man who has taken his decision, he sprang to his feet and passed into his bedroom. A little later a rakish young workman, with a goatee beard and a swagger, lit his clay pipe at the lamp before descending into the street. "I'll be back some time, Watson," said he, and vanished into the night.

OCTOBER 28

"A SCANDAL IN BOHEMIA" (1891)

It was close upon four before the door opened, and a drunken-looking groom, ill-kempt and side-whiskered, with an inflamed face and disreputable clothes, walked into the room. Accustomed as I was to my friend's amazing powers in the use of disguises, I had to look three times before I was certain that it was indeed he.

OCTOBER 29

THE SIGN OF FOUR (1890)

"I think that you might offer me a cigar too," he said.

We both started in our chairs. There was Holmes sitting close to us with an air of quiet amusement.

"Holmes!" I exclaimed. "You here! But where is the old man?"

"Here is the old man," said he, holding out a heap of white hair. "Here he is—wig, whiskers, eyebrows, and all. I thought my disguise was pretty good, but I hardly expected that it would stand that test."

OCTOBER 30

"THE MAN WITH THE TWISTED LIP" (1891)

Holmes stooped to the water jug, moistened his sponge, and then rubbed it twice vigorously across and down the prisoner's face.

"Let me introduce you," he shouted, "to Mr. Neville St. Clair, of Lee, in the county of Kent."

Never in my life have I seen such a sight. The man's face peeled off under the sponge like the bark from a tree. Gone was the coarse brown tint! Gone, too, was the horrid scar which had seamed it across, and the twisted lip which had given the repulsive sneer to the face! A twitch brought away the tangled red hair, and there, sitting up in his bed, was a pale, sad-faced, refined-looking man, black-haired and smooth-skinned, rubbing his eyes and staring about him with sleepy bewilderment.

OCTOBER 31

THE HOUND OF THE BASKERVILLES (1902)

A hound it was, an enormous coal-black hound, but not such a hound as mortal eyes have ever seen. Fire burst from its open mouth, its eyes glowed with a smouldering glare, its muzzle and hackles and dewlap were outlined in flickering flame. Never in the delirious dream of a disordered brain could anything more savage, more appalling, more hellish be conceived than that dark form and savage face which broke upon us out of the wall of fog.

NOVEMBER

"It was a wild night. The wind was howling outside, and the rain was beating and splashing against the windows. Suddenly, amidst all of the hubbub of the gale, there burst forth the wild scream of a terrified woman."—*Helen Stoner*

"The Adventure of the Speckled Band" (1892)

NOVEMBER 1

"Do not think of revenge, or anything of the sort, at present. I think that we may gain that by means of the law; but we have our web to weave, while theirs is already woven."

NOVEMBER 2

"You are sure that she has not sent it yet?"

"I am sure."

"And why?"

"Because she has said that she would send it on the day when the betrothal was publicly proclaimed. That will be next Monday."

"Oh, then we have three days yet," said Holmes, with a yawn.

NOVEMBER 3

"Run down, my dear fellow, and open the door, for all virtuous folk have been long in bed."

NOVEMBER 4

"Circumstantial evidence is a very tricky thing," answered Holmes, thoughtfully. "It may seem to point very straight to one thing, but if you shift your own point of view a little, you may find it pointing in an equally uncompromising manner to something entirely different."

NOVEMBER 5

"Recognizing, as I do, that you are the second highest expert in Europe—"

"Indeed, sir! May I inquire who has the honour to be the first?" asked Holmes with some asperity.

"To the man of precisely scientific mind the work of Monsieur Bertillon must always appeal strongly."

"Then had you not better consult him?"

"I said, sir, to the precisely scientific mind. But as a practical man of affairs it is acknowledged that you stand alone. I trust, sir, that I have not inadvertently—"

"Just a little," said Holmes.

NOVEMBER 6

"THE ADVENTURE OF THE SIX NAPOLEONS" (1904)

"The affair seems absurdly trifling, and yet I dare call nothing trivial when I reflect that some of my most classic cases have had the least promising commencement. You will remember, Watson, how the dreadful business of the Abernetty family was first brought to my notice by the depth which the parsley had sunk into the butter upon a hot day."

NOVEMBER 7

"THE RED-HEADED LEAGUE" (1891)

"As a rule, when I have heard some slight indication of the course of events, I am able to guide myself by the thousands of other similar cases which occur to my memory. In the present instance I am forced to admit that the facts are, to the best of my belief, unique."

NOVEMBER 8

"THE ADVENTURE OF THE EMPTY HOUSE" (1903)

It was indeed like old times when, at that hour, I found myself seated beside him in a hansom, my revolver in my pocket, and the thrill of adventure in my heart. Holmes was cold and stern and silent. As the gleam of the street-lamps flashed upon his austere features, I saw that his brows were drawn down in thought and his thin lips compressed. I knew not what wild beast we were about to hunt down in the dark jungle of criminal London, but I was well assured, from the bearing of this master huntsman, that the adventure was a most grave one—while the sardonic smile which occasionally broke through his ascetic gloom boded little good for the object of our quest.

NOVEMBER 9

"A SCANDAL IN BOHEMIA" (1891)

"Wedlock suits you," he remarked, "I think, Watson, that you have put on seven and a half pounds since I saw you."

"Seven!" I answered.

"Indeed, I should have thought a little more. Just a trifle more, I fancy, Watson."

NOVEMBER 10

"THE ADVENTURE OF THE NOBLE BACHELOR" (1892)

"Draw your chair up, and hand me my violin, for the only problem we have still to solve is how to while away these bleak autumnal evenings."

NOVEMBER 11

"The Press, Watson, is a most valuable institution, if you only know how to use it."

NOVEMBER 12

"THE ADVENTURE OF
THE SOLITARY CYCLIST" (1903)

Holmes's quiet day in the country had a singular termination, for he arrived at Baker Street late in the evening, with a cut lip and a discoloured lump upon his forehead, besides a general air of dissipation which would have made his own person the fitting object of a Scotland Yard investigation. He was immensely tickled by his own adventures and laughed heartily as he recounted them.

"I get so little active exercise that it is always a treat," said he. "You are aware that I have some proficiency in the good old British sport of boxing. Occasionally, it is of service; to-day, for example, I should have come to very ignominious grief without it."

NOVEMBER 13
"THE ADVENTURE OF THE DEVIL'S FOOT" (1910)

Holmes paced with light, swift steps about the room; he sat in the various chairs, drawing them up and reconstructing their positions. He tested how much of the garden was visible; he examined the floor, the ceiling, and the fireplace; but never once did I see that sudden brightening of his eyes and tightening of his lips which would have told me that he saw some gleam of light in this utter darkness.

NOVEMBER 14
THE SIGN OF FOUR (1890)

"The main thing with people of that sort," said Holmes as we sat in the sheets of the wherry, "is never to let them think that their information can be of the slightest importance to you. If you do they will instantly shut up like an oyster. If you listen to them under protest, as it were, you are very likely to get what you want."

NOVEMBER 15
"THE BOSCOMBE VALLEY MYSTERY" (1891)

"It was a confession," I ejaculated.

"No, for it was followed by a protestation of innocence."

"Coming on the top of such a damning series of events, it was at least a most suspicious remark."

"On the contrary," said Holmes, "it is the brightest rift which I can at present see in the clouds."

NOVEMBER 16

"THE ADVENTURE OF THE BRUCE-PARTINGTON PLANS" (1908)

All the long November evening I waited, filled with impatience for his return. At last, shortly after nine o'clock, there arrived a messenger with a note:

Am dining at Goldini's Restaurant, Gloucester Road, Kensington. Please come at once and join me there. Bring with you a jemmy, a dark lantern, a chisel, and a revolver.—S. H.

NOVEMBER 17

"THE ADVENTURE OF THE PRIORY SCHOOL" (1904)

"I must take the view, your Grace, that when a man embarks upon a crime, he is morally guilty of any other crime which may spring from it."

NOVEMBER 18

"SILVER BLAZE" (1892)

"One true inference invariably suggests others."

NOVEMBER 19

"THE ADVENTURE OF THE
BRUCE-PARTINGTON PLANS" (1908)

In the third week of November, in the year 1895, a dense yellow fog settled down upon London. From the Monday to the Thursday I doubt whether it was ever possible from our windows in Baker Street to see the loom of the opposite houses. The first day Holmes had spent in cross-indexing his huge book of references. The second and third had been patiently occupied upon a subject which he had recently made his hobby—the music of the Middle Ages. But when, for the fourth time, after pushing back our chairs from breakfast we saw the greasy, heavy brown swirl still drifting past us and condensing in oily drops upon the window-panes, my comrade's impatient and active nature could endure this drab existence no longer. He paced restlessly about our sitting-room in a fever of suppressed energy, biting his nails, tapping the furniture, and chafing against inaction.

NOVEMBER 20
"THE FINAL PROBLEM" (1893)

"As you are aware, Watson, there is no one who knows the higher criminal world of London so well as I do. For years past I have continually been conscious of some power behind the malefactor, some deep organizing power which forever stands in the way of the law, and throws its shield over the wrong-doer. Again and again in cases of the most varying sorts—forgery cases, robberies, murders—I have felt the presence of this force, and I have deduced its action in many of those undiscovered crimes in which I have not been personally consulted. For years I have endeavoured to break through the veil which shrouded it, and at last the time came when I seized my thread and followed it, until it led me, after a thousand cunning windings, to ex-Professor Moriarty, of mathematical celebrity."

NOVEMBER 21
"THE FINAL PROBLEM" (1893)

"You have probably never heard of Professor Moriarty?" said he.

"Never."

"Ay, there's the genius and the wonder of the thing!" he cried "The man pervades London, and no one has heard of him. That's what puts him on a pinnacle in the records of crime. I tell you, Watson, in all seriousness, that if I could beat that man, if I could free society of him, I should feel that my own career had reached its summit, and I should be prepared to turn to some more placid line in life."

NOVEMBER 22

THE VALLEY OF FEAR (1915)

"I thought you told me once, Mr. Holmes, that you had never met Professor Moriarty," [asked Inspector MacDonald.]

"No, I never have."

"Then how do you know about his rooms?"

"Ah, that's another matter. I have been three times in his rooms, twice waiting for him under different pretexts and leaving before he came. Once—well, I can hardly tell about the once to an official detective."

NOVEMBER 23

"THE FINAL PROBLEM" (1893)

"I was sitting in my room thinking the matter over when the door opened and Professor Moriarty stood before me.

"My nerves are fairly proof, Watson, but I must confess to a start when I saw the very man who had been so much in my thoughts standing there on my threshold. His appearance was quite familiar to me. He is extremely tall and thin, his forehead domes out in a white curve, and his two eyes are deeply sunken in his head. He is clean-shaven, pale, and ascetic-looking, retaining something of the professor in his features. His shoulders are rounded from much study, and his face protrudes forward and is forever slowly oscillating from side to side in a curiously reptilian fashion."

NOVEMBER 24
"THE FINAL PROBLEM" (1893)

"You know my powers, my dear Watson, and yet at the end of three months I was forced to confess that I had at last met an antagonist who was my intellectual equal. My horror at his crimes was lost in my admiration at his skill."

NOVEMBER 25
"THE ADVENTURE OF
THE NORWOOD BUILDER" (1903)

"From the point of view of the criminal expert," said Mr. Sherlock Holmes, "London has become a singularly uninteresting city since the death of the late lamented Professor Moriarty."

"I can hardly think that you would find many decent citizens to agree with you," I answered.

"Well, well, I must not be selfish."

NOVEMBER 26
"SILVER BLAZE" (1892)

"See the value of imagination," said Holmes. "It is the one quality which [Inspector] Gregory lacks. We imagined what might have happened, acted upon the supposition, and find ourselves justified. Let us proceed."

NOVEMBER 27
"THE ADVENTURE OF WISTERIA LODGE" (1908)

The whole inexplicable tangle seemed to straighten out before me. I wondered, as I always did, how it had not been obvious to me before.

NOVEMBER 28
"THE ADVENTURE OF
THE GOLDEN PINCE-NEZ" (1904)

It was a wild, tempestuous night, towards the close of November. Holmes and I sat together in silence all the evening, he engaged with a powerful lens deciphering the remains of the original inscription upon a palimpsest, I deep in a recent treatise upon surgery. Outside the wind howled down Baker Street, while the rain beat fiercely against the windows. It was strange there, in the very depths of the town, with ten miles of man's handiwork on every side of us, to feel the iron grip of Nature, and to be conscious that to the huge elemental forces all London was no more than the molehills that dot the fields.

NOVEMBER 29

"THE ADVENTURE OF THE SPECKLED BAND" (1892)

Round his brow he had a peculiar yellow band, with brownish speckles, which seemed to be bound tightly round his head. As we entered he made neither sound nor motion.

"The band! the speckled band!" whispered Holmes.

I took a step forward. In an instant his strange headgear began to move, and there reared itself from among his hair the squat diamond-shaped head and puffed neck of a loathsome serpent.

"It is a swamp adder!" cried Holmes; "the deadliest snake in India. He has died within ten seconds of being bitten. Violence does, in truth, recoil upon the violent, and the schemer falls into the pit which he digs for another."

"My dear Holmes," said I, "this is too much. You would certainly have been burned, had you lived a few centuries ago."

DECEMBER

It was a bitter night, so we drew on our ulsters and wrapped cravats about our throats. Outside, the stars were shining coldly in a cloudless sky, and the breath of the passers-by blew out into smoke like so many pistol shots.

"The Adventure of the Blue Carbuncle" (1892)

DECEMBER 1

It was pleasant to Dr. Watson to find himself once more in the untidy room of the first floor in Baker Street which had been the starting-point of so many remarkable adventures. He looked round him at the scientific charts upon the wall, the acid-charred bench of chemicals, the violin-case leaning in the corner, the coal-scuttle, which contained of old the pipes and tobacco.

DECEMBER 2

"The most difficult crime to track is the one which is purposeless."

DECEMBER 3

It was not, I must confess, a very alluring prospect. The old house with its atmosphere of murder, the singular and formidable inhabitants, the unknown dangers of the approach, and the fact that we were putting ourselves legally in a false position all combined to damp my ardour. But there was something in the ice-cold reasoning of Holmes which made it impossible to shrink from any adventure which he might recommend. One knew that thus, and only thus, could a solution be found. I clasped his hand in silence, and the die was cast.

DECEMBER 4

"THE ADVENTURE OF THE MAZARIN STONE" (1921)

The prize-fighter, a heavily built young man with a stupid, obstinate, slab-sided face, stood awkwardly at the door, looking about him with a puzzled expression. Holmes's debonair manner was a new experience, and though he vaguely felt that it was hostile, he did not know how to counter it.

DECEMBER 5

"THE ADVENTURE OF CHARLES AUGUSTUS MILVERTON" (1904)

"You know, Watson, I don't mind confessing to you that I have always had an idea that I would have made a highly efficient criminal."

DECEMBER 6

"Once or twice in my career I feel that I have done more real harm by my discovery of the criminal than ever he had done by his crime. I have learned caution now, and I had rather play tricks with the law of England than with my own conscience."

DECEMBER 7

The day was just breaking when I woke to find the long, thin form of Holmes by my bedside. He was fully dressed, and had apparently already been out.

"I have done the lawn and the bicycle shed," said he. "I have also had a ramble through the Ragged Shaw. Now, Watson, there is cocoa ready in the next room. I must beg you to hurry, for we have a great day before us."

DECEMBER 8

"But I am prepared to bet that you will not guess the form that my exercise has taken."

"I will not attempt it."

He chuckled as he poured out the coffee.

"If you could have looked into Allardyce's back shop, you would have seen a dead pig swung from a hook in the ceiling, and a gentleman in his shirt sleeves furiously stabbing at it with this weapon. I was that energetic person, and I have satisfied myself that by no exertion of my strength can I transfix the pig with a single blow. Perhaps you would care to try?"

"Not for worlds."

DECEMBER 9

THE VALLEY OF FEAR (1915)

"Porlock is important, not for himself, but for the great man with whom he is in touch. Picture to yourself the pilot fish with the shark, the jackal with the lion—anything that is insignificant in companionship with what is formidable: not only formidable, Watson, but sinister—in the highest degree sinister. That is where he comes within my purview. You have heard me speak of Professor Moriarty?"

"The famous scientific criminal, as famous among crooks as—"

"My blushes, Watson!" Holmes murmured in a deprecating voice.

"I was about to say, as he is unknown to the public."

"A touch! A distinct touch!" cried Holmes. "You are developing a certain unexpected vein of pawky humour, Watson, against which I must learn to guard myself."

DECEMBER 10

"THE PROBLEM OF THOR BRIDGE" (1922)

"But what were his relations with the governess, and how did you discover them?"

"Bluff, Watson, bluff!"

DECEMBER 11

"THE ADVENTURE OF WISTERIA LODGE" (1908)

"There are no better instruments than discharged servants with a grievance, and I was lucky enough to find one."

DECEMBER 12

"THE ADVENTURE OF THE
MISSING THREE-QUARTER" (1904)

"I have heard your name, Mr. Sherlock Holmes, and I am aware of your profession—one of which I by no means approve."

"In that, Doctor [Armstrong], you will find yourself in agreement with every criminal in the country."

DECEMBER 13

"I have not all my facts yet, but I do not think there are any insuperable difficulties. Still, it is an error to argue in front of your data. You will find yourself insensibly twisting them round to fit your theories."

DECEMBER 14

"But you had retired, Holmes. We heard of you as living the life of a hermit among your bees and your books in a small farm upon the South Downs."

"Exactly, Watson. Here is a fruit of my leisured ease, the *magnum opus* of my latter years!" He picked up the volume from the table and read out the whole title, *Practical Handbook of Bee Culture, with Some Observations upon the Segregation of the Queen.* "Alone I did it. Behold the fruit of pensive nights and laborious days when I watched the little working gangs as once I watched the criminal world of London."

DECEMBER 15

THE VALLEY OF FEAR (1915)

"I said that I would play the game fairly by you, and I do not think it is a fair game to allow you for one unnecessary moment to waste your energies upon a profitless task. Therefore I am here to advise you this morning, and my advice to you is summed up in three words—abandon the case."

MacDonald and White Mason stared in amazement at their celebrated colleague.

"You consider it hopeless!" cried the inspector.

"I consider your case to be hopeless. I do not consider that it is hopeless to arrive at the truth."

DECEMBER 16

"THE ADVENTURE OF THE RED CIRCLE" (1911)

"Why should you go further in it? What have you to gain from it?"

"What, indeed? It is art for art's sake, Watson. I suppose when you doctored you found yourself studying cases without thought of a fee?"

"For my education, Holmes."

"Education never ends, Watson. It is a series of lessons with the greatest for the last. This is an instructive case There is neither money nor credit in it, and yet one would wish to tidy it up."

DECEMBER 17

"The pressure of public opinion can do in the town what the law cannot accomplish. There is no lane so vile that the scream of a tortured child, or the thud of a drunkard's blow, does not beget sympathy and indignation among the neighbours, and then the whole machinery of justice is ever so close that a word of complaint can set it going, and there is but a step between the crime and the dock."

DECEMBER 18

"I consider that a man's brain originally is like a little empty attic, and you have to stock it with such furniture as you choose. A fool takes in all the lumber of every sort that he comes across, so that the knowledge which might be useful to him gets crowded out, or at best is jumbled up with a lot of other things so that he has a difficulty in laying his hands upon it. Now the skilful workman is very careful indeed as to what he takes into his brain-attic. He will have nothing but the tools which may help him in doing his work, but of these he has a large assortment, and all in the most perfect order. It is a mistake to think that that little room has elastic walls and can distend to any extent. Depend upon it, there comes a time when for every addition of knowledge you forget something that you knew before. It is of the highest importance, therefore, not to have useless facts elbowing out the useful ones."

DECEMBER 19

"THE RESIDENT PATIENT" (1893)

"However, wretch as he was, he was still living under the shield of British law, and I have no doubt, Inspector, that you will see that, though the shield may fail to guard, the sword of justice is still there to avenge."

DECEMBER 20

"THE FINAL PROBLEM" (1893)

"I think that I may go so far as to say, Watson, that I have not lived wholly in vain," he remarked. "If my record were closed to-night I could still survey it with equanimity. The air of London is the sweeter for my presence. In over a thousand cases I am not aware that I have ever used my powers upon the wrong side. Of late I have been tempted to look into the problems furnished by nature rather than those more superficial ones for which our own artificial state of society is responsible. Your memoirs will draw to an end, Watson, upon the day that I crown my career by the capture or extinction of the most dangerous and capable criminal in Europe."

DECEMBER 21

I could tell by numerous subtle signs, which might have been lost upon anyone but myself, that Holmes was on a hot scent. As impassive as ever to the casual observer, there were none the less a subdued eagerness and suggestion of tension in his brightened eyes and brisker manner which assured me that the game was afoot.

DECEMBER 22

"I have worked with Mr. Holmes before," said Inspector MacDonald. "He plays the game."

"My own idea of the game, at any rate," said Holmes, with a smile. "I go into a case to help the ends of justice and the work of the police. If I have ever separated myself from the official force, it is because they have first separated themselves from me. I have no wish ever to score at their expense. At the same time, Mr. White Mason, I claim the right to work in my own way and give my results at my own time—complete rather than in stages."

"Why do you not solve it yourself, Mycroft? You can see as far as I."

"Possibly, Sherlock. But it is a question of getting details. Give me your details, and from an armchair I will return you an excellent expert opinion. But to run here and run there, to cross-question railway guards, and lie on my face with a lens to my eye—it is not my *métier*. No, you are the one man who can clear the matter up. If you have a fancy to see your name in the next honours list—"

My friend smiled and shook his head.

"I play the game for the game's own sake," said he.

"Look here, Holmes, this is simply impossible. This is a desperate man, who sticks at nothing. He may have come to murder you."

"I should not be surprised."

"I insist upon staying with you."

"You would be horribly in the way."

"In *his* way?"

"No, my dear fellow—in my way."

"Well, I can't possibly leave you."

"Yes, you can, Watson. And you will, for you have never failed to play the game. I am sure you will play it to the end."

DECEMBER 25

"I suppose that I am commuting a felony, but it is just possible that I am saving a soul. This fellow will not go wrong again. He is too terribly frightened. Send him to gaol now, and you make him a gaol-bird for life. Besides, it is the season of forgiveness. Chance has put in our way a most singular and whimsical problem, and its solution is its own reward. If you will have the goodness to touch the bell, Doctor, we will begin another investigation, in which also a bird will be the chief feature."

DECEMBER 26

"There is nothing in which deduction is so necessary as in religion," said he, leaning with his back against the shutters. "It can be built up as an exact science by the reasoner. Our highest assurance of the goodness of Providence seems to me to rest in the flowers. All other things, our powers, our desires, our food, are all really necessary for our existence in the first instance. But this rose is an extra. Its smell and its colour are an embellishment of life, not a condition of it. It is only goodness which gives extras, and so I say again that we have much to hope from the flowers."

DECEMBER 27

"THE ADVENTURE OF THE BLUE CARBUNCLE" (1892)

I had called upon my friend Sherlock Holmes upon the second morning after Christmas, with the intention of wishing him the compliments of the season. He was lounging upon the sofa in a purple dressing-gown, a pipe-rack within his reach upon the right, and a pile of crumpled morning papers, evidently newly studied, near at hand. Beside the couch was a wooden chair, and on the angle of the back hung a very seedy and disreputable hard felt hat, much the worse for wear, and cracked in several places. A lens and a forceps lying upon the seat of the chair suggested that the hat had been suspended in this manner for the purpose of examination.

"You are engaged," said I; "perhaps I interrupt you."

"Not at all. I am glad to have a friend with whom I can discuss my results."

DECEMBER 28

"Now, Watson, confess yourself utterly taken aback," said he.

"I am."

"I ought to make you sign a paper to that effect."

"Why?"

"Because in five minutes you will say that it is all so absurdly simple."

DECEMBER 29

A STUDY IN SCARLET (1887)

"I shall have him, Doctor—I'll lay you two to one that I have him. I must thank you for it all. I might not have gone but for you, and so have missed the finest study I ever came across: a study in scarlet, eh? Why shouldn't we use a little art jargon. There's the scarlet thread of murder running through the colourless skein of life, and our duty is to unravel it, and isolate it, and expose every inch of it."

DECEMBER 30

"But what I can't make head or tail of, Mr. Holmes, is how on earth *you* got yourself mixed up in the matter."

"Education, Gregson, education. Still seeking knowledge at the old university. Well, Watson, you have one more specimen of the tragic and grotesque to add to your collection. By the way, it is not eight o'clock, and a Wagner night at Covent Garden! If we hurry, we might be in time for the second act."

DECEMBER 31

"There's coffee on the table, Watson, and I have a cab at the door."

Index of Sources

To compile these quotations, we drew on a number of editions of Holmes stories, including the three wonderfully illustrated volumes of *The New Annotated Sherlock Holmes*, edited by Leslie S. Klinger (New York: W. W. Norton & Company, 2005–6), the compact and authoritative Oxford World's Classics editions, and, thanks to Google Books (friend to all contemporary literary detectives), a number of collections of the issues of the *Strand* in which the stories were first published.

"The Adventure of the Dancing Men," January 9, January 27,
    March 25, December 28

"The Adventure of the Devil's Foot," January 14, February 18,
    February 22, March 14, March 16, June 1, September 26,
    November 13

"The Adventure of the Dying Detective," January 30, February
    26, April 11, April 27, June 13

"The Adventure of the Empty House," February 8, March 19,
    April 29, May 5, June 5, July 21, November 8

"The Adventure of the Engineer's Thumb," June 22

"The Adventure of the Golden Pince-Nez," January 5, Novem-
    ber 3, November 28

"The Adventure of the Mazarin Stone," March 29, April 7,
    June 12, August 9, September 21, October 18, December 1,
    December 4, December 24

"The Adventure of the Missing Three-Quarter," February 19,
    February 21, March 21, May 23, July 13, December 12

"The Adventure of the Noble Bachelor," June 6, November 10

"The Adventure of the Norwood Builder," April 17, June 29,
    November 25

"The Adventure of the Priory School," March 26, November
    17, December 7

"The Adventure of the Red Circle," February (general),
    February 17, March 15, March 18, April 20, May 8, June 10,
    December 16, December 30

"The Adventure of the Second Stain," March 28, April 19, May
    31, June 18

"The Adventure of the Six Napoleons," February 7, February
    28, June 27, June 30, November 6, November 11, December
    31

"The Adventure of the Solitary Cyclist," May (general), Sep-
    tember 9, November 13

"The Adventure of the Speckled Band," March 1, March 7,
    April 3, April 8, May 2, May 18, May 26, June 2, June 8, July
    16, July 20, July 24, August 4, September 7, September 29,

October 7, October 20, November (general), November 29

"The Adventure of the Three Students," February 2

"The Adventure of Wisteria Lodge," March (general), March 27, August 1, September 5, September 15, September 17, November 27, December 3, December 11, December 13, December 21

"The Boscombe Valley Mystery," January 25, February 10, March 11, March 17, March 24, June 3, June 25, July 5, July 12, August 6, August 31, November 4, November 15

"The Cardboard Box," April 25, April 28, August (general)

"A Case of Identity," January 26, February 1, March 3, March 10, May 1, May 11, June 4, August 17, October 11

"The Crooked Man," October 13

"The Disappearance of Lady Frances Carfax," January 10, February 9, March 13, May 14, July 18, August 22, September 13

The Extraordinary Adventures of Arsène Lupin, Gentleman-Burglar (by Maurice Leblanc, translated by George Morehead), February 29

"The Final Problem," April 24, May 3, May 4, July 29, September 4, September 14, October 8, November 20, November 21, November 23, November 24, December 20

"The Five Orange Pips," January 4, January 12, February 3, February 11, March 30, April 2, July 31, August 15, September 20, September 28, October 19, November 1

"The Giant Rat of Sumatra," referenced as the source for our April 1 quote, is a case mentioned in "The Adventure of the Sussex Vampire," but the story of that case was never published. The origin of this familiar noncanonical line is disputed.

"The 'Gloria Scott,'" September 2

"The Greek Interpreter," January 11, March 12, July 10, August 23, August 25, August 27, October 16

"His Last Bow," August 2, December 14

The Hound of the Baskervilles, January 19, April 15, April 21,

April 23, May 16, May 20, May 28, June 26, June 28, July 3,
    July 23, July 25, July 28, August 3, August 14, August 30,
    October 2, October 4, October 31, November 5
"The Man with the Twisted Lip," January 15, April 26, April
    30, June 11, June 15, September 25, October 14, October 25,
    October 30
"The Musgrave Ritual," February 25
"The Naval Treaty," January 13, February 23, April 5,
    September 1, October 6, December 2, December 26
"The Problem of Thor Bridge," March 23, May 29, October
    (general), December 10
"The Red-Headed League," January (general), January 17,
    January 31, March 22, March 31, July 26, August 5, August
    11, August 20, September 24, October 9, November 7
"The Reigate Squires," February 24, March 2, April 10, April
    14, July 2
"The Resident Patient," January 23, December 19
"A Scandal in Bohemia," February 15, March 20, April 4,
    May 13, July 1, July 27, August 12, September 30, October
    12, October 24, October 26, October 28, November 2,
    November 9, November 30
The Sign of Four, January 3, January 20, February 5, February
    14, March 8, April 16, May 21, May 27, June (general), June
    20, July 7, July 15, July 22, August 10, August 13, August 18,
    August 21, September (general), September 3, September
    8, September 11, September 16, September 23, October 1,
    October 10, October 17, October 23, October 29, November
    14
"Silver Blaze," January 18, February 13, May 22, July 9,
    September 27, October 3, November 18, November 26
"The Stock-Broker's Clerk," April 6
A Study in Scarlet, January 1, January 6, January 16, January
    24, February 4, February 27, March 4, March 9, April 9,
    May 25, May 30, June 14, June 17, June 21, June 23, June 24,

July 8, July 11, July 30, August 8, August 16, December 18, December 29

The Valley of Fear, April 13, April 18, May 15, June 9, July 4, July 17, July 19, August 7, August 19, September 18, November 22, December 9, December 15, December 22

"The Yellow Face," May 6, May 12, July 6

About the Editors

Levi Stahl is the marketing director of the University of Chicago Press and the editor of *The Getaway Car: A Donald E. Westlake Nonfiction Miscellany.*

Stacey Shintani is a project manager at One Design Company in Chicago and, like Holmes in his retirement, a beekeeper.

beautiful ENTOURAGE

book one of the beautiful entourage series

E. L. TODD

Fallen Publishing

Beautiful Entourage

Cover Design provided by Dinoman Designs

Editing Services provided by Final-Edits.com

Copyright © 2015 by E. L. Todd

All Rights Reserved

ISBN-13: 978-1511714594

ISBN-10: 151171459X

Rhett & Aspen

Rhett

Spring was approaching, and New York City was beginning to thaw from the ice that gripped it by the throat. With every passing day, the patches of snow melted and became smaller. Eventually, they disappeared altogether. The only reason I noticed this was because I hated winter. The bite from the cold sunk into my bones and made me stiff. My hands became cramped because they were frozen, and playing basketball with my friends became impossible. We could use the court at the gym, but of course, it was always booked.

I checked my phone to see the time. It was half past five and Troy hadn't arrived. I was sitting in a booth at our usual bar. My beer sat in front of me, untouched. The foam was heavy on top.

I hated foam.

Like I usually did when I had nothing to do, I checked my emails and text messages, wondering if I missed anything.

Sitting around and doing nothing was difficult for me. I always had to be doing something. If I wasn't productive, it was a waste of time. Some people said I had an astounding work ethic. But most people would say I didn't have much of a life.

Troy finally walked inside then spotted me. He wore a long sleeve gray shirt with a thick black jacket on top. His dark jeans faded into his black boots. Once he walked inside, he ordered a beer from the bartender, who flashed him a smile of interest, and then he joined me in the booth. "Hey, man."

I nodded to him. "How's it going?"

He held up his finger to silence me while he downed half his beer in a single drink. He returned the glass to the table, even though a coaster was right next to it, and then released a satisfied smile. "I could live off beer. Seriously."

"Nothing else?" I asked, humoring him. "Water is negligent?"

"Water is in beer, right?"

"True."

"Then I could do it."

"Food is pretty important," I said. "It would be difficult to live without."

"Then let me rephrase what I said." He took another drink before he continued. "I could live off beer and forgo any other liquid."

"You'd be drunk all the time."

He shrugged. "I'm better company anyway."

The corner of my lip upturned in a smile even though I wished it wouldn't. "How'd it go the other night?"

He rubbed his palms against his face. "Ugh..."

"That bad?" I asked with a laugh.

"Like you wouldn't believe."

I finally took a drink of my beer. "Spill it."

"So, we get to the wedding and everything is going smooth. She introduces me as her boyfriend, and I keep my arm around her waist, doing my job. Her friends show their interest, and I hear some of them whisper to one another about how cute I am."

"Sounds good so far..."

Troy held up a finger. "Wait for it."

I drank my beer again.

"We get through the ceremony and dinner. I meet her parents and they like me. Everything was going great. But then we ran into her ex."

"Isn't he the reason she hired you as her escort?"

"Yeah," Troy said. "Apparently, he cheated on her with her friend and she wanted to prove she was over him."

"Did it work?"

"The guy came at me swinging."

"What?" I asked incredulously. "He didn't say a word? He just attacked you?"

"I don't know, man." He finished his beer then waved at the bartender for another. "I turned and he was barreling down on me."

"What happened?"

"What do you think happened?" he snapped. "I beat the shit out of him." He pointed to his face. "I can't damage this. This is my livelihood right here. No guy is going to mess it up."

I nodded in agreement. "And then?"

"People broke us apart but he was in bad shape. They called an ambulance because he had a concussion. My date attended to him with tears in her eyes. Long story short, they got back together."

"Well, at least it had a happy ending," I said with a laugh.

"I guess," he agreed. "But once a cheater, always a cheater. She made a mistake."

"That's not always the case."

A sarcastic laugh escaped his lips. "If a guy doesn't have the balls to be upfront about his intentions, then he isn't going to be upfront about any aspect of his life. He prefers to hide in the shadows and cover up his mistakes. Every behavior is connected to every other behavior. If someone is a liar, then they'll lie about everything. If someone is a cheater, they won't respect any partner they have. I'm telling you, I know."

I suspected his philosophy had something to do with the bad break up he had a few years ago. "You're right. I'm not disagreeing with that. But I think some people can change. It's rare but it happens."

"I've never seen it," he said seriously.

"Maybe you need to look harder."

The bartender brought his second beer. "The glass just came out of the freezer." She gave him a playful smile, and I swear I saw her bat her eyelashes.

"Thanks, Brooke," Troy said with a smile. "You always take care of me."

She stood there for a moment, like she expected something to happen. "Well, let me know if you need anything else."

"I will," he said. "Thank you."

When she was gone, I shifted my gaze back to him "She's into you." I rested my arm on the back of the booth then looked out the window.

"I know." He took a drink then rested his elbows on the table.

"Not interested?"

He shook his head. "Nah." Troy was quiet about his personal life. If he were seeing someone, he probably wouldn't tell me about it. It was ironic since we'd been best friends for years. After his last serious girlfriend, he hadn't been hot on the dating scene. "What's new with you?" he asked.

"Nothing, really."

"Any escort dates gone haywire?" He drank half his beer in a single gulp.

I'd never been able to keep up with him. "No, I escorted this girl for a long time so her family would get off her back. Then that ended."

"Why?" he asked. "Didn't need you after the holidays?"

"No. She breached the contract."

He shook his head slightly and gave me a knowing look. "If I had a nickel every time the contract was breached, I wouldn't even need this job."

I chuckled slightly. "You're right about that."

"So, what was it? Sex? Kissing?"

"Neither," I said. "She told me she was in love with me."

He sighed in an irritated way. "She hoped you felt the same way?"

"Unfortunately."

"This is what I don't get." He started talking with his hands, his usual move when he was extremely passionate about something. "All women think we're going to change our minds. That we make the rules in order to break them. It's like it makes them want us *more*."

"There are worse problems than having women wants us," I said with a grin.

"But we're running a business here," he said. "It's an exchange of goods. We act like perfect boyfriends or whatever they want us to be and they pay us. Then we go our separate ways. We're an escort service, not a boyfriend service."

I agreed with him completely and utterly. But I also understood emotions could be complicated. "I think they grow attached to us and want our services to continue indefinitely. That's all."

"Whatever the case may be, it's annoying." He finished his second beer. "Delicious."

I was still on my first one. "If I didn't know you so well, I'd say you had a drinking problem."

"It's only two beers."

"Are you telling me you aren't about to order a third one?" I challenged.

He narrowed his eyes at me, irritated I could predict his behavior so well. "No, I'm not."

I laughed. "Damn liar."

"Who cares how many beers I drink?"

"I do," I said honestly. "I don't want you to stumble into a gutter then get your skull run over by the city bus."

"Like you wouldn't rejoice if that happened." He looked out the window.

"I admit the world would be a better place. But I would care—a little."

He rolled his eyes. "Shut the hell up, Rhett. You're nothing without me."

That was true. Having someone to confide everything to without judgment was nice. He didn't always reciprocate but I knew it wasn't personal. Not everyone had friends they considered to be family. I was one of the lucky few. "I wouldn't say that, but I would sorely miss you."

"That's better," he mumbled. "Have you had that date yet?"

I met a girl through mutual friends and we were going out tomorrow. "Not yet."

"She's pretty cute. I hope you score."

I shrugged, not really caring if I did or not.

"You don't sound excited."

"Every time I tell a date what I do for a living, they get weird about it."

He clanked his empty glass against mine. "I hear ya."

"I'm not a prostitute," I argued. "There's not even kissing involved. As soon as I say the word escort, jealousy and rage burns in their eyes. Then it goes nowhere."

"Just lie," he said. "Say you're a...cab driver or something."

"A cab driver?" I asked incredulously.

"Do you not know what a cab driver is?" he asked. "They drive around the city and—"

"I know what a cab driver is, Troy."

"Good. Tell them you do that."

"I'm sure girls love that..."

"Ooh!" He snapped his fingers. "CIA operative. Chicks are into that."

I gave him a serious look. "Do I look like a CIA operative?"

He shrugged. "I wouldn't know. I've never seen one before."

I finished my beer and let the comment go. "Hopefully I'll at least get laid."

"Dry spell?"

"Not really," I said. "But anytime I go on a date, I hope that's where it will lead."

"And if it doesn't?"

I shrugged. "If I like her, I'll ask her out again. If not, that's the end."

"You know, we could just become a real escort service and charge women big bucks to make them come."

"A glorified prostitute?" I asked.

"We don't use real names so what does it matter?"

"Could you really do that for a living?" I asked. "Because I want to get married and have kids someday. I'd be pretty ashamed if that's how I made my living. At least this is friendly more than anything else."

He shrugged. "The money would be amazing..."

"I'll pass." I gave him a pointed look. "I know you would too."

"Maybe...maybe not." He eyed the bar then turned back to me. "So, how much are you going to judge me if I order another beer?"

"Not at all," I said seriously. "Like always."

He clanked his empty glass against mine again. "I knew you were my friend for a reason."

***

I sat at the table near the window and waited for my date to arrive. I offered to pick her up but she insisted on meeting at the restaurant. I didn't ask any questions. Whatever the lady wanted, the lady would get.

She finally entered through the main doors and searched for me in the crowded room. Silverware scratched against plates and quiet chatter created the backdrop for the evening. Low burning candles sat at every table, and chandeliers glowed dimly from the ceiling.

I stood up so she would see me. I wore slacks and a collared shirt, wanting to be formal but not overbearingly stiff. My hands were in my pockets and I waited for her to notice me.

When she did, she headed my way, a nice smile on her lips. "I apologize for being late."

"No need for apology." I greeted her with a hug then pulled out the chair for her. I knew every manner that ever existed, and I knew how to act like a gentleman since it was my job. Now it was second nature to me.

"Thank you." She sat down then put her purse down on the chair beside her.

I sat across from her. "I ordered a bottle of wine. I hope you like red."

"I like anything with alcohol," she said immediately.

"Then we'll get along just fine." I didn't know Laura very well. We were barely on a first name basis. But she seemed cool. And, of course, she was pretty.

We made small talk about sports and TV shows. She used to play the violin when she was young but quit when she entered high school. Soon after, cheerleading consumed her life. And then in college, all she did was study. I told her a little bit about myself, skipping over the fact I was an escort, and tried to stick to safe topics.

Like always, I was fairly bored. Laura was very nice and beautiful but I didn't feel that pull that should come naturally in romance. It seemed to be impossible for me to feel a connection with anyone. It was odd because I got along with everyone I met. I wasn't judgmental and I didn't think anyone was beneath me. But I just didn't feel anything—period.

She brought up her job even though I didn't ask. She was a jewelry saleswoman for a place in Soho. It seemed like she enjoyed it. She was knowledgeable about diamonds and distinguishing their quality. It was a subject I knew nothing about.

"What do you do?" she asked. "Troy never told me."

Lying would be the easy way out. I could make up something, we would finish dinner, and then I would probably get laid. She was clearly interested in me, and her leg kept grazing mine under the table. She looked into my blue eyes like it was too hard to look away. "I'm an escort." I said it simply and didn't beat around the bush.

She stared at me like she hadn't heard me. "Sorry?"

"I'm an escort," I repeated. I wasn't ashamed of it and I didn't care if people judged me for it.

"Like...you have sex with people for money?" Disdain was in her voice. All the interest she had completely disappeared.

"No, never," I said calmly. "People mainly hire me so they can pretend they have a boyfriend. It gets family members off their backs or it makes their exes jealous. While there's handholding and innocent touches, there is no kissing or anything else physical involved. It's very professional."

She nodded slowly. "I see..."

Yeah, I lost her.

Some girls didn't care and thought it was interesting. Others, like this one, immediately hated the idea. I could see it in her green eyes and the rigidness of her shoulders. "I've been doing it for a while. It's also a companion service. I have one client that I meet at the park once a week and we play checkers. I do various things like that, not just pretending to be someone's love interest."

She nodded again. "Okay..."

I was immediately irritated but I didn't show it. What I did for a living wasn't that odd. It wasn't traditional, I admit that, but it didn't make me a bad person. If people understood what I did, the fact I actually help people, they wouldn't look down on me like this.

Fortunately, dinner was finished and the tab was sitting at the edge of the table. I slipped the money inside so we could go our separate ways and never see each other again.

She held her silence, her lips pressed tightly together in agitation.

Laura liked the rest of me, my hobbies and my personality. But all that was irrelevant compared to how I made a living. I tried not to take it offensively. Everyone was different, and some people just couldn't handle something so unique. "Well, it was nice to meet you, Laura." I stood up to embrace her.

She grabbed her purse and turned away. Without saying thank you for the meal or the evening, she walked out. Never once did she look back. The last thing I saw was her blonde hair as it disappeared out the door.

E.L. Todd

Aspen

Every year since I could remember, Harper and I gave each other flowers on our birthdays. We always left them on the doorstep in the morning, so as soon as the other woke up, the start of our birthday, no matter how old we felt, would make our day start off right.

I walked into the floral shop on the corner of fifth and Lankershim and perused the arrangements. Most people spent a long time choosing birthday cards because they had to be just right. Half an hour could pass and they wouldn't realize how much time they had wasted until they checked the time. That's how I was when I picked out flowers for my best friend. They had to be perfect.

They couldn't be the same color as last year, and they couldn't be the same flower either. I doubt Harper would even know since she wasn't a flower expert and didn't have the best memory, but that didn't matter. It was important to me.

I browsed through the rows and examined the various arrangements. I preferred to get her something in a vase so it would be ready to place on her kitchen table once she noticed them on her doorstep. She didn't even need to add water.

Deep maroon petals caught my eye when I heard a voice that immediately sent my body into defensive mode.

"We have to have lilies," the woman said. "Roses are tacky and overdone. I can't count the number of weddings I've been to this year alone where the roses were overkill." She had the voice of a fashion girl who flicked her wrist with every word she said. Without looking at her, I knew she was wearing a three hundred dollar pair of shoes and a purse that could pay someone's monthly mortgage.

I was in the back of the store, blocked in. If I moved, I would be seen over the arrangements of flowers.

"What does John like?" another girl asked. It was Casey, her best friend.

I hated hearing his name. It was like a poison dart just penetrated my skin and impaled me with a deadly substance. My heart palpitated as the memories swept through me. But now I saw them behind my eyes with nothing but regret.

"Oh, John doesn't care." I actually imagined her flipping her blonde hair over one shoulder. "He'll do whatever I say. No questions asked." She said it like it was something to be proud of, that her man was either too weak or too stupid to question her. I wasn't sure why I was ever with John to begin with. I preferred a man with a backbone.

I needed to get out of there. Her voice was like nails on a chalkboard. My ears burned with every spoken word. How did John put up with the sound of her voice? I guess it didn't matter because he probably only listened to her when her back was on a mattress and he was thrusting inside her.

"Would you like to look at our arrangements?" the florist asked.

You've got to be kidding me. Now what do I do?

"Yes, let's do it," she said.

Okay, I could try to sneak out like a coward or I could just hold my ground. Honestly, I just wanted to flee, and if I could slip out without being noticed, I would. But that didn't seem possible.

I turned my head sideways and pretended to be particularly interested in a vase of roses since I knew she wouldn't look at them. It seemed like a safe place to try and obscure my face.

"Most of these are ugly," she mumbled to Casey. But if I heard it, so did the florists. And that was pretty rude.

The fact she was so abrasive and inconsiderate made me question myself. I could talk shit about her all I wanted, but when it came down to it, John preferred her over me. So, I obviously had worse flaws. But I didn't know what they were because he never told me.

"These are okay," she said when she stopped a few feet away from me. "What do you think, Cass?"

I touched the rose gently like I was seriously considering it.

"Is there anything I can help you with, miss?" the florist asked.

Goddammit, leave me alone. "No, just browsing." I kept my face turned the opposite way.

"Pardon?" she asked, clearly not hearing me since I hadn't looked at her when I spoke.

"I'm okay," I said a little louder.

"Like, oh my god." When my arch nemesis said those words, I knew exactly why. "Casey, guess who's here?" Her whispers turned to excited taunts.

I'd been found. And there was nothing I could do about it.

"Hey, Aspen." She said it enthusiastically, like she was absolutely delighted to find me cornered and alone. "Just buying yourself some flowers? To cure the blues?"

"I bet she's sending them to herself too," Casey said. "To make it seem like a surprise."

I'd met a few bitches in my day, but these women were the queens. I turned to them and mustered a fake smile. "I'm buying flowers for my best friend. It's her birthday." These bullies couldn't intimidate me if they tried.

"Oh, how lovely," Isabella said with a fake smile. Her blonde hair framed her face and her perfect body was highlighted by the skin-tight dress she wore. Any time I saw her, whether it was in the morning or late at night, she was dressed like a celebrity. "At least you have someone to spend time with."

"Yeah, it's nice to have a friend that won't say mean things the second you turn your back, not that you would know what that's like."

"Well, you can't be talking about John since all he did was complain about you when he was cheating on you with me," Isabella snapped.

"Ooh," Casey said. "Good one."

That was cold, ice-cold. I kept a stoic face and pretended like she didn't slap me in the face with a tennis racket. "And he'll complain about you to the next mistress he finds when he grows tired of you."

"Well, I'm not a shitty lay," Isabella argued. "So he won't get tired of me."

Knowing John paraded our personal life to anyone who would listen hurt most of all. And the fact he complained about it, said whatever he said about moments I found personal and beautiful was enough to make me cry. But I kept it together, refusing to give this witch that satisfaction. "Have fun choosing your flowers for the big day. But make notes for the ones you'll have for your divorce." I casually walked away, keeping my head held high.

"Don't let the door hit your fat ass on the way out."

I stopped before I walked out. "If you fit through it, then I should be fine." I gave her a smile as rage contorted her face. She opened her mouth to speak but I walked out before giving her the chance to make herself look even more ugly than she already was.

***

As the assistant director of Refined Oil and Gas, I was tied up a lot. I didn't take lunch very often because I simply didn't have the time, and breaks were unheard of. But at least the time went by fast.

I handled all the finances, averted legal processing, and controlled the distribution of oil and energy. I was also in charge of research, and currently, we were working on new methods of clean energy. While oil was extremely profitable, the company wouldn't survive years down the road when climate changes were unavoidable or we simply ran out of resources. My boss didn't always agree with me, but I knew it was the best move.

His resistance to research was financial. It cost a lot of money to recruit college students to the research program. We found scientists all over the world, especially India and paid them big bucks to make us big bucks.

My boss was narrow-minded, and investing in something that wouldn't be cashed in until his lifetime had come and gone was all he cared about. It didn't matter if he had kids or something else to work toward. He was a very selfish man.

And he was my father.

My intercom went off. "Mr. Lane wants to see you in his office."

"Thank you, Cindy." I left my office then walked to his side of the building. His office was as big as an average house. It was covered in floor-to-ceiling windows, and he had a putting golf course inside. Whenever he was on speakerphone, he putted the golf ball around.

After I knocked, he ushered me inside. He was sitting at his desk, his jacket hanging over the back of his chair. Suspenders covered his shoulders to keep his pants up. He'd always been overweight since I could remember. But he never bothered to take care of himself or join a gym, despite my encouragement.

"How's your day going, Dad?"

He ignored the words entirely. "Why am I just hearing about a two million dollar investment into the research program?"

We already discussed this—countless times. But I kept my cool. "We can't expect our scientists to discover something without the right equipment. They petitioned to me several times that their lab tools and instruments were worn down and old. They need the best to discover the best."

He rubbed his temple then his eye as he usually did when he was extremely annoyed or about to scream. "Aspen." His voice reverberated off the walls and echoed long after he spoke. "I gave you this money for clean energy, but yet, they haven't discovered anything. They're just taking their checks and fooling around."

"I check on them daily, sir. I assure you, they're working hard. Most of them work overtime without pay."

He waved away my words. "This is a waste of resources, Aspen."

"No, it's not," I said calmly.

"Oil is where the money is."

"And oil won't always be around." I realized I was getting irritable. "Sir," I added.

"That's not my problem."

I had this conversation too many times to count. "With all due respect, it is your problem. This company won't survive the future without adapting and evolving. We must change with the world. Climate change is the biggest problem we face."

"Climate change is bogus." He lit a cigar and inhaled it.

Sometimes I wanted to quit. But I knew the company would be mine soon and I wouldn't have to argue with him anymore. I could add more funding to research and make this company stronger. But while he was still around, all he cared about was money. "Two million dollars is negligible to your net worth."

"But I've already put millions of dollars into this program with no return on my investment."

"Because these things take time," I said calmly.

He groaned and rubbed his temple again. He was in a particularly bad mood.

"Dad, they'll discover something soon, and people will pay any price to have it. Just remember that." Money was the only language he understood.

"You better hope so." He opened his drawer then browsed through some papers. Then he tossed a newspaper on his desk. "Have you read it?"

I looked at it but didn't pick it up.

"I asked you a question, Aspen." He stared at me with cold and unforgiving eyes. I didn't see any part of myself inside him. It was like I was adopted, which was what I hoped for sometimes.

He pushed it closer to me. "John and Isabella's wedding announcement. You should give it a read."

I kept a stoic face and pretended his words didn't cut me to the bone.

"Do you realize how embarrassing this is for me?"

My eyes narrowed on his face but I didn't explode. I didn't yell all the things I wanted to yell. I kept my cool and acted like the insults meant nothing to me. They were hollow bullets that went right through me.

"You become engaged to John and then he leaves you for someone else? Now he's marrying her?"

I didn't have anything to say. It wasn't my fault. I had no idea John was cheating on me. If I'd known, I wouldn't have stuck around. I wouldn't have accepted his marriage proposal.

"To your own cousin?" he demanded. "Now the whole world knows about it and thinks you're a fool—that I'm a fool." He grabbed the newspaper and ripped it into pieces, his anger directing his actions. "It's humiliating."

My breathing increased but I didn't show a single emotion.

"Please don't tell me you're going to cry." He gave me a disgusted look. "I told you to never cry in my presence."

"I'm not crying." My voice was low so I cleared my throat and spoke up, "I'm not crying."

"Good. Because it's annoying. Maybe that's why John left."

I averted my gaze and remained strong.

He was quiet for a long time, rubbing his temple like he was fighting off a headache. "I've been thinking...a lot about this fiasco."

I held my breath.

"I really don't think it's a good idea for you to be the face of this company. You brought me shame once. You'll do it again."

Knives stabbed each lung and I couldn't breathe. It was a death threat, a promise to ruin everything I worked for. I believed in this company and knew it could change the world. I was the person needed to commandeer this ship into prosperity. How could he take that away? "Sir, I'm more than qualified—"

"It's not about your qualifications. You do a great job—behind the scenes. I need someone that represents strength. You haven't even had a boyfriend in over a year. You just work all the time. When the American people look at you, they don't see a strong leader. They see a weak one who can't even keep the loyalty of a man. How will you keep the loyalty of a million people?"

His words were cutting me right where it hurt. But I kept my voice steady. "My personal life has nothing to do with my work ethic. And what happened between John and I wasn't my fault. He was the lying sleazebag, not me."

"Image is everything, Aspen. When will you realize that?" His voice was cold. "Unless you regain my trust and your image, I can't give you the company when I retire. You can keep your position indefinitely but I won't trust the company in your hands. I'm sorry. I wish things were different."

I didn't believe that for one second. I wanted to argue and scream. I wanted to knock his desk over then push it out the window. My hands balled into fists and I restrained myself from exploding with profanities and threats. I took a deep breath and stilled those emotions, understanding that arguing would get me nowhere.

"You're dismissed, Aspen." He took another puff of his cigar then turned back to his computer.

I stayed there for a moment, thinking of all the things I wanted to say to my father, my worst critic. But every feeling and emotion was irrelevant. I could scream at the top of my lungs but he would never hear me. I'd suspected it for a long time but never accepted it as truth—until now.

My father didn't care about me—at all.

***

"I'm so sorry I'm late." I arrived at the restaurant late because I cried when I got home then fell asleep. I didn't even have time to shower so I just threw on whatever I could find. I washed my face but I had a feeling nothing could dissolve my tearstains.

"It's totally fine." Harper held up her drink. "Some old guy bought me a Mai Tai. So, I was entertained."

I forced a chuckle. "Who says you can't have a good time alone."

"Who said anything about alone?" She shook her glass at me. "This was my best friend until you showed up. And we had a great time."

"I hope I'm not interrupting anything," I teased.

"I can juggle both of you." She put her drink down then gave me all her attention. "Thank you for the flowers. They were beautiful—like always."

"I hope they jump-started your day."

"They totally did," she said. "They're sitting on my kitchen table right now. I may not have a man, but I have a girl who loves me more than any man ever could."

"I'll drink to that." I held up an invisible glass then clanked it against hers. "Speaking of love…" I grabbed the small bag beside me then handed it to her. "Happy Birthday."

"You shouldn't have," she said. "You already got me flowers."

"Shut up," I said with a laugh. "Don't act like you don't want it."

"You're right," she said mischievously. She pulled out the tissue paper then found a picture frame. "Awe, this is when we saw David Letterman."

"It's a good picture," I said. "You look incredible."

She eyed the picture and smiled. "My tan looks amazing."

I laughed then tapped the bag. "There's something else."

She grabbed another picture frame but it was empty. She stared at it in confusion for a moment before she spotted the tickets inside. "You got tickets to see Kevin Hart?"

"Yep."

She screamed loud enough for everyone in the restaurant to hear. "Oh my god! I love him."

"I know you do." We watched his specials on Netflix at least twenty times.

"He's the most hilarious guy on the planet," she said. "Like, ever."

"And we'll take a picture there and put it in the picture frame."

"Awe." Her eyes crinkled in affection. "That was so sweet."

"I knew you would like it."

She came around the table and hugged me. "No. I love it."

I returned her warm embrace, feeling better than I had all day. It was nice to be in the arms of someone who loved me, someone who cared. I had a million problems on my plate but

I kept them to myself since it was her birthday. I wasn't going to bring her down with my baggage.

She returned to her side of the table. "This calls for fajitas!" She snapped her fingers like a Latin dancer.

"This is an Italian place," I said, trying not to laugh.

"Actually, I had a *few* Mai Tais. I forgot to mention that…" She snapped her fingers again.

"Well, we can try ordering them anyway." The thought was amusing. I could picture the waiter's expression as we made a ridiculous demand. He would regret waiting on our table.

She picked up the menu and scanned the selections. "What's the most fattening, greasy thing on here?"

I picked up my own. "The lasagna looks deadly on the waistband."

"Then that's what I'm getting." She threw her menu down. "It's my birthday so I get to be a pig today."

"So classy," I teased.

"Like you aren't going to order lasagna too." She gave me a pointed look then sipped her Mai Tai.

Actually, I was. "You know me too well."

"I'm like your boyfriend. I just don't put out."

"Unfortunately," I said with a chuckle.

"Pay for my dinner and I'll consider it." She winked at me.

"Flowers, show tickets, and dinner man you're difficult to get into bed."

"Now you know why I'm single."

The waiter came to our table and took our order.

"Two of the greasiest slices of lasagna please." Harper handed the menus to him.

His lips upturned in a smile. "I'll make sure the cooks prepare it to your specification."

"You can just pour grease on top if it's not enough," I said. "We'll still love it."

He chuckled. "You got it, ladies. Any special occasion?"

"It's my best friend's birthday," I said. "And she looks more beautiful than ever before."

Harper flipped her hair over one shoulder with an expression that clearly said, "Oh stop."

"In that case, the next round is on me," he said. "Happy Birthday."

"Wow...thank you," Harper said.

The waiter walked away, and Harper leaned forward to stare at his ass like it held the secrets to the universe. "He's got a nice behind."

I laughed. "Go for it."

She shrugged. "I'm just going to go home and be depressed anyway. May as well have a man to distract me."

"Wait, hold on." I raised my hand. "I buy you all these pretty things and I don't get anything? But he buys you a drink and you're going to put out?"

"Hey." She pointed at me. "When you get an ass like that, we'll talk."

A deep chuckle escaped my throat. "You're right. I can't compete with that."

"Not that you aren't immensely attractive," she said. "If I were a guy, I'd do you."

I flipped my hair over one shoulder just as she had done and gave her the same expression. "Oh stop."

She slapped the table with her hand as she laughed. Then she took another drink. "So, how was your day? I feel like all we're talking about is me."

"It's your birthday. We're supposed to talk about you."

"True," she said. "But I'm boring. So how was your day?"

Absolutely and completely horrendous. "Fine." I downed my water so I had something to do.

"Just fine?" she asked. "Normally when I ask you a question, you won't shut up."

The drawback to having a best friend was how well they knew you. Harper could read me better than I could read myself. This was dangerous because I didn't want to ruin her birthday with my bullshit. I could wait until tomorrow to drop my problems on her shoulders. "Well, I got a new plant for my office. It really lightens up the place." I kept a straight face and pretended to be normal.

Her eyes narrowed in suspicion.

Goddammit. "For lunch, I ate a salad. I don't know what I was thinking. I hate salads for a reason, and the leafy lettuce and low-fat dressing was disgusting. I should have gotten a burger instead. What was I thinking?"

Harper still wasn't buying it. "Aspen, what happened?"

Why did she have to know me so damn well? "It's fine, really. I just had a long day."

She leaned closer over the table and examined my face like I was a painting on display. "Have you been crying?"

"No!"

"Aspen, you better tell me right now or I'm going to drag it out of you."

"It can wait until tomorrow."

She rolled her eyes. "Aspen, I don't care about my birthday and you know that. The only reason I celebrate it is because you force me to. If I had it my way, I'd be drinking in my apartment alone until midnight." She got that fiery look in her eyes like she wanted to rip me apart. "Now spill it, chicka."

"Honestly, it can wait," I said. "We're having a good time."

She gave me a pissed look, the one she gave before she threw a tantrum. "Don't make me cause a scene. I'll do it."

I sighed and rolled my eyes at the same time. "Fine."

She leaned forward and prepared to listen to my story.

I told her everything, from bumping into that witch Isabella to the argument I had with my father. I released the air from my lungs when I was finished.

"Ohmygod!" Harper slammed her fists on the table. "Talk about a day from hell."

"Hell is an understatement."

"You should have broken that pretty nose of hers."

I was more of a lover than a fighter. "Not worth my time. I don't think it would make me feel better either."

"What does he see in her? She's a total skank."

She mentioned he said I was terrible in bed. I admit I wasn't the adventurous type. John was my first so I didn't have much experience. I was shocked he would hold that against me. It really hurt my feelings, even though it shouldn't, so I kept it from Harper. I was embarrassed because I knew John was right. "Well, you like what you like, right?"

"But I'm more pissed off at your father. I've never heard of such a cold tyrant in my life."

I shrugged, unsure what to say.

"All he cares about is how it affects him. Has he ever asked how you felt?" She was practically yelling. "His daughter was dumped for some other girl and all he cares about is his image. It wasn't even your fault. John was the jackass, not you."

"Dad doesn't see it that way."

"And it has nothing to do with your work ethic. It's not fair!" She slammed her hand on the table again. She was more upset about it than I was.

"He's never been an emotional guy. All he cares about is money, and apparently, me being humiliated publicly hurts his bank account in some way."

"I'll take him out," she said seriously. "I'll smack him right in front of the media and see how that affects his bank account."

A laugh escaped my lips involuntarily. The idea of Harper, a hundred pound woman at five feet in height, smacking my father around was extremely amusing. "I'd pay good money to see that."

"Teach that tyrant a lesson..." She shook her head while the anger bubbled in her eyes.

The waiter brought the dishes. "Extra greasy, just as you asked."

"You did good," I said. "Expect a good tip."

Harper looked at her plate. "There's so much cheese. I'm going to be constipated for a month but I don't even care."

I tried not to laugh at her bluntness.

The waiter seemed amused, with a slight smirk on his lips. "Maybe we can get breakfast tomorrow with lots of coffee and fiber to help you out."

I liked this guy. He was playful and not stuck up, but he wasn't trashy either.

"I like your thinking," Harper said with a flirty look.

"I get off at ten," he said. "Do you have plans?"

"Well, I was supposed to head to space in my rocket shuttle but I could reschedule it," Harper said.

"That's generous of you," he said affectionately.

"Oh wait!" She smacked her forehead. "I can't. I'm with my girl tonight. She needs me. Tomorrow?"

"No." I waved her words away. "It's fine, really. Go out with him."

"But—"

"She'll be ready at ten," I said to the waiter.

He smiled. "I look forward to it, Harper." Then he walked away.

She gave me that look I'd known for years. "I can go out with him tomorrow."

"No." I wouldn't budge on this. "There's nothing you can do anyway. My life isn't fabulous right now but that's no one's fault."

"It's John's fault, actually," she said with anger.

"Whatever," I said, brushing it off. "Honestly, I want you to go out with him. He's got a nice ass and all. Consider him my final present."

Her lips stretched into a slow smile. "You're sure?"

"Absolutely," I said firmly.

"Okay." She let the topic drop. "Back to me bitching about all of this, why don't you just quit? You have an MBA. You could work somewhere else."

The thought crossed my mind many, many times. "I can't. That company is important to me."

"Why?"

"It has all the resources to research clean and sustainable energy. We could find something better than solar power that could be used in all sorts of machines, whether it's nuclear plants or buses. Climate change is a serious problem, and my father's company has the ability to make a huge change. If we find something better, other companies could follow in our footsteps—all over the world. It's not about money or power. It's about the future."

She smiled. "When your eyes glow and your cheeks redden, I know you're particularly passionate."

I was slightly embarrassed I was so easily readable but I let it go. "I can't just leave. The only reason there's any research at all is because of me. If I walk out, my dad will shut it down and drill for more oil. Since his life is almost over, he only cares about immediate returns. The future generations mean nothing to him. I can't walk out. It's not an option."

She grabbed her glass and clanked it against mine. "It's people like you that make me believe in humanity. I'm proud of you."

Her touching words made me blush. "I'm just doing what I think is right. I want to have kids someday. This affects them. And my grandchildren...and my great grandchildren...and the whales, polar bears, and Oregon birds. It affects us all."

She released a sigh. "This conversation just got extremely depressing."

I laughed even though it wasn't funny. "I'm sorry. I have a way of doing that..."

"Well, what are you going to do?" she asked. "How are you going to change his mind?"

I'd been thinking about it all day. "I'm going to have to get a perfect boyfriend to make up for what John did. When he sees I can have a stable relationship with a successful man, his image of me will improve and he'll reconsider."

She nodded. "That makes sense. Where are you going to find a boyfriend? Online dating?"

I'd lost faith in the institution of relationships. Perhaps I hadn't moved on from what John did to me and I was still a little bitter about it, but regardless, I wasn't ready for a relationship. "I don't know. I'm not in the right place for a relationship right now and I don't want to waste some guy's time. That wouldn't be fair."

She took a bite of her lasagna and spent a whole minute chewing it because it was so big. When she finally swallowed it, her eyes widened. "I have a perfect idea!"

"What?" I asked eagerly.

"Hire an escort."

All the energy I had disappeared. "A male prostitute? Harper, you've had some crazy ideas but this has to be—"

"No." She held up her hand. "My friend hired this guy to take to her friend's wedding because her ex would be there. She just paid him to act as her date. There's no sex or anything like that at all. They don't even offer sex. They are super professional. And apparently, the guy was smoking hot."

I'd never heard of that before.

"Hire a guy to act as your boyfriend for a while. When your dad gets off his high horse and stops acting like a smelly douchebag—"

"Smelly douchebag?"

Harper ignored the interruption. "Then you can stop paying for his services. Once the company is legally yours, then your dad can't do anything about it. The guy doesn't get hurt because it's just business, and you don't have to deal with a real boyfriend since you aren't ready for one. Dude, it's perfect."

"Dude?"

"Did you listen to a word I said?" she demanded.

"I did."

"What do you think?" she asked.

31

I ate a few bites of my lasagna while I considered her proposal. "I don't know...paying some guy to be my boyfriend is a little...pathetic."

"You aren't making him be your boyfriend," she argued. "He's just a figurehead. It doesn't make you pathetic. It's not like you actually have feelings for the guy and pay him to make you feel good. It's not like that all. People do this all the time."

"I don't know..."

She pulled out her phone and started texting someone. "I'll ask her what the company was called."

"Don't tell her it's for me!"

"I won't," she hissed. "If she asks, I'll say it's for me." She put her phone down then returned to eating.

I picked at my food, unable to believe I was actually considering this.

Her phone vibrated on the table and she snatched it like a snake. Her eyes narrowed as she read the message.

"What did she say?"

"It's called Beautiful Entourage." Her eyes were glued to her screen. "She said the guy was worth every penny and he was a total sweetheart. She would do it again in a heartbeat. And she thinks her ex was jealous." She looked up at me. "Dude, do it."

"Since when did you start calling me dude?"

"Aspen, do it. How much fun would it be to have eye candy everywhere you go?"

"A little weird, actually."

"I bet his ass looks amazing."

I felt guilty when I wondered how amazing it looked.

"I'm making you do this," she said. "This is going to happen."

"You just want to see how hot he is."

"Do not!" She feigned innocence.

I gave her a look that said, "Bullshit."

"Okay, fine. Maybe..."

"You got a date tonight with a guy with a great ass. Don't get greedy on me."

She twirled her hair playfully. "True..."

"I'll think about it, okay?"

"You better think about it," she said. "And if your answer is no, I'm just going to change it. So save us both some time by just saying yes."

I pushed the Mai Tai closer to her. "Drink up and finish your greasy lasagna."

She gave me an affectionate look. "You know me so well, bestie."

"Better than you know yourself."

E.L. Todd

Rhett

I just got home when my phone rang. It was Mrs. Robinson, the woman who lived across the hall from Chase. Anytime I saw her name on my phone, I dreaded taking the call. I forced myself to remain calm before I answered. "What's he done now?"

"You really need to consider putting him in assisted living."

That wasn't an option. "What happened?"

"He's in the laundry room, cowering in the corner and shaking uncontrollably. I can't get him to move or do anything. You'll need to come down here."

I held back the irritation deep in my throat. "Thank you for calling me. I'll be there in a second." I hung up without waiting for her reply.

I put my shoes back on then left my apartment. He was just a few blocks from me, far enough away that I had some privacy but close enough for me to reach him quickly when the need arose.

When I entered the building, I headed to the basement where the laundry room was located. As soon as I walked inside, I found Chase sitting in the corner. His knees were pulled to this chest and he covered his head with his arms like boulders were crashing down on him.

Mrs. Robinson stood a few feet away. "He's been like that for half an hour."

"Is he hurt?" I asked.

"No."

I saw the pile of his laundry on the washer. The clothes didn't even make it inside before he freaked out. Chase had episodes often, and sometimes I didn't know how to handle them. I did my best, but I knew it wasn't enough.

"Rhett, is that you?" Chase called from under his arms.

"It's me." I came beside him then touched his arm. "Buddy, there's nothing to be scared of."

"The shadows, they're here." He trembled under my touch.

"Chase, they won't hurt you." My brother had sciophobia, the fear of shadows. Sometimes it was hilarious, but other times, like now, it was just sad. "They're only the absence of light, not physical."

"They still hurt me."

"They don't hurt you." I kept my voice gentle.

"I was trying to do my laundry when someone turned on the light...and then they moved in."

Mrs. Robinson gave him a sad look. "Your brother needs help, Rhett."

"I'm not going to a hospital," Chase said forcibly. "You can't make me."

"No one is taking you to a hospital, Chase." He needed to hear that so he would stay calm. I stood up then turned off the light. "There are no more shadows, Chase. You can relax now."

There was dim light through the small window near the ceiling. I could barely distinguish him and it took a moment for my eyes to adjust.

"Are you sure?" he asked hesitantly.

"I can barely see two inches in front of my face."

He removed his hands and looked around. He breathed a sigh of relief then turned to me. "I want to go back to the apartment."

"Sounds like a good idea."

He grabbed his night vision goggles then put them on over his face.

Mrs. Robinson gave me that look she always gave me. It clearly said, "This is *not* normal."

I ignored the look then grabbed his clothes and put them in the hamper.

Chase wrapped a blanket made out of foil around his body. "Okay, let's go." His head was covered and he held onto my arm so I could guide him. Together, we walked up the floors until we entered his apartment.

The place was covered in glow-in-the-dark lights. They marked the floor and the hallways. Various lights were on cabinets, giving enough light to see without casting any shadows. The windows were completely covered with black shutters, obscuring any light.

Chase threw off the blanket once he was inside. "I feel better now..."

I set the laundry basket on the counter. "What happened, man?"

"I was doing my laundry in the dark when this lady turned on the light. I couldn't reach my light-guarder and the room started to spin. The shadows were about to get me when you arrived."

I'd tried telling him, on numerous occasions, that his fear was absurd and fake. But no amount of logic would change his mind. When I tried to admit him to a psychiatric ward, he tossed, turned and screamed for help. It was so painful to watch that I took him home and didn't make the attempt again. He wasn't a danger to himself or anyone else so I didn't see what the harm was. "I'll do your laundry at my place then bring it back."

"Thanks." He sat on the couch, and then acting like everything was totally normal, turned on the TV. "Want to watch the game?"

I held back any irritation I had, knowing his sickness was real. "Sure."

"There's beer in the refrigerator."

I grabbed two then sat beside him. He had the hookups for a washer and dryer in the apartment but I purposely didn't buy him the appliances so he would be forced to join the rest of society downstairs. I brought him groceries but made him do some errands on his own. After sunset, he went out, but it was always with an anxious heart. The times I could get him out in the daylight were times when I talked him into it and promised the shadows wouldn't get him. I even lied and said I had a Shadow Sword that would defeat them instantly if they tried to harm us. That usually did the trick.

Chase was normal in every other way. He loved sports, movies, and music. He played guitar and loved women. Somehow, he got dates, usually finding them online. When they came to his apartment, they thought he was just extremely eccentric. He never mentioned his fear of shadows, and if he did, they would probably find it endearing because he was so charismatic. He was a good-looking guy and had a weight room in the apartment. I was always afraid he would get hurt lifting weights in limited light but it never happened.

"Seriously, where do they find these refs?" he asked. "On Craig's list?"

I laughed then drank my beer.

My brother was a computer programmer and he was very gifted at it, so he didn't have to leave the apartment. But he didn't make much money because no one wanted to hire someone who refused to ever come into the office. So, I supported him. I didn't resent him for it. It was better than us living together. I refused to let that happen. I couldn't live in the dark.

"I think I'm going to get you a washer and dryer," I said.

"You don't have to do that," he said immediately. "I'll just go in the middle of the night when everyone is asleep."

That wasn't a way to live. "I don't mind."

"You do enough for me as it is." He drank his beer then set it on his thigh.

"Well, I'm going to do it anyway."

He stared at the TV for a while before he turned to me. "Thanks, man."

"Yeah."

"What's new with you?"

"Nothing, really."

"How'd that date go?" he asked.

"It didn't work out," I said vaguely. "How about you?"

"Liz and I stopped seeing each other last week."

His relationships never worked out, but I suspected Chase wasn't looking for something serious. He seemed content with his life as a single guy, but like everyone else, he had needs. "You okay?"

"I'm fine," he said. "It ran its course. She comes over once in a while for sex then leaves."

"Well, that's convenient," I said with a chuckle.

"Works out for me," he said with a grin.

We watched the game for the next hour, and the beers were depleted. After a while, I got used to the odd lighting in the apartment. In a weird way, it was comfortable. But I couldn't do it for more than a few hours at a time. "I should go. I got to get this laundry done."

Chase walked me to the door. "Thanks. I'll come by tomorrow night and grab it."

"I'll drop it off," I said. "Don't worry about it." I grabbed the basket on the counter but he stopped me.

He pulled me into a hug and patted me on the back. "Thanks, brother. I really don't know what I'd do without you."

I returned the embrace then held him close. Other people might see Chase as a freak but he wasn't. He was just someone who was different. He was still the same person underneath, fun, loyal, and funny. "No problem."

"I'll see you tomorrow," he said. "You want to watch the game?"

"Sure. I'll bring a pizza."

"You're bringing the laundry," he said. "I'll order the pizza. It's the least I can do."

I nodded. "That sounds good."

He opened the door and stayed behind it, steering clear of the lighted hallway. "See ya."

"Bye, Chase."

Aspen

I couldn't believe I was doing this.

After long consideration, I realized this was the best decision for me. It would help me get the company, no one would get hurt except my bank account, and it was convenient.

Beautiful Entourage was difficult to find. I found the location using the GPS on my phone but I wound up in front of a Chinese restaurant. I checked the address several times, wondering if I got the wrong information.

When I couldn't figure it out, I decided to call the number.

A woman answered. "Beautiful Entourage, where we'll find your next date for your special event. I'm Danielle. How may I help you?"

"Uh, hi." I didn't expect the person who answered to be so formal. "I'm having a tough time locating your office."

She chuckled. "In front of the Chinese restaurant?"

At least I wasn't the first one to get lost. "Yes."

"If you turn to the right, you'll see a staircase. We're on the second floor. We really need to put a sign out there or something."

"It wouldn't hurt," I said with a laugh.

"Come on up. I've got a cup of coffee with your name on it. It must have been a tiring journey."

"I'll see you soon." I hung up then headed to the staircase. I climbed it to the top then stepped inside. It was contrastingly different from the Chinese restaurant down below. It had elegant hardwood floors and floor-to-ceiling windows. Light jazz music played in the background, and there was a water cooler along with a table covered in coffee supplies. Leather couches were positioned in the lobby.

"I'm Danielle." A woman in a pencil skirt approached me with her hand outstretched. "Sorry about the Oregon Trail we put you on."

I laughed as I shook her hand. "It's okay. It burned extra calories."

She looked me up and down. "Like you need to burn extra calories."

I didn't know what to say to that so I looked around. "This place is nice."

"A lot of people are surprised. I think they expect to walk into a brothel or something." She chuckled then approached her desk. "Take a seat. How do you prefer your coffee?"

"Black, please."

"Coming right up."

I sat down and looked at her elegant desk. There was a pot of flowers, and the surface of the wood was so shiny I could see my reflection. There were no picture frames and her area looked bare. But it was also classy at the same time.

She set the coffee down then rested her folded hands on the desk. "I didn't catch your name."

"Aspen."

"Pretty," she said. "How can I help you, Aspen?"

I felt embarrassed that I was there. Did she think I was a loser who couldn't get my own dates?

Danielle spotted my unease. "I can tell this is your first time."

"A friend told me about it and encouraged me to give it a shot."

"Well, tell me what you need first. We'll go from there."

I told her about my issue with my father but left out John since that was mortifying. "He just wants me to be more *proper*."

She nodded. "We've had similar situations to that. You aren't the first." She gave me a smile then pulled out a few papers. "We can help you."

"That's good."

"There are a few things I need to make clear, however." She turned serious. "I'm very protective of my men. This is not a hookup location or a dating service. These men are to act as escorts, nothing more. If you're looking for something romantic, I suggest you check eHarmony."

"I understand."

"They have strict rules. If you break them at any time, the contract is void. You will not get a refund and you will be prohibited from using our services again."

Wow, they were really professional. I wasn't expecting that. "What are the rules?"

She handed me a list. "You need to check each one before you sign at the bottom." She started to name off the rules. "You are not paying your escort for sex. If you expect sex, demand it, or attempt to seduce them with substances or drugs, we will take legal action."

My eyes widened. "Like rape?"

"Men can be raped too, Aspen." She had a no-bullshit look in her eyes.

That was disturbing. "I understand." I checked the box.

"There will be no kissing. Breach of contract will terminate the service in the same way."

I checked the box.

"The only affection permitted is handholding, his arm around your waist, and a kiss on the cheek. Nothing more."

"Okay." I checked the box.

She continued through the list. There were various rules, like no smoking during the duration of the date and no dishonesty. Then she concluded the final rule. "In the event that you feel something more for your escort and you express that, the service will be terminated."

"Why?" I asked.

"It's a conflict of interest," she said. "Some of my escorts have relationships with clients that last for years. Feelings can develop, and naturally, that makes things complicated. The escorts don't want to be put in that situation, especially since they are hurting their client. This is a business, Aspen, and we run it as such."

I checked the box and indicated my understanding.

"Finally, these men have the right to keep their personal lives private. You will not have their real phone number and you will not know their address. In the event you attempt to stalk them, there will be legal consequences."

How amazing were these guys? They made women turn crazy? Try to rape and stalk them? I actually felt bad for them even though I had no idea who they were. "Well, you don't have to worry about that with me. I respect everyone, no matter how beautiful they may be."

She nodded. "You don't strike me as the crazy type." She flashed me a grin. "I'm not worried."

I signed the bottom and handed it back to her.

"So, what do you prefer?"

I cocked an eyebrow. "How do you mean?"

"Blond? Brunette? Tall? Really tall?"

"Uh...I have no preference. I'm sure any of them are fine."

"You're easy," she said. "Women can be picky."

I just wanted someone my dad would like. So, I was pretty low-maintenance in that regard.

She pushed a paper across the desk toward me. "Here is the price breakdown. The more dates you purchase, the cheaper each date becomes."

My eyes widened when I looked at the number. *Damn, these guys were making a killing.*

Danielle read my mind again. "I assure you, they are worth every penny. Your family will love them, your girlfriends will be jealous, and your ex will be totally envious. They are all wonderful, each and every one."

I made decent money working for my father and I didn't have a lot of expenses. I didn't own a car and I didn't have a fetish for expensive things, like shoes and purses. If this secured my position as the CEO of my father's company, it was worth the price. "Can I put it on a credit card?"

"You may."

I handed it over and she processed it. "You have secured five dates. When, and if, you need more, just let me know."

"It'll always be the same guy, right?"

"Yes."

"But if he has other clients, how does he work around that schedule?"

"I take care of all that," she said. "Don't worry about it. You'll have him when you need him. But you need to give us three days notice."

"I can do that," I said.

"Just give me a few moments and I'll make the selection." She typed on her computer for a while and made notes on her notepad.

I sipped my coffee and looked through my phone.

Harper texted me. *Are you there?*

Already made the payment.

Yes! I could hear her scream through the text message.

Danielle turned to me. "How do you feel about tattoos? Like them? Hate them?"

"I'm indifferent to them," I said. "As long as they can't be seen under his clothes."

"Okay." She returned to her computer. "Any other special requests?"

"Like what?"

"Accents? Dialects?"

I could pick his accent? "American is fine."

"Okay." She made a few more notes. "Rhett will be your escort. He'll meet you for coffee tomorrow at Starbucks at noon sharp."

"But I don't need him then..." That was quick. This woman was like a puppeteer.

"This meeting is free. You're just going to get to know each other so when he attends an event with you, it's not obvious you've never met."

That made sense. "Okay, I'll be there."

She stood up then shook my hand. "It was a pleasure meeting you. Call me if you need anything."

"Thank you." I couldn't believe I actually agreed to this.

"Have a wonderful day."

I walked out, feeling a little dizzy.

I was actually doing this.

***

I was nervous even though I shouldn't be. The meeting was no different than a work conference. It was just a conversation, an open dialogue about the arrangement I paid for.

There was no reason to be nervous.

I had a backbone when it came to my job. I could be fearless and cold. Unless it was my way, there wasn't a way at all. But in my personal life, I was calmer. I was stressed about work as it was, and there was no reason to increase that level of stress outside the office.

I found a table in Starbucks and sat alone. A girl near me had headphones on and she looked like she was studying. Judging her age, she was in college. A table away, there was a couple talking quietly. Their meeting seemed awkward. Perhaps they were old lovers. The blender behind the counter would go off and catch my attention. I forgot about it once the noise was gone, but it caught my attention again as the loud noise pierced my ears.

I wore a green dress with strappy white sandals. My brown hair was over one shoulder and I felt the earrings hang from my lobes. I didn't want to look like crap when I first met him. Sitting alone didn't bother me, but I grew tired of the stares directed my way. Was it that odd I was sitting alone?

The door opened and someone stepped inside. It was a man dressed in black slacks and a gray collared shirt. His chest was expansive and his stomach was tight. I couldn't see through his clothes, but it was clear his frame was covered in muscle.

He was tall, at least six feet or more. A Rolex was on his wrist and he wore shiny dress shoes. A black tie hung from his neck. As he came inside, he glanced around.

Penetrating blue eyes met mine, and realization seemed to flash in them. They were bright, reminding me of the clear blue sea found off the coast of Mexico. The warmth reflected in them was like a tropical beach, playful and inviting. His eyes caught my attention because they were not only beautiful, but deep.

He had a strong jaw, reminding me of Clint Eastwood or a star from a western film. His skin was fair but had a slight tint to it, like he was outside often. His mouth contained thin lips but they stretched into an alluring smile as he looked my way. Wide shoulders led to a formidable chest. I stared at each feature over and over again, hoping I didn't miss anything.

Was that him?

Rhett came my way, passing the other tables as he went. He was clearly headed for me.

Ohmygod, it was him. Damn, he was gorgeous. I definitely underpaid.

Rhett reached my table with an aura of welcome. "You must be Aspen." He stared into my face, and his eyes examined every inch of me as mine did to him. They flashed a lighter shade of blue as he watched me. Then they faded back to their natural color. He extended his hand to shake mine. "I'm Rhett. It's nice to meet you."

I snapped out of my moment of gawking then shook his hand. "It's a pleasure." My voice was surprisingly steady for how hard my heart was beating.

He sat in the seat across from me with perfect posture, and his shoulders were straight. They expanded past the chair, showing his obvious strength and power. I stared at them for a moment before I forced myself to stop. "How are you?" he asked.

The beautiful creature had manners too? "Well. You?"

"Great," he said. "Thank you."

"I apologize if I seem nervous. I've never done anything like this before." I could only imagine the look on my face. I probably looked like a love-struck teenager at a New Direction concert.

"I understand," he said. "A lot of my clients are uncomfortable in the beginning. It's normal."

I nodded.

"Can I get you some coffee?"

"Sure. Thank you."

"What would you like?"

"Earl grey tea is fine."

"Coming right up." He rapped his knuckles on the table quietly then walked away.

Don't look at his ass. Don't look at his ass. Don't look at his ass.

Harper's voice came into my head. "You better look!"

"No!" I mentally screamed to shut her up.

"Do it," she yelled.

I turned my gaze and snuck a peek. *Damn, it was nice.* I quickly turned away again when I realized how hypocritical my behavior was. I hated it when men stared at my ass. Here I was doing it to someone else. But I admit, I was more understanding of men's behavior after seeing Rhett.

He returned with the drinks. "Not a fan of coffee?"

"I am but I already had plenty today."

"Caffeine addict?" he asked. "I'm the same way."

"It's a sickness, really."

"The world runs on coffee," he said. "Without it, the sun would probably burn out."

"Literally." I took a sip then returned it to the table.

"Aspen is a beautiful name." Rhett said it randomly, like it was on his mind the entire time but he didn't know when to say it.

"Thank you."

He took a drink of his coffee then set it down. "Danielle told me about you but I'd like to hear a few things from you."

"Sure."

"So, your father won't give you his company until you get a boyfriend?"

"Yes," I answered.

His eyes shifted away, like he was deep in thought. His eyes were always stunning, hypnotizing, but like a mood ring, they changed depending on his emotional state. Now they were darker as he remained quiet. Then he turned his gaze back to me. "With all due respect, that's hard to believe. What does your relationship status have to do with taking over an energy company?"

I really didn't want to mention John. That catastrophe followed me everywhere I went and I just wanted to forget about it. The fewer people who knew, the less often I would be reminded of it. If I told Rhett, he would pity me or think less of me, just like everyone else. I didn't need charity, even if it was in the form of wordless thoughts. "I haven't been consistent about dating and my father wants me to be more invested in my marital future. He wants to make sure I choose someone that will represent his image well. A single woman running a company doesn't always get public approval. He insists a woman with a husband and family is better." I made all that up on the spot and hoped he would believe it. If he really was interested in me, all he had to do was Google me or my father and he'd get all the dirt. But judging the fact he asked that question, he had no idea of my public disgrace.

"I see," he said. "Does that mean you intend to keep a long relationship with me? Having me act as your husband?"

"No," I said immediately. "I just want him to see that I have good taste in men. We don't need to take it that far."

He nodded. "Okay." He sipped his coffee again, and while he drank, his eyes were focused on me. I wondered what he was thinking, what he thought of me, but I didn't ask. "Danielle told you the rules of this arrangement?"

"She did," I said with a nod. "I'm sorry you have to establish rules at all. It's unfortunate you have to protect your dignity in such a strict way. You deserve more respect than that."

He examined me with crystal blue eyes like an x-ray machine. It seemed like he could see inside me, see my thoughts as well as my soul. His body suddenly became rigid, but after a moment passed, he relaxed again. "I appreciate your words."

I nodded.

"You and I will get along well," he said. "I can tell."

"I hope so."

"So." He ran his fingers through his hair in a sexy way, although I'm sure it wasn't intentional. He was just naturally suave and cool, and every little thing he did was attractive. It was hard to believe I was sitting across from a man so beautiful. "Tell me about your job."

I explained my position and my plan to invest in clean energy despite my dad's objections. "He may not agree with me, but the utilization of fossil fuels needs to end. A lot of companies make high profits off it, but is sacrificing the earth really worth it?"

He leaned over the table and rested his elbows on the surface. "You sound like a hippie."

"I am a hippie," I said proudly.

A slow smile stretched his face then disappeared. His eyes brightened during the action, making him sexy and adorable at the same time. How did someone pull that off? "I meant it in a complimentary way. Not enough people care about big issues like that. We toss our refuse in the landfill and never think twice about it. We throw our cigarettes anywhere and just assume they'll disappear. There are a lot of problems in the world that deserve a conversation."

We'd only been talking for a few minutes but it was clear Rhett was highly intelligent, logical, and of course, charismatic. Like a politician, he attracted your admiration and made you feel loyal to him even though you hardly knew him. He was trustworthy, easy to believe in. He spoke eloquently, choosing the right words at the right time. And he listened, making him a good conversationalist. Most of the time, people weren't listening. They were just waiting for their chance to speak again.

"I admire you for your passion," he said. "I wish there were more people like you."

His words made me feel warm. Heat blazed through my extremities and made me feel slightly weak. I didn't know him well, but I already felt my stomach tighten in excitement just from being near him. No wonder why women wanted more than he was willing to give. Now I didn't blame them. "I care about the future and the generations that will be here after my time ends. I think that's something we should all care about, the continuation of our race."

He nodded in agreement. "I'll definitely work hard to get your father's approval. I have to get you in the seat of power."

It was a very sweet thing to say and I doubt he even realized it. "I appreciate it."

"Can I ask you something?" He sipped his coffee then set it down.

"Sure." What did he want to know?

"Why have you decided to use an escort service? I apologize in advance if this offends you, but you're a beautiful woman and I doubt you have trouble finding men to spend time with."

Beautiful woman? Me? I never thought I was ugly, but I didn't think this ridiculously handsome man had the same standards I did. Compared to the women he must sleep with, I had to be a troll. Perhaps he was just flattering me to make me feel more comfortable around him. He was a salesman, in a complicated way, and it was his job to sell himself, to me and everyone else. "I didn't want to use someone for my gain. I would feel terrible if I dated someone just for appearances. It wouldn't be fair to him. This way, no one gets hurt."

"But you must date often, right? If you really liked the guy, I doubt he would mind being your poster boy."

"Well...I don't date much." I wasn't sure why I was telling him that. He was just so hypnotic. It was easy to spill secrets and insecurities. We were practically strangers but I already felt like he was a friend.

"Any reason why?" he asked.

I pulled out the tea bag from my cup and set it on the napkin. "It's just not for me."

Rhett seemed to understand this was a topic not up for discussion because he didn't ask any more questions. "What are your father's hobbies?"

"Cars, golfing, and beautiful women. Oh, and of course, money." I said everything quickly, knowing the answer to that question like the back of my hand.

"Women?" he asked. "Are your parents divorced?"

"My mom passed away years ago."

His eyes fell in sadness. Perhaps he was pretending to care because it was his job but he seemed sincere. "I'm very sorry to hear that." He didn't ask how she passed away and I was relieved. I didn't like talking about it.

"My dad will never remarry but he still enjoys female company. He loves to take them on luxurious vacations and out to dinner in his fancy car. They're usually half his age and more interested in his money than his personality, but I don't think he cares. He likes the attention. Or perhaps he's just senile."

He felt the rim of his cup with his thumb. "You don't strike me as a spoiled rich girl."

"Because I'm not," I said immediately. "My dad didn't give me much. I earn my salary and have always worked for everything I've achieved. He didn't ever just hand me money or gifts. I was taught to work hard. That's the one thing I do appreciate about my dad. However, he'll make me work for everything I have but he'll pay for some chick's boob job. It doesn't make much sense to me." I stared into my tea, seeing the dregs at the bottom. "But, in the end, I'm glad it worked out the way it did. I wouldn't take his money even if he offered it."

Rhett watched me with his full attention. He hung on every word, making me feel like we were friends who'd known each other for years.

I realized I was babbling and droning on about my daddy issues. "I'm sorry. I said too much and made you uncomfortable."

"No, not at all," he said. "This is the stuff I like to know. It will make it easier for me to help you. I'm sure you assume an escort service is just men taking women out on fake dates, but it's actually a lot more than that. We help people get through their issues, the real reason why they need us at all."

"Yeah?" I asked. I didn't challenge him. I just wanted him to elaborate.

"Yeah," he said. "I have a client I've been working with for years. He's a sixty-two-year-old man."

I raised an eyebrow.

"I play chess with him a few times a month in the park. That's all we do. Play chess. He talks about his kids, whom he never sees, and I try to persuade him to reach out to them. He tells me other things too. Overall, he just wants me as a friend. He pays for my company, but in reality, I would do it for free."

"Then why don't you tell him that?"

He gave me a playful look. "I need eggs, butter, milk, and cheese."

"Dairy products?"

He chuckled. It was a beautiful sound. It was hearty and full of joy. His chest rumbled as he did it, and his lips broke out in a smile that made the sun darken in comparison. "I meant food in general, which includes dairy products."

Seeing him laugh made me smile. It was infectious. "It's nice your escort services apply to more than fake romances."

"We're a friend service more than anything else. It's just unfortunate the friendships can't continue when the service ends."

I didn't ask him why they ended. "Do you enjoy what you do?"

"Very much. Some people look down on me because they assume I'm a glorified prostitute, but I'm not. I stopped trying to change people's opinions a long time ago. They can think what they want. People will judge me no matter what I do. I may as well do what I want."

"Words to live by," I noted. "How long have you been doing this?"

"A few years," he answered.

"How did it come about? It's such an unusual profession."

"I started when I was in college. A friend needed a date to a wedding, and after that, her friend asked me to do something similar. It snowballed from there and I started charging them for it. Then I got my friends together and we decided to make it into a company. It's been very successful."

I assumed he went to college. He seemed educated and knowledgeable. "Where did you go to school?" I asked, being curious about this unnaturally attractive man.

"New York."

"What did you study?" I knew I should let him ask the questions but I found him so interesting I couldn't stop.

"Business," he answered. "I worked in an office for a credit card corporation for a while. But, I was very unhappy there. It was mindless, and I did the same tasks over and over. I was restricted to my cubicle and it was far too quiet."

"Then why did you work there to begin with?"

He rubbed the back of his neck while he pondered my question. The curiosity was harmless, but it must mean something to him. "I'd rather not say. But, I quit when I couldn't handle it anymore and continued the escort business. In the end, it makes me happy. I enjoy it."

"Does it affect your personal relationships?"

He seemed uncomfortable again. He pressed his lips together like he was debating whether to answer or not.

"I apologize," I said. "It's none of my business."

After a long pause, he spoke. "It's difficult. A lot of women don't like the fact I take other women out and hold their hands and pretend to be their boyfriend. It's understandable. However, I wish they realized how professional it was." He shrugged.

"I'm sorry to hear that."

"You can't have it all, right?"

Actually, he could. He had the looks, the intelligence, and the charm. "Have you done modeling?"

His eyes turned back to me then he quickly looked away. A light coloring filled his cheeks. Then a grin broke out on his face. He turned back to me, the redness still in his face.

I loved seeing him smile. I'd never been so moved by the simple gesture before. A smile from John never gave me butterflies the way it did with Rhett.

"That's a flattering thing to say," he said. "But no, I've never modeled and I don't plan to."

"Well, it's always an option."

"It's not for me," he said simply.

"So, all the men you work with are your friends?"

"Yes," he answered. "One has been my best friend since grade school, and the others are guys I met on the journey."

"Then work must be a lot of fun."

"It is." The smile reappeared. "We don't interact often. But we have stories to tell—a lot of stories."

"Are you going to tell them about me?"

His eyes turned serious as he regarded me. He rubbed his chin before he returned his hand to the table. "I will."

"And what will you say?" I had no idea why I asked that. It just came out. My boldness surprised even me.

"That you're beautiful and a delight to talk to."

I smiled and tucked a strand of hair behind my ear.

"You have nice eyes."

Had he ever looked at his own? They were breathtaking. "I like yours."

"I've always loved green eyes. They're so bright and noticeable. Most people have blue or brown eyes. But it seems like no one ever has green ones."

"I've never noticed."

"Now you will," he said. "So, when is my first outing as your man?"

His last words made my body tense. I wasn't sure why. "There's a work party this weekend. It's a silent auction fundraiser for charity."

"I thought your dad wasn't generous with his money."

"He never donates any himself," I said. "But he throws the party for tax purposes."

He nodded. "I understand. What evening?"

"Saturday."

"What would you like me to wear?"

"I get to decide?" I asked incredulously.

"You're paying me. I'm at your mercy." He gave me a playful look.

"A suit."

"What color?"

"Black," I said.

"I can do that," he said. "Would you like me to pick you up or meet you there?"

"You can pick me up." I didn't want to risk anyone seeing our meeting on the sidewalk.

He pushed his napkin toward me. "Write down your address and I'll pick you up. What time?"

"It begins at seven."

"I'll be there at six thirty."

I wrote down the address then slid it back to him.

He pocketed it. "Thank you, Aspen."

I liked it when he said my name. The baritone of his voice made it come out sexy, even though he didn't do it intentionally. Some people were naturally sexy. I was naturally not sexy. "Thank you for doing this."

"It's my pleasure," he said. "We'll get you that company."

"I hope so."

"And when we do, you better save the world."

I stared into his eyes and almost forgot to speak. "I intend to."

***

"Tell me what happened!" Harper walked through my door without knocking.

I was sitting on the couch eating a bowl of cereal for dinner. "Uh, hi?"

"Uh, hello?" She jumped onto my couch. "So, what's he like?"

I put down the cereal and turned to her. "Okay, you know how that waiter had a nice ass?"

"Yes..." She leaned forward in excitement.

"Well, this guy's ass is a million times nicer than that."

She smacked my arm. "Lucky!"

"He was dreamy. Like, wow."

"Like, really wow?"

"Like, whoa." I realized we sounded like teenage girls but I didn't care.

"It's a shame they don't offer sex," she said with a sigh. "I'd tell you to go for it."

"He wouldn't be nearly as dreamy if he did perform sexual favors for money."

"If a guy is hot, he's hot," she said. "No ifs, ands, or buts about it."

Harper always saw things in black and white. I was more of a shades of gray type of person.

"I told you it was a good idea."

"I haven't introduced him to my father yet. It could be a disaster."

"I find that extremely unlikely," she said. "If he charmed you in five minutes, imagine what he could do to everyone else in an hour."

"Well, since my father is straight, I doubt Rhett will have the same effect on him as he did on me."

"Rhett?" she said. "That's his name?"

"Yeah."

"Even his name is hot."

"I know. I wonder if that's even his real name."

"I bet his real name is even hotter, like Jasper or something."

"Maybe," I said with a chuckle.

"How awesome would it be if you two fell in love?" She clapped her hands excitedly.

"Whoa...hold on there. Let's not get carried away."

"It could happen."

"It won't," I said firmly. "He made it clear he doesn't date clients."

"Maybe the right girl hasn't come along..." She nudged me in the side playfully.

"This guy looks like he belongs on a billboard. There's no way he'd be interested in me. I'm not fascinating, and I couldn't even keep John around."

She pointed her finger in my face and gave me a catfight look. "Don't you ever say that again! That's not true and you know it. John was just a weasel. You think he won't do the same thing to Isabella that he did to you? He will, and she'll hate her life. Do not let a man determine your value. Ever. That's a sisterhood promise."

She was right.

"My best friend is sexy as hell, has a great ass, and is the coolest person on the planet. You belong on a billboard long before this Rhett guy does."

"You'll change your mind once you see him."

"Okay...maybe I will. But you still deserve your own billboard. Don't let John make you doubt yourself. He's just one shrimp in a sea of sharks. He's nothing but a bottom feeder, munching on whatever is left over. His opinion is irrelevant."

"You're right." Harper was always right. "Thanks for being my best friend."

"It's my job to tell you when you're being stupid. And you're being damn stupid."

I smiled. "Thanks. So, how'd it go with waiter boy?"

"It was okay," she said. "He was decent in bed."

"Did he...you know?"

"Just say it, Aspen." She rolled her eyes. "Did he make me come? Yes. But only once."

"Only once?" I asked incredulously. I was lucky if John made me come at all. In our entire relationship, I think it happened three times. And it was in the beginning when the hormones were new for me. After that, it was pretty quiet down below.

"My future husband will know how to make me come more than once. That's one of my requirements."

"That's oddly specific...and difficult to fulfill."

"Hey, if it's meant to be, it's meant to be."

"You're putting a lot of pressure on him."

She picked up my bowl of cereal and took a few bites. "Uh...gross."

She returned it to the coffee table. "What? I've used your toothbrush before."

"When?" I demanded.

"The other day when I slept here."

I cringed. "Harper!"

"What?" She feigned innocence. "Your immune system will be indestructible."

I shook my head, thoroughly grossed out.

"Anyway," she said. "I'll tell you a secret about female sexuality. Are you listening?"

"What else am I doing?" I said sarcastically.

She ignored the jab. "Women need to be extremely comfortable and aroused in order to climax. So, really, the pressure isn't on him. If we meet and he's the one, I'll be so into him that he won't have to do much other than last five minutes. So, it's not too much to ask for."

As someone without much sexual experience, I couldn't argue with that. "Let me know when that happens."

"Oh, you'll be the first to know. Actually, the second. I'll make sure he knows when I give him a nice pat on the back."

I chuckled. "So, you aren't going to see that waiter again?"

"Probably not. He was cute and fun but I don't see it going anywhere."

"Well, back out on the prowl."

"Does Rhett have a brother?" she asked.

I shrugged. "I don't know much about him."

"You were at coffee for an hour. Something was said."

"We didn't talk about his family," I said. "Mostly work related stuff."

"Did you tell him about John?"

"No way," I said immediately. "I go out of my way to not humiliate myself in front of hot guys. At least, I make the attempt."

"It's not humiliating," she argued.

"That my fiancé left me for my cousin?" I asked incredulously. "It's extremely humiliating."

Harper didn't argue for once. "You know what would be fun?"

"Hmm?"

"If you took Rhett to some function where Isabella is. She would eat her heart out if she saw him. He would put John to shame."

The idea of making Isabella, and admittedly, John, jealous did excite me. But I knew that was childish. "I'm not going out of my way to do that. I need Rhett for my father, nothing else."

"Well, it doesn't hurt to kill two birds with one stone."

I had a quick daydream of Rhett going with me to a family party. John stood at the edge, watching the way Rhett held me close and danced with me. Isabella grew angry and yelled at John for staring. Then he broke off his engagement to her in front of everyone and marched over to me. He pushed

Rhett away and asked me to take him back. Instead, I kissed Rhett.

The dream faded away and a smile was on my face. "Yeah...maybe."

Rhett

I arrived at her doorstep with an arrangement of lilies. Roses were too romantic so I never got those. They didn't send the right message. I knocked on the door then adjusted my tie.

Aspen opened the door wearing a black gown covered in shiny glitter. Every time she moved, her dress sparkled like the stars in the universe. The dress was low-cut but I didn't look. Her hair was curled in big, open waves. Unlike the other day, her face was covered in makeup. She reminded me of a Victoria's Secret model on the runway. "Are those for me?"

I was dumbstruck, staring at her and unable to stop. Her beauty was obvious to me the first time I saw her, but now I was astounded by her transformation. She was beautiful without even trying, and when she did try, she outshone every woman in the world. What did a gorgeous girl like her need me for? "They are." I recovered from the shock and handed them to her. "I hope you like them."

She took them with a smile. "They're beautiful." She inhaled their scent and kept staring at them. "Wow."

I was glad she liked them but I was surprised how much she appreciated them.

She stepped back inside her apartment then pulled a vase from under the sink. She inserted the flowers then filled it with water. Then she placed it on her kitchen table. "Perfect," she said. "It's nice to have flowers even when it's not my birthday."

"Is that a popular gift?" I asked.

"Harper, my best friend, always gets me flowers on my birthday. I do the same for her. It's a tradition we've been doing for a long time."

"That's touching." The idea of someone going out of their way to make Aspen smile made me happy. "Are you ready?"

"Yeah." She grabbed her clutch and tucked it under her arm.

We walked out together then took a cab to the hotel. Aspen looked out her window and watched the traffic on the other side of the road.

I caught myself looking at her for an unusually long time. Then I focused my gaze out the window.

When we arrived, I helped her out then put my arm around her waist. "Is this okay?"

"More than okay." She gave me a warm smile then walked forward.

The dinner was held at a fancy hotel, and there were people standing outside greeting each other. Aspen either didn't recognize anyone or didn't feel like talking because she headed straight to the entrance.

The event was held in a ballroom, and once we walked inside, I realized just how pristine it was. Chandeliers hung from the ceiling, flutes carried on trays moved through the crowd, and everyone was decked out in their finest.

"Nice party," I said.

"It looks nice on the outside, but beware, everyone is extremely boring."

"They are?"

"We produce and sell oil," she said. "It's definitely not interesting."

I liked her sarcasm as well as her positive energy. She had a good balance to it. She was fun to be around but she wasn't overbearing. Most girls I escorted either spoke too much or too little. Aspen spoke just the right amount. "Can I get you a drink?"

"Sure."

I stepped away from her and grabbed two flutes of champagne. When I handed the glass to her, she immediately took a long drink. "Nervous?" I asked with a smile.

She looked into my eyes then released a faint chuckle. "Do I make it obvious?"

"Why are you nervous?" I asked.

"I just hope Dad doesn't see through my plan."

"I'd be impressed if he did."

She gave me another dazzling smile before she took another drink.

It was very rare for me to escort a woman who was more attractive than I was. Aspen wasn't necessarily a woman you would see on the cover of a magazine, but that wasn't a bad thing. Her eyes were shaped liked almonds, blending well into her face. The deep green color reminded me of freshly mowed lawn in the summer. I could even smell the grass. She was taller than the average woman. Being six two made short girls difficult to dance with and hold. Aspen was about five seven so that was a nice change. She had the confidence of a businesswoman that wouldn't take no for an answer, but she also had the gentleness of a school counselor. She was lighthearted and fun, but she also had layers of depth. I was talented at reading people, and I think I pinned her down.

The greatest thing about her was her obvious disinterest in me. She didn't drool when she stared at me like she was inspecting a piece of meat. She didn't look into my eyes and melt into a puddle on the floor. She wasn't enchanted like most women. She was indifferent. She said she wasn't dating so I knew she wasn't looking for romance. It made my life a lot easier. I hated rejecting women and making them cry. I hated being the bad guy. With Aspen, I didn't have to worry about that.

My absolute favorite quality about her was her empathy. She sympathized with me, understanding that it was difficult for me to command respect from people when I told them what I did for a living. And she also understood that most women viewed me as a piece of ass. All they cared about was the package I came in, nothing else. And when I was seduced with roofies or other substances, it didn't feel good. I had a new respect for women in that regard. They were constantly preyed upon because they were small and desirable. They were hardly respected as human beings.

"What are you thinking?" she asked.

Her deep voice brought me back to the present. "How beautiful you look tonight." It was the truth, in a way. I went off on a tangent but the thoughts stemmed from her appearance.

"You really are worth every penny." She clanked her glass against mine then took a drink.

"I would have said it whether you paid me to or not."

"You're smooth," she said playfully.

I knew she was dodging the compliment because she was used to men giving it to her, not because she didn't believe me. She and I were alike in that respect. There were days when I wanted to wear a mask just so I could walk the world unnoticed. Aspen would do the same.

"Hey, watch this." A guy a few feet away picked up a flute from a passing tray, and my eyes could hardly believe it as he poured the champagne on the waiter's head. The guy bust up laughing, finding the action extremely humorous.

Did that just happen?

The waiter had the grace not to yell or start a fight. He held the tray without dropping it then wiped the liquid away with his sleeve.

"Hilarious, right?" The guy wore a tuxedo with a lime green bow tie. His face was covered in a full beard and his hair was long and unkempt. He looked like a homeless person who mugged someone outside the charity event.

Two guys stood beside him and they chuckled along, acting like two mindless cronies.

I wanted to intervene and do something but I honestly had no idea what was going on. Why would an attendee at a black tie party dump champagne on a waiter? It didn't make any sense. Did the waiter do something?

"Jerome, give me your glass." The guy reached for it and prepared to throw it again.

Whatever the reason they were throwing drinks, it was uncalled for. I took a step to intervene but it was too late.

Aspen marched over, her back perfectly straight, with the strength of a Roman soldier. Her gown trailed behind her, and her dress glittered as she moved. She carried herself with grace and confidence.

"When will you grow up, Lance?" She snatched the glass from him before he could throw it. "Don't embarrass Dad like this."

"Why don't you take a chill pill?" he countered.

"Good one," she said sarcastically. "Still using taunts from sixth grade. That's really impressive."

He narrowed his eyes at her and looked like he might hit her.

"No one is forcing you to stay," she said. "Just leave if you're going to be nothing but a nuisance to everyone."

"Do you ever get tired of being a bitch?" he snapped.

My fists clenched at my sides.

"Another good one," she said sarcastically. She turned away and walked back to me, her head held high and her shoulders back.

Lance grabbed another drink then prepared to throw it on Aspen.

I ran to him then knocked the glass down. "Touch my girlfriend and I'll break your arm."

The crowd noticed us and turned in our direction.

I gripped his arm then pinned it behind his back. Without hesitation, I kicked his knees out from under him, using my martial arts training. "Do you understand me?" I leaned toward his ear as I whispered.

"Fine," he said in an aggravated voice. "Now get off me."

I released him then turned away.

Aspen sighed when I reached her. Irritation was on her face, and the green color of her eyes became more prominent. Even though she was angry, her eyes looked more beautiful. "I really hate him sometimes."

"Who is he?"

"My brother."

I cocked an eyebrow, unable to believe it. "Are you sure?"

Her body relaxed from the drama and she chuckled. "Unfortunately."

I turned back and watched him march off with his gang. "That guy?"

"Yes. He's a typical loser who only cares about himself. He's childish, immature, and just a pain in the backside. I'd kick his ass if we weren't in public."

"Why is he here?"

"He works for the company, mainly busywork."

I found it hard to believe that guy could be serious for even a moment.

Aspen read my mind. "Dad employs him just because Lance is his son. For some reason, he turns a blind eye to everything he does. The employees used to complain about him because he was so disruptive and harassed the girls, but Dad dismissed all of their claims. Now they don't even bother. It's ironic since Dad screams at me for every little mistake I make, and most of them are completely out of my control, but his first born son can do no wrong."

The more I got to know her, the more I realized she had to put up with a lot of shit.

"I'm sorry." She rubbed her temple quickly then dropped her hand. "I'm babbling about my problems again."

"No." I pulled her closer to me and moved my hands to her hips. "These are the things I like to know about."

Her playful attitude returned. "You're like a therapist."

"I've never thought about it that way, but yes, I suppose I am."

She rested her head against my chest for a moment.

I was suddenly aware how close we were to one another. I wasn't sure why. Her hair was styled perfectly and I didn't want to mess it up so I didn't rest my chin on her head like I wanted to. I just held her there.

"Aspen?"

She and I turned at the sound of her name.

E.L. Todd

"What was the commotion about?" He was an older man with white hair and a thick mustache. He wore glasses that made him look constantly angry. His suit looked expensive, and he carried himself like he owned the room and everything in it. I assumed this was her father. And I didn't like him at all. Even if I knew nothing about the man, I wouldn't like him. His body language, mannerisms, and tone of voice told me everything I needed to know.

Aspen's eyes were greener than ever before. "Your son thought it would be fun to dump drinks on the waiter's head."

"Nonsense," he said. "That couldn't be right."

How blind was this guy?

"Nonsense?" she asked incredulously. "I saw him do it."

"I'm sure it was a mistake," he said. "There's no reason to get riled up."

Aspen took a deep breath and controlled her anger. I could tell it took all of her strength not to snap. She was barely holding on. I brought her closer into my side to remind her I was there for support.

Her father caught the affection. "Who are you?" he asked rudely.

I brushed off his abrasiveness, extending my hand to shake his. "It's a pleasure to meet you, Mr. Lane. I'm Rhett, Aspen's boyfriend."

He eyed my hand before he took it. "Aspen's boyfriend?"

"We've been dating for a while," she said. "I've been eager for you to meet him and thought now was a good time."

He eyed me up and down, practically getting my measurements.

I spoke before he could say something to piss off Aspen. "Your daughter tells me you're an accomplished golfer. Just the other day, I finished with a seventy-two for an eighteen-hole course. It's my best score so far."

"Seventy-two?" His eyes narrowed and his voice was full of awe. "Where?"

"The New York Country Club."

"That's impressive," he said. "You've golfed for a long time?" All the irritation he had for Aspen had disappeared.

"My whole life," I said. "I buy new clubs every year since I wear them out so often."

"Me too," he said. "I'm glad I'm not the only one. But I admit, I just love shopping for golf supplies."

I released a fake laugh. "You and I are one and the same, sir."

Mr. Lane was in a very good mood now. "What do you drive?"

Aspen said cars were another weakness. "I drive a Jaguar. But I also have an Indian motorcycle for those rare occasions I want to venture out of the city and into the wide open spaces."

"New York can get claustrophobic at times," he said. "I have a house in Connecticut so I can breathe in the fresh air."

"That's a smart idea, sir." At least he and I were getting along.

Mr. Lane snapped at a waiter. "Get this man a scotch."

I didn't like the way he spoke to the waiter but I didn't voice it.

"You're a scotch man, right?" he asked.

"Through and through," I answered.

The waiter handed me the glass and I downed it.

Mr. Lane smiled. "You drink like a real man." He drank his own.

Aspen stood silently beside me, like she didn't exist.

I kept my arm around her so she wouldn't feel completely left out.

"What do you do?" Mr. Lane asked me.

I had a cover story, thanks to the help of a friend in a high place. "I own a company that supplies parts exclusively to GMC motors."

His eyes were wide. "They make a killing."

"They do, sir. It's a great team to be a part of." I figured if he knew I worked in business, he would like me, and perhaps that would help in Aspen's favor. But it was ridiculous she had to have a boyfriend at all when it was clear she could take care of herself.

He took another drink of his scotch. "What are your other interests?"

"I'm an entrepreneur. I'm always trying to find new ways to make money." That wasn't true at all. I made a killing working as an escort but the money wasn't important to me. I just said what he wanted to hear.

He chuckled then clanked his glass against mine. "You got a good head on those shoulders."

"Thank you, sir."

"Come with me." He put his arm around my shoulder and pulled me away from Aspen. I felt bad Aspen was being forgotten like dust on the top of the refrigerator but I was doing what she paid me to do. Her father seemed to like me and that's all that mattered.

He and I sat at the bar and talked about golf. We discussed difficult tactics, different clubs, and even what brand of balls we used. I'd been golfing for a long time, so it worked out in my favor when Aspen said her father loved to play. And I did drive a Jaguar and a motorcycle. Perhaps he and I were more alike than I cared to admit.

He introduced me to his colleagues and I made small talk with them. They were just as stiff as Mr. Lane and all reeked of scotch.

"I need to go bid on the silent auction," he said. "I hope you'll be making your way over there sometime this evening."

"I will. That vacation to Hawaii sounds tempting."

He laughed and patted my shoulder before he walked away.

I breathed a sigh of relief when he was gone. How did Aspen put up with that shallow and selfish man on a daily basis? She deserved a medal from the President of the United States.

She appeared out of thin air. "How'd it go?"

I relaxed when I recognized her. "He likes me. Mission accomplished."

"You know, my father likes anyone with money. He'll know you're lying about GMC."

"No, he won't," I said. "I know the CEO. He'll cover for me."

"He will?" she asked in surprise.

"When you're in this business, you meet all kinds of people." I shrugged then finished my scotch.

"You undercharge, you know that?"

I chuckled. "After doing this for so long, it becomes second nature."

"Hopefully, my dad comes around and decides to give me the company. He's being a real pain in the ass about it."

"I don't understand," I said. "How did you turn out so amazing but your father is...not the best?" I tried to be sensitive since it was her father I was bad-mouthing.

"The words you're looking for are smelly douchebag."

"Smelly douchebag?" I said with a laugh.

"And I don't have an answer to that question. I suppose it's because he spoiled Lance and made me work for every dime I had. Or maybe he has a mental disorder. Probably both." She rolled her eyes in irritation.

"For what it's worth, I think you're pretty amazing for putting up with their bullshit."

"Thank you." She put her hands on her hips. "It's about time someone said it."

I chuckled then put my arm around her waist. "Now what?"

"I want to ditch," she said. "Get some ice cream."

That was the most random thing I ever heard. "Ice cream?"

"Yum...with chocolate syrup and whipped cream."

It sounded like she'd been thinking about it for a while. "Can we do that?"

"No." She deflated like a balloon. "Let's stay for dinner then hightail it out of here. My dad might want to talk to you again. You guys discussed golf, cars, and money. Now women is all that's left."

"That would be an interesting conversation..."

We took our seats at the table near the front of the stage, and plates were set in front of us. I put my hand on Aspen's thigh and noted how toned it was. Her legs were thin but they were tight. I wondered if she was a runner.

Her father took a seat at the table and so did her brother.

Lance glared at Aspen across the table.

She ignored him.

"So, what's this about you pouring booze on a waiter?" Mr. Lane asked his son.

Lance shot Aspen a hateful look, clearly pissed she tattled on him when she hadn't. "Aspen was the one who knocked me into him. Then she tried to pour champagne on me but got the waiter instead."

Did he really think anyone would believe that?

Mr. Lane gave Aspen a dark look. "Is that true?"

"Absolutely not." She kept her voice low so no one else would hear. "Lance brought his annoying friends along and they were just being jerks."

It didn't seem like her father believed her. "You need to stop picking on your brother. It's always something with him. Just let it go."

Aspen looked outraged.

Lance grinned like an idiot.

Was this a joke? Did the owner of a billion dollar company really believe his punk-ass son just because he was a boy?

"You should just fire her, Dad," Lance said seriously. "She's an embarrassment."

Aspen looked like she might explode.

Her dad started to eat like the conversation no longer interested him.

I knew I should stay out of the argument because it wasn't my place but I couldn't let Aspen be knocked around like a punching bag. "Sir, Lance did pour champagne on that waiter. It was an unprovoked attack. I saw the entire thing."

Their father turned his gaze on Lance. "Rhett says you're lying. What do you say to that?"

"Who cares what he says? He's just a punk."

I stared him down without blinking. This guy was a scumbag.

"I do," Mr. Lane said. "And you're suspended from work without pay for two weeks."

I tried not to smile in victory.

Aspen didn't hide her joy. "Asshole..." she mumbled.

"What the fuck?" Lance said. "That's not fair."

"Do not cuss," Mr. Lane hissed. "We're in public."

Lance opened his mouth to speak but was cut off.

"You want me to make it three weeks?" Mr. Lane threatened.

It was pathetic that Lance had to be disciplined like a child.

Lance threw his napkin down and marched off.

Mr. Lane ate like nothing just happened.

Aspen turned to her father. "When I say something you don't believe me. But when Rhett, a guy you hardly know, says Lance is acting like a child, you believe him?"

He sighed. "Don't get started, Aspen."

She turned away like she'd been slapped in the face.

I held her hand under the table and tried to comfort her. It was ridiculous she had to put up with this. Of the three of them, she was the most responsible and logical one. "Think about that sundae we're going to get," I whispered in her ear.

Somehow, she found the strength to smile. "With a cherry on top."

I smiled at her, glad she didn't let her woes weigh her down. "I'll give you mine so you'll have two."

"You practically just gave me your soul."

"Well, make sure you enjoy it."

She squeezed my hand. "Oh, I will."

***

She and I left the fundraiser the moment they announced the last winner of the silent auction. Without saying goodbye to her father or spitting on her brother, which was an impressive feat, we slipped out and reached the crowded sidewalk.

"Geez, that was torture." She tucked her clutch under her arm and walked beside me, keeping her grace despite the sky-high heels. Her shoulders were back and her spine was perfectly straight. She turned heads as she walked.

"Good thing I got paid for it," I said as I nudged her in the side playfully.

She laughed then nudged me back. "Well, you got ripped off."

"It wasn't so bad," I said. "There was a full bar, dinner, and I got to spend the night with a beautiful woman."

She gave me a slow smile then faced forward. "You're sweet."

"And not just because I'm paid to be sweet."

"You wouldn't tell me otherwise even if it were true."

"No, probably not," I said.

We entered a small ice cream parlor a few blocks away then approached the glass that protected the ice cream from coughs and sneezes.

She touched my arm gently then leaned toward my ear, like she was going to share a secret with me. "You know those scenes on TV when the mother or father goes to the room where they keep all the babies in the hospital after they're born, and they stare in amazement at how beautiful their child is?"

"Yeah." I had a feeling I knew where she was going with this.

"That's how I feel every time I get ice cream." She tapped the glass with her fingers then gave me a smile that clearly said she wasn't ashamed.

I chuckled. "Were you obese as a child?"

"No. Somehow, I learned restraint."

"Well, don't hold back tonight."

"I won't," she said. "After that terrible evening, I need a monster size. Alcohol fixes most people. But my poison is ice cream."

"At least it's less detrimental than alcohol."

"What's your poison?" she asked.

I put my hands in my pockets as I thought of a response. "Running."

She stared at me blankly. "Running?"

"Whenever I'm really upset, I'll go for a long run. The endorphins you release during intense physical activity minimize pain."

She rolled her eyes then looked away. "Lame…"

"How is that lame?"

"A poison is something you abuse, something you shouldn't use as a crutch. Your poison is healthy, so it's lame."

"I never thought doing the smart thing would make me lame."

"Well, it does."

"Why don't you try it sometime?" I asked.

She gave me that look that clearly said, "You're crazy."

"What?" I asked with a laugh. "I can tell you work out."

"I run," she said. "But I have to force myself to go. And for a full hour before that I try to make excuses to get out of it. *Like, I have to do the dishes. I have to make the grocery list. A nap doesn't sound bad…*"

I tried not to laugh. "For what it's worth, I'm not judging you."

"Oh, I feel so much better now," she said sarcastically.

I laughed even though I didn't want to. When she was away from the stress of her dysfunctional family, she was really cool. She made me laugh more times than I could count.

The guy behind the counter approached her. "What can I get you?"

Her eyes lit up like a child. "Monster sundae with rocky road and extra fudge." She said it quickly like she'd been eager to order for a while.

"You got it," he said. "Two spoons?"

"Uh, no..." She shot me an apprehensive look then turned back to the guy. "That's just for me."

"Oh." He seemed embarrassed by the assumption. "And you, sir?"

"I'll have the same," I said. "And one spoon."

"Wow, you're going to eat all of that, Mr. Perfect?" she asked.

"When did I ever say I was perfect?" I countered.

She made her voice deep and imitated me. "When I'm upset, I run. I founded a successful company all on my own. Modeling? That's beneath me..."

I knew she was kidding so I wasn't offended. "You hit the nail right on the head."

"I know." She moved to the register and opened her wallet.

I quickly handed the guy a twenty. "Keep the change, man."

"Why are you paying?" she asked. "I hired you for the evening."

"I may be working but I'm still a gentleman," I said. "And you needed a treat after that night." I carried our sundaes to a table then took off my jacket to get more comfortable.

She eyed my shirt for a moment before she dug into her sundae. She didn't eat it slowly or with tiny bites like most women. She scarfed it down, eating it before it started to melt. I couldn't count the number of times I took a girl out for ice cream and her cup melted because she ate so slowly or didn't eat it at all.

"Who taught you to eat ice cream?" I asked.

"Pardon?"

I nodded to her sundae. "You know your way around a spoon."

"I usually get ice cream with Harper, and if I don't eat fast, I don't eat. You catch my drift?"

"I think so," I said with a smile.

She finished before me, and then she eyed the cherry sitting in my bowl. She gave me a look that said, "That's mine."

I dropped it in her bowl. "It's all yours, sweetheart."

She ate both of her cherries. "Delicious. I could eat a whole bottle of these."

"They sell them at the grocery store."

"But that's a slippery slope," she said. "First it would be the cherries...and then it would be the ice cream...and then it would be the chocolate syrup. Before I knew what happened, there would be an ice cream bar in my house."

"Harper and I would be there all the time," I said.

She laughed loudly, her eyes watering.

I didn't think my comment was that funny.

She dabbed her wet eyes with a napkin. "Sorry. I just imagined the three of us sitting in my apartment with a real ice cream bar. I found it hilarious for some reason."

I ate my ice cream while I smiled, which was hard to do. "I'm glad I could make you laugh. I think it's better than any poison."

"And it's a good workout for the abs. If I didn't laugh, I'd be all flab."

I doubted that. "So, what's next?"

She dropped her plastic spoon in her empty cup. "Well, he liked you—a lot. That's a good start. Honestly, I feared he wouldn't. But you handled it very well."

"When you have something in common, it's easy to find something to talk about," I said. "And people usually like people they can relate to."

"True."

"Hopefully this moves you in the right direction."

"I think it will." Her eyes looked distant, like she was thinking about something deep and complex. Then she turned her eyes on me, the trance broken. "Thank you so much. It's nice to feel in control again."

Her sincerity caught me off guard. "No problem." I held her gaze, entranced by the green eyes that were so vibrant they looked fake.

"As soon as that company is mine, I won't have to stress about him anymore. I can make the right decisions for everyone. And I'm going to fire that pathetic excuse I call my brother."

"Yeah...Lance was a peach."

She chuckled but it was in a sad way. "If you can believe it, he was worse when he was younger."

"No, I can," I said without hesitation.

She laughed again. "It's embarrassing..."

"Hey, we don't choose our family, right?" I said, trying to make her feel better.

"Actually, we do," she said seriously. "Harper is my family and I've chosen her. We don't share the same blood or ancestors but our minds are more alike than anyone else. For the holidays, my dad usually goes somewhere tropical with a date, or two, and I have no idea what my brother does, probably hires a prostitute for the night. I usually spend it with Harper and we have a grand time."

Aspen was unique in the sense she wasn't a selfish prick like the rest of her family, but the aspect I admired most was her attitude about it. Clearly, the circumstance bothered her but it didn't eat her alive. She had a positive outlook and refused to let it crush her soul. It was a rare and admirable characteristic.

"I hope I meet her somewhere down the road."

"She'll pop up at some point." She looked over her shoulder like she expected to see her. "And when we least expect her."

"How long have you known each other?"

"Since...I don't even remember," I said. "Elementary school? I fell on the slide and she ran over to me. My finger was swollen and painful. She grabbed a small branch that fell out of a tree and moved it around like a wand. Then she whispered a spell and fixed it. Well, at least I thought she did. Like a placebo effect, the pain went away. We've been best friends ever since."

I smiled involuntarily. "That's a cute story."

"What about you?" she asked. "Do you have a best friend?"

"Five, in a way."

"Five?" she asked in surprise.

"Well, I'm closer to one more than all the others. His name is Troy. And if he heard me say the other four were also in my inner circle, he would throw a fit."

She chuckled. "Harper is the same way."

"We've been friends since we were small. The rest is history."

"Is he an escort?"

"Yep, as well as the remaining four."

"I remember you mentioning him now."

"He's a good guy," I said. *The best, actually.*

"You guys must never run out of things to talk about."

"Nope." That was definitely true.

"Does he like escorting?" she asked.

"Not lately." I smiled at the most recent story he shared. Aspen caught the grin. "Ooh...spill it."

"He escorted this girl to a wedding where her ex would be. They were there for about five minutes when her ex came at him in a bloody rage."

"Ohmygod. What happened?"

"Troy busted his jaw." I wish I could have seen it.

"Yikes..."

"He didn't get a scratch but he can't afford it. He says his face is too pretty."

"That could have turned out worse," she said. "Good thing it didn't."

"We're all trained in some form of self-defense. I know some martial arts but my specialty is boxing."

"Why am I not surprised?"

"You should try it," I said. "I know a lot of girls who do kickboxing. They enjoy it."

"My pepper spray and keys will suffice."

I held up my hands. "I know not to mess with you..."

She kicked me playfully under the table. Her calf brushed against mine and it was soothing more than anything else. Then she pulled back and gave me a warning look.

"You taught me a lesson," I said sarcastically.

"There's more where that came from."

Aspen's playful attitude was refreshing. Our meeting didn't feel like a date at all. It felt like we were friends, and we'd been friends for a very long time.

"I'm ready whenever you are." She stacked our cups on top of each other.

I stood up then tossed our trash in the garbage. "We should get out of here before we order another round."

"The guy behind the counter would judge us."

"I'm pretty sure he already judged you," I teased.

She nudged me in the side.

I laughed then rubbed my ribs like she actually hurt me.

We walked back to her apartment, both of us walking particularly slow. I wasn't in a hurry for the night to end and she seemed to feel the same way.

When she crossed her arms over her chest and rubbed her biceps, I knew the nighttime chill had gotten to her. I removed my jacket then placed it over her shoulders. It blanketed her like a trench coat.

"Thank you." She pulled it closer around her.

"It looks better on you than it does me."

"Are you saying I look like a dude?"

"Prettiest dude I've ever seen."

"Well, in that case…" She grinned then faced forward. "So, do you have any siblings?"

I thought of Chase and his ridiculous paranoia. "One younger brother."

"What's he like?"

"Smart, friendly, considerate, and funny."

"You want to switch brothers?" she asked seriously.

If only she knew. But I would take my brother over hers any day. Sometimes his phobia ruined my night, and paying his rent and bills got old. But he was still a great person who appreciated everything I did for him. I enjoyed spending time with him even though I had to pretend I carried an undefeatable Shadow Sword. "Never."

"Smart choice," she said. "You couldn't handle Lance."

"I'd smash his face in a few times." I wasn't joking. He was a classic jerk, someone who deserved to have his skull cracked against the concrete in front of a group of spectators. He didn't understand the foundation of what a real man was. Pouring champagne on a waiter was pathetic and tasteless.

"I'd help you," she said. "I've slapped him before. But nothing I do knocks any sense into his empty brain."

"Your father seems stern. I'm surprised he lets him get away with whatever he wants."

"My father is very old. My mother was twenty years younger than him. The only reason why Lance and I exist is because she insisted she needed to have children."

Knowing her father never wanted her must have been difficult.

"Anyway, since he comes from an older generation, he doesn't believe women should be in the workplace at all. He's the most sexist pig I've ever met."

"Then how did you get a job there?"

"I volunteered in order to prove myself. When he realized I was making his life a million times easier, he hired me as an assistant director. But never once has he thanked me for all I've done. Most of the people on the payroll are men but when the company was investigated for sexism, he was forced to hire more women. That's the only reason why they're there, and of course, they are all in low positions, like clerks and secretaries." She rolled her eyes. "Would you judge me if I said I hated him?"

"Not in the slightest."

"Good. I absolutely loathe the man."

"Now I understand why he ignores Lance's obvious flaws."

"Because he has a penis between his legs." She actually growled at the end of her sentence.

I found the action cute. "Did you just growl?"

"I growl when I get really angry. If I ever growl at you, run."

"I'll remember that."

"Whenever I growl at Harper, she just growls back."

"She sounds fearless," I noted.

"Crazy is a better word."

I rubbed the back of my neck. "So, your father will give you the company if you have a man in your life? Does that mean he wants him to work for the company as well, to supervise you?"

She looked away. "Probably."

I never felt worse for Aspen. She was doomed to disappoint her father no matter what she did.

We arrived at her apartment and she unlocked the door. "I get you until midnight, right?"

"Yep."

"Well, I want the most bang for my buck. Come in."

I walked inside then eyed the flowers I brought. They lightened up the room.

"Want to play Battleship?"

Did she just ask me that? "Battleship?"

"Yeah. You've never played it?" She picked up the box from the couch and looked at me.

Seeing a beautiful woman in a floor length gown that sparkled, along with elegantly curled hair and just the right amount of makeup, holding a child's game was naturally disconcerting. It was the last thing I expected her to say. "I just wasn't expecting you to ask."

She narrowed her eyes at me. "Do you suck?"

"No," I said defensively.

"Do you want to play then?" She sat on one end of the couch and pulled her station into her lap.

I sat on the opposite corner then got my pins ready. "Ladies first."

"E1?"

I cocked an eyebrow. "Hit."

She grinned then put the red pen in her station.

"A3."

"Miss. E2?"

"Hit," I said in irritation.

She put the pin in with a slight smirk on her lips.

"B9?" I asked.

"Miss." She was clearly enjoying this. "E3?"

"You've sunk my battleship." Aspen kicked my ass right from the beginning.

She flipped her hair over one shoulder. "And that's how it's done."

I stared at her, watching her outline contrast against the sight of the city through the window. She was the perfect specimen to represent a real woman, one whose beauty outshined others without any effort. She had the smile of a model for a toothpaste commercial, and she had the legs of a swimsuit model. But her beauty underneath was more powerful than anything else. And now she was playing a game like a child, completely oblivious to all her charms.

I didn't know what to make of it.

***

"Duuuuude." Troy bellowed into the phone the instant I answered. "Party at Cato's. Get your ass over here."

"Hello to you too."

"Don't be a bitch and just get over here." He hung up without waiting for a response.

It was hard to tell when Troy was drunk because he acted exactly the same sober or wasted. But if he was at a party, he was probably drunk.

I headed to Cato's apartment on the east side with a pack of beer in my hand. When I walked up the stairs, I heard the deafening sound of the bass from his stereo. If I could hear it from here, then his neighbors weren't going to get much sleep tonight.

The door was open so I walked inside and moved past the crowd. Ice chests littered the ground in the kitchen so I tossed the beers in the first one I could find. I popped the lid on one and downed it like water.

"Duuuuude!"

I turned at the sound of Troy's voice. "When did you start calling me dude all the time?"

"Dude, shut up and talk to me." He wore a gray t-shirt with jeans that hung low on his hips.

"Which one do you want me to do?" I asked. "Shut up or talk to you?"

"Well, you just talked so I'm going to go with the second one."

I grinned. "Asshole."

He laughed then clapped my arm. "So many hot chicks here."

"I just walked in."

"Well, they're everywhere so just keep your eyes peeled."

90

I took another drink of my beer.

"Hey, how'd it go with Laura? Are her tits real?" Troy always spoke his mind, to anyone.

"It didn't work out."

"I could tell she was snooty. If she leaned her head back any further, her nostrils would act as teacups."

"We had a great time but when she found out I was an escort, she walked out without saying a word to me."

"Seriously?" He looked thunderstruck. "She's hot but not *that* hot."

I shrugged and drank my beer.

"Whatever. Her tits weren't even that nice anyway."

"I wouldn't know."

"I can tell." He waved his fingers in front of his eyes. "I got x-ray, bro."

A blonde in heels walked past us to the refrigerator.

Troy eyed her then turned to me. "She's cute. Go for her."

"I didn't even see her face."

"Who cares?" he said. "Her ass looks great. That's all that matters."

She walked by again and Troy did something I've never seen before.

He pulled his keys out of his pocket then threw them over his shoulder. They made a loud clank against the tile when they landed. It was heard over the music.

She stopped and turned around, noticing the sound.

"Did you drop these?" Troy asked as he picked them up.

She stared at them suspiciously. "No..."

"Good. Because they're mine." He positioned her in front of me then walked off.

I wasn't mad because the sight was so humorous. "I'm sorry about that."

She relaxed as she looked at my face, obviously liking what she saw. Her eyes took me in, and they settled on my shoulders for a long time before they returned to my face. "I've never seen you before."

"I'm Rhett." I extended my hand to shake hers.

She didn't take it. Instead, she came closer to me, her chest almost touching mine. "Trixie."

"It's nice to meet you," I said politely.

"Likewise." She twisted a strand of hair in her fingers while she batted her eyelashes at me.

"So, what music do you—"

"Are we going to make out or what?"

Cato knew the sluttiest girls. I wasn't sure where he found them. Most of them were models, so I assumed they would have the confidence to play hardball. Sometimes it was nice to find an easy kill, a beautiful woman who would let me fuck her without having a single conversation about anything somewhat important, but I wasn't in the mood tonight. And she was too skinny for my taste. "I actually need to be somewhere..." I moved around her.

"Dick," she hissed.

I turned back to her. "If what you're selling is always free, no one is going to want it."

Her eyes narrowed in offense.

I kept walking and moved through the crowd. I really was a dick to her, but I wouldn't be a nice guy to a bitch. If she wanted me to respect her, then she needed to respect me.

When I reached the living room, Cato was doing a kegstand.

Troy recorded it on his phone. "He's not going to remember this tomorrow. I got to document it."

I turned my head while I watched him. "Impressive."

"You want to go next?"

"You think I want to suck on the same hose Cato is using?" I asked. "He probably has syphilis or something."

He nodded. "Word." He ended the recording then pocketed his phone. He eyed me for a moment. "Where's that blonde I hooked you up with? Did you fuck her already?"

"Yeah...I was in and out of there in two minutes."

He clapped my shoulder. "Aren't there for the ladies, huh?" He wiggled his eyebrows.

Sometimes he didn't get sarcasm.

"I wasn't into her. She was too skinny and her breath reeked."

"Like what?" he asked.

"Like beer and vomit mixed together."

"Gross." He cringed. "But you don't need to kiss her while you screw her."

"Why don't *you* screw her?" I demanded.

He shook his head. "I'm not going to screw a girl that smells like vomit."

I stared at him incredulously. "Then what makes you think I want to?"

"Well, that date didn't go well, right? Which means you didn't get laid."

"I can get laid whenever I want and you know that." I drank my beer then watched Cato lay on the ground after he inhaled a trough of beer.

He looked around the room. "You have your pick of the crop."

I glanced around and saw a lot of pretty girls. But I just wasn't in the mood for any of them.

"How did work go the other night?"

"Good," I said. "It was pretty fun, actually."

"Fun?" he asked in surprise. "Did you just say that?"

"Yeah. We went to this fundraiser, and that was pretty lame, but then we got ice cream and played Battleship. She kicked my ass five times in a row."

"Battleship?" He looked at me like I was crazy. "Did you go on a date with a twelve-year-old boy?"

I shook my head and released a quick laugh. "No, she was actually really hot."

"Hot?" he asked. "Like, how hot?"

"I'd say a nine point five or a ten."

He whistled. "Damn, you got any pictures?"

"No, sorry."

"Damn," he said. "Why did I get stuck with a girl with a psycho ex but you get a hot chick who likes Battleship?"

"The world works in mysterious ways…"

He shook his head then downed his beer. "I don't get paid enough for this shit."

"Half a million a year isn't a salary to bitch about."

He stared at me with an angry look. "The guy went straight for the money maker." He pointed at his face.

"There are plenty of plastic surgeons in the city."

"I'm all natural, bitch. Maybe you should get some fake tits."

I laughed, loving how mad he was getting.

"Are you escorting this girl again?"

"Yeah. She's trying to take over a company from her father but he wants her to have a serious boyfriend."

He rubbed his chin. "That's weird."

I shrugged. "The guy was a total dick so it doesn't surprise me."

"Did he like you?"

"He showed me more love in twenty minutes than he showed his daughter her entire life." It worked me up when I thought about it.

"So, she has daddy issues?" He smirked like he had a plan on his mind.

"We can't date women we escort. You know that."

"Well, if she's that hot and cool, then that's a different ball park. Secondly, I'm not escorting her. *You are*. So, she's fair game."

I knew he was joking so I didn't rise. "You couldn't get her."

"You bet your ass I could."

"She said she isn't dating right now. I can tell she's picky about the men she spends time with. There's no way she'd pick you."

"All I'd have to do is turn on the charm and she'd melt right in my hand."

I shook my head. "She's out of your league, man."

"No one is out of my league, dude."

"Well, this girl is."

"Now I have to see this chick. Get me a picture."

"No," I snapped. "I'm not going to take a picture of her like a creeper."

"Do it when she doesn't know. Set up a camera in her apartment."

I gave him a look I'd been giving him since we were kids. "You want me to break the law and get thrown in jail?"

"Hey, some girls are worth going to jail for."

"I'm done talking to you." I turned away.

"Wait." He grabbed my arm. "Does she have a big mouth?"

I gave him a confused look. "Why?"

"Girls with big mouths give great head."

I rolled my eyes but laughed at the same time. "You're going to hell."

"And you're coming with me."

Aspen

The hours passed quickly since I had so many things to do at the office. My assistant informed me I had a meeting with investors in an hour, and on top of that, I had a pile of paperwork on my desk.

As busy as I was, I kept thinking about my night with Rhett. If he weren't there, that evening would have been unbearable. He lightened the mood and didn't make me feel alone. Most of the time, John just made me feel worse.

What did I ever see in him?

When the fundraiser ended and we got out of there, the night really picked up. Getting ice cream and playing Battleship was fun. We had a lot of laughs and had a great time. Spending the evening with a beautiful man who had a great personality was worth every cent. Even though we just met, I felt like I'd known him forever. He reminded me of a Disney prince, which made me wonder if he was real from time to time.

The fact my father liked him was a great relief. Now he would get off my back about John and my good image would be restored. My dad wouldn't talk about it anymore and the scandal would remain in the past, where it belonged. While my dad still didn't value any contribution I made to the company, at least he didn't look at me like I was something stuck on the bottom of his shoe.

My assistant spoke over the intercom. "Mr. Lane would like to see you, miss."

"Thank you, Jane." I sighed then rubbed my temple. My dad played golf in his office and acted as a figurehead while I worked my ass off. I was the real worker behind the company. Why couldn't he walk down here and speak to me? Why did he have to call for me like I was a dog? I took a deep breath and let the emotion pass. I'd become a master at controlling my emotions, thanks to the abuse of my father. An excellent punching bag, taking swings and moving with the inertia.

After I talked myself down, I walked to his office.

Like I expected, he was hitting a golf ball around on the fake green.

I hate him. I hate him. I hate him. "You wanted to see me, sir?" The last conversation we had in this office hung above my head like a cloud.

You better not cry. You know how I feel about that.

I held my hands together at my waist and regarded him with a stoic expression.

Dad put down his club then abandoned his ball on the green. He crossed his arms over his chest while he regarded me like I was a stranger, not his flesh and blood. "You didn't tell me you had a boyfriend."

Why would I? It's not like we're pals. "I didn't want to say anything until I knew we were serious."

He nodded then paced around the room. "I like him, Aspen. He's a good man. I don't know how you landed him but I'm glad you did."

My eyes narrowed in offense. *I don't know how you landed him.* What the hell is that supposed to mean?

"He golfs, knows his cars, and comes from money."

"Yes, the only qualities that matter." My voice was full of sarcasm but I doubt he picked up on it.

"And, I must admit, he's a very good-looking chap. Where did you meet?"

"Coffee shop."

"I don't know how you charmed him but you did something right. It's clear he's really into you."

He didn't know how I charmed him? "Surely, you must realize I don't look like a troll and I'm a very pleasant person." It took all my strength not to rip his head off.

He ignored my statement altogether. "I want to golf with him this afternoon. Set it up."

That was short notice. I had to give Rhett's office seventy-two hours notice in order to book a date with him. That seemed unlikely. "I'll let you know."

He picked up his club again. "Let me know as soon as possible."

I wanted to beat him over the head with that damn club. "Of course, sir." I walked out.

"Aspen?"

I turned before I closed the door.

"Where are those faxes I asked for an hour ago?" he demanded.

"I emailed them to you fifty-nine minutes ago. If you were at your desk, you would have noticed." I shut the door and didn't even feel bad for snapping. The dickhead deserved it.

***

I called Danielle with hesitation. She laid down the rules already and I signed that contract. She said seventy-two hours and I doubt she would make an exception. I'm sure Rhett had other clients he had to attend to, and if not, he had a life.

She answered. "Beautiful Entourage. How may I help you?"

"Hey, Danielle. It's Aspen."

Her voice picked up in excitement. "How are you? Is Rhett performing to your satisfaction?"

"He's amazing," I blurted without thinking.

"He's quite popular with the ladies."

"Shocking..."

She chuckled. "What can I do for you?"

I knew I shouldn't even bother but I had to try. "I know you said you needed seventy-two hours notice but I was wondering if I could use Rhett this afternoon to play golf with my dad..."

There was a pause on the other end. "I'm sorry, Aspen. Rhett has other obligations, and plans his weeks accordingly. You're paying for a high quality date, not someone who can change their life around to accommodate you. He's not a dog."

"That's not what I was implying at all," I snapped. I had a long day so my tolerance was low. I could yell at Danielle but I couldn't yell at my father. "I just thought it wouldn't hurt to ask. Geez..."

Danielle breathed into the phone. "I'm sorry. I didn't mean to come off rude. Like I said before, I'm protective of my boys and I don't let people walk all over them."

"That's not what I'm trying to do. I thought if Rhett was free, by chance, it wouldn't be a big deal."

"I'll give him a call," she said with a sigh. "But don't expect this treatment again."

"Thank you," I said. "I appreciate it."

She hung up.

I got back to work, and half an hour later, my cell phone rang. "Hello?"

"Rhett is able to accommodate you. Just let me know the details when you have them."

I was surprised it actually worked out. "I will. Thank you." I hung up. Wow, I got lucky. I assumed Rhett already had another date to fulfill, and if not a date, he didn't want to pick up an extra shift, so to speak.

My phone rang again but it was a number I didn't recognize. I decided to answer it, curious whom the number belonged to. "Hello?"

"E3."

My lips stretched from ear to ear. His voice was deep and smooth, and it contained a hint of amusement. His face came into my mind, and I imagined that smile I was so fond of and his bright eyes. "Miss."

"I always miss," he said with a laugh.

I loved listening to the sound of his voice. I'd pay big money just to have his voice on a CD that I could play over and over, as stalker-ish as that made me sound. "This is a nice surprise. I thought I wasn't supposed to have your phone number?"

"It's okay to break the rules once in a while," he said. "And you don't strike me as the crazy type so I think we're good. Besides, Danielle can be a real mood killer."

I laughed into the phone. "She just cares about you."

"A little too much," he said. "She's the mother hen of our company. I've seen her pull a chunk of some girl's hair right out of her scalp, and then slap her hard across the face."

"Damn..."

"Don't mess with her. If you need me for something like this, just call me."

"Won't she be upset you gave me your number?"

He paused for a while. "It's my decision, not hers. So, your father wants to go golfing, huh?"

"I'm so sorry…"

"Hey, it's what you're paying me to do. And he's not that bad…to me at least."

"It's going to be so boring and all he'll talk about is cars and money…" I rolled my eyes just thinking about it. "You'll fall right asleep."

"How about you come along and keep me company?"

"My father didn't invite me."

"Who cares?" he said. "Tell him I invited you. Do you know how to golf?"

"Damn straight, I know how to golf."

He chuckled into the phone. "Feisty…I like it. So, come with us then. We'll get ice cream afterwards."

"Are you trying to make me fat?" I said in a teasing way.

"Like you could ever get fat," he countered. "You weigh what? A hundred and fifteen pounds?"

"One twenty, thank you very much." I was surprised he guessed my weight so well.

"My apologies," he said with a laugh.

"And that can change with enough sundaes."

"I'll believe it when I see it," he said. "So, when am I golfing?"

"Two hours. Can you make it?"

"I'll be there. Should I meet at the office or the country club?"

"Meet here," I said. "Let me know when you're in the lobby and I'll retrieve you. The building is a little confusing."

"Will do. See you then."

"Bye."

"Bye."

"Wait," I said.

"Yeah?" he asked.

"Thanks for doing this. I'm sure you have a million other things you'd rather be doing."

His voice came out quiet. "Actually, I'd rather help you."

***

Rhett was standing in the lobby wearing dark brown slacks with a black polo. Even in golf clothes, he was eye-catching. His shoulders were broad and noticeable, and the tightness of his shirt outlined his powerful chest and slender waist. His pants hung low on his hips and a belt was woven through the loops. I stared at him for a second, forgetting why I was there to begin with.

"Nice lobby," he said. He put his hands in his pockets and examined the tile floor and expansive counter where the receptionist stood.

I suspected he looked away because my obvious gawking made him uncomfortable. I needed to learn to hide my attraction to him better. "The elevator is this way…"

We stood side by side as the elevator rose.

"How's your day going?" he asked.

"It's okay." I crossed my arms over my chest so I wouldn't be tempted to touch him.

"That bad, huh?"

"My father is just being a dick, nothing unusual."

He put his arm around my waist and pulled me into his side.

My spine shivered involuntarily and I wanted to melt right then and there. Having a ridiculously handsome guy touch me like he loved me was every girl's dream. I smiled like an idiot, living in the moment.

"You got me, remember?" he said. "You aren't alone."

"I suppose."

The doors opened and we walked down the hall together. A few people in the office turned our way when they saw Rhett with his arm around my waist. I knew what they were all thinking.

Why is he with her?

Whatever. They were jealous because they weren't me.

Rhett looked around as we walked. "Fancy..."

"Your office is pretty nice too."

"But it's only one story. This has to be...fifty stories?"

"Well, we employ a lot people."

"I'll say."

We reached Dad's office and I knocked.

"Come in," he called.

Rhett opened the door and let me enter first.

I gave him a smile because I couldn't help it. He was so charming and thoughtful. John never went out of his way for me.

Dad's eyes lit up when he spotted Rhett. "There's the man I wanted to see." He shook his hand then patted his back. "Ready to hit the green?"

"I'm always ready, sir."

"Excellent, my boy," Dad said. "Let's go." He turned to me. "You can hold down the fort while I'm gone?"

I would hope so...since I do it every damn day. "Yeah—"

"Actually, I invited her along," Rhett said. "I've never seen her golf. Is that okay, sir?"

"Sure," Dad said. "Why not?"

Rhett grabbed my hand and walked out with me. When we made it to the lobby, Dad turned to Rhett. "Where are your clubs, kid?"

"In my car," he answered. "Should we carpool?"

"You tell me," he said. "Have you ever been inside a Bentley?" A mischievous look was on his face.

"No, sir. I never have," Rhett said.

"Then you're in for a surprise."

Rhett and I retrieved his clubs from his trunk then joined my father in the parking garage. When Rhett opened the passenger door for me to sit down, Dad intervened.

"You need to sit up front, kid. Otherwise you don't get the full experience. Aspen has been in this thing a million times."

Actually, I'd been in it twice. But whatever.

"Good idea, sir." He opened the back door for me to get inside.

I kept a stoic expression as I got in, not wanting to snap at my dad while he was warming up to Rhett.

For the entire drive, they discussed the Bentley and how shiny and pretty it was. I just stared out the window and tried not to fall asleep. How could my father care so much about something that didn't matter, but be totally oblivious to something as paramount as clean and renewable energy? I tried not to think about it because it made me want to slash his tires and key the doors.

When we arrived at the course, it was a beautiful day. The sun shined in a cloudless sky, and the green had its own distinct smell. Golf carts were scattered throughout the course, and a slight breeze moved through my hair. Since my golf clubs were at home, I had to rent a set. If I had my own, I would play better but it wasn't a big deal. It didn't matter what clubs I used. I was still a better golfer than my dad even though he would rather say he was a transvestite than admit I was good at anything.

Rhett continued the boring conversation with my father but touched me whenever affection was permitted. When we began our eight-hole course, Rhett turned to me. "Ladies first."

I grabbed my driver then stood over my ball. I carefully planned out my swing and how I intended to hit the ball.

Dad and Rhett discussed tax loopholes, something my father was particularly interested in. Rhett kept up in the conversation, and I was surprised he knew so much about the topic. He owned a business himself but it was small, not a billion dollar corporation like my father's. But there didn't seem to be anything he wasn't knowledgeable about. He was one of the brightest men I'd ever met.

They totally ignored me so I took my time lining up the shot. The hole was over a slight hill and dangerously close to a sand pit. The slight breeze also played a factor into my calculations. When I had everything set up, I pulled my driver back then hit it with a predetermined amount of force.

The ball flew through the air then hit the green with a thud. I swear I could hear it even though it was impossible. I shielded my eyes from the sun as I examined my ball. It rolled slightly, heading right for the hole. Then it dropped inside. I smiled to myself, proud of my golfing abilities.

Take that, Dad.

"Did you just make that shot?" Rhett asked in surprise. His eyes were wide and his jaw was hanging.

"Yep." I put the driver over one shoulder and put one hand on my hip. "Watch out, Tiger Woods."

"That was amazing." Rhett couldn't control his shock. "I've never seen that happen in my life, except at the Masters Tournaments. How did you...?" He couldn't wrap his mind around it. "I'm sorry." He put down his club and started to clap. "That deserves a round of applause."

Rhett was already making this day better. At least he acknowledged my accomplishments and acted like they actually mattered. Dad was never impressed with anything I did. I could win the Nobel Prize and he wouldn't give a damn.

"Isn't that amazing, sir?" Rhett asked. "You raised a fine daughter."

"Yeah..." He pressed his lips together like they were chapped. "She's a decent golfer for a woman."

"For a woman?" Rhett asked incredulously. I could tell he was combating his anger, sick of the way my father treated me like garbage. The fact I didn't have a penis dangling between my legs somehow made me worthless. "She's a great golfer—period."

I put my hand on his arm, silently reminding him why I hired him in the first place.

Dad put his ball down and got ready to swing. "The first hole is always the easiest one."

Rhett took a deep breath but didn't explode. He did a great job hiding his irritation, but I could tell he was struggling. The more time he spent with my father, the more his tolerance started to wane. I wasn't sure how I put up with it my entire life.

Dad made his swing and the ball glided across the course. It landed near the flag but didn't sink in.

"So much for it being the easiest hole..." Rhett muttered under his breath.

I squeezed his arm again.

He sighed then put his ball down and made his hit.

The afternoon was spent with them bonding while I stood there awkwardly and tried to decide what color to paint my nails. Pink? Nah, I did that color last time. French tips? But that was so old...

When the game was over and scores were tallied, I was in the lead by five points. Rhett came in second, and of course, Dad came in last.

"Good game." Dad shook Rhett's hand. "You have a great swing. Who taught you to golf?"

"My uncle."

"He must be a fine golfer."

"He does alright," Rhett said with a smile. "Nothing compared to me."

Dad chuckled. "We need to do this again sometime. It's nice to play with someone who knows their way around the course."

Uh, hello? Do I not exist?

Rhett gave me a sad look but didn't voice his thoughts.

When we returned to the office, my shift was long over. I'd have more work to do tomorrow, but I refused to go back in there and pick up where I left off. I had enough of the office for one day.

"Thank you for inviting me, sir." Rhett shook Dad's hand.

"Of course," he said. "I want to see more of you. You're a fine young man."

"Why, thank you, sir," Rhett said gracefully. "That means a lot."

Dad nodded to me without speaking then got back into his car and drove away.

Rhett gave me a look of admiration when Dad was down the street. "How do you not poison his scotch?"

I sighed. "I don't know. But I'm asking for a raise tomorrow."

***

After we returned his clubs to his trunk, we headed to the nearest ice cream parlor. I needed a big-ass sundae, like, right this second.

After we sat down with our treats, Rhett spoke. "Where did you learn to golf like that? You obviously didn't learn from your father."

"I hired a golf pro a few years ago. It's a long story." I shoveled the ice cream into my mouth, grateful for the cool, crisp taste.

"I'm yours for the afternoon so I have the time." He ate his ice cream slowly, like he wasn't really hungry. He probably just came because he knew I needed something fattening in my stomach pronto.

"Well, this was years ago when I was stupid," I said bluntly.

"Stupid?" he asked with a hint of a smile. "You don't strike me as the stupid type."

"Wait to cast judgment until you hear the story. Believe me, you'll think I'm stupid when I'm finished."

"I'm still skeptical but I'll keep an open mind." His blue eyes looked into my face, waiting to hear the story. They were so deep that I wanted to fall inside and never crawl out.

"Years ago, I was at a point in my life when I was desperate for his approval. I would get his coffee before he asked for it, work overtime every day just so he wouldn't have to lift a finger, and I went above and beyond to make this man notice me. Since he loves golf so much, I assumed if I impressed him with my skills, he would pay more attention to me. Then he would invite me to golf with him and it could be an activity we did together."

His eyes softened while he listened to me, and I knew he pitied me.

"So, I paid someone to teach me. I practiced every day, and he praised me as I got better. It came to a point where he had nothing left to teach me. He said if my father wasn't impressed, he was totally blind."

"Then what happened?" he asked quietly.

"I invited my dad golfing, and after he saw me play, he asked if I was a dyke."

His eyes widened then narrowed in confusion. "Sorry?"

It was such a ridiculous thing to say. I didn't blame Rhett for being completely confused by it. "He asked if I was a dyke or a lesbian. Why would I be so good at a man's game unless I was trying to be a man myself?" I shook my head in disapproval. "A woman good at sports? Oh, there must be something wrong with her then. He's despicable. Sometimes I wish he would crash in that stupid car of his and die." I realized my words after I said them and guilt washed through me. It was such a cold thing to say and I felt terrible. I let my anger get carried away. "I didn't mean that...I take it back."

Rhett stopped eating his ice cream and gave me all his focus. "I wouldn't blame you if you didn't take it back."

"My father has his flaws and there are a million things I hate about him but...he's never hurt me physically and he hasn't killed anyone so he doesn't deserve that."

"Evil doesn't come in black and white. It comes in shades of gray."

I was grateful Rhett was so understanding. I knew how ugly I was being right then.

"He doesn't treat you right and you don't deserve that," he said seriously. "I hope he realizes that someday."

"He never will." There wasn't a doubt in my mind.

"Sometimes only catastrophic events are strong enough to change someone's way of thinking."

"If I was lying in the hospital from a terrible accident, he wouldn't blink an eye over it. He wouldn't even visit me." I pretended to be indifferent to the words I was saying, but as I said them, I felt terrible. And I knew it was because everything I said was true. "If I didn't care about this company so damn much, I would never speak to him again. He wouldn't call me either."

"I wish there was something I could do." His voice came out quiet and hollow, like he was in as much pain as I was.

"You're already doing it, Rhett. You're already in his good graces. He even told me this afternoon that he 'doesn't understand how I landed you.'" I got a chunk of fudge on my spoon and shoved it into my mouth like I was starving.

"Who the hell says that to his daughter?" he demanded. "You're so amazing. What man wouldn't be proud to call you his daughter?" An incredulous look came into his eyes and he dropped his gaze.

"Beats me..."

"Sometimes it's hard to believe that people have such a weird way of thinking. Why your father treats you that way is beyond my understanding. It makes me wonder why he is the way he is."

I'd never thought about it. To me, he was just born an ass.

"Do you have any theories?" he asked.

"About what?" I asked.

"Why he behaves that way."

I swirled the nuts around in my cup. "I've never given it much thought. I know he grew up poor and made his own way in life. But I would assume that would make him humble, not a monster. I never knew my grandparents, so maybe they were abusive to him or something."

"Maybe you should ask him…"

"My father and I never discuss anything besides work. It's just not possible for us to talk about anything else."

"What was your mom like?"

I didn't like thinking about her, but not because I disliked her. She was an amazing woman, and I still missed her every day. She was warm and always made me feel loved. But that was why I didn't like to think about her. Because I missed her so much. "She was the best mom in the whole world."

He regarded me seriously. "I'm glad you had her to balance out your father."

"Yeah…she was great." I stared at my ice cream and suddenly lost my appetite.

"Was he like that when she was around?"

"I wasn't working with him when she was alive so I didn't know him as well. He was never around, always working. We never had a relationship and he never tried to have one. When I got older, that's when he took it upon himself to insult me at every given opportunity."

He considered my words for a long time. "Everyone's behavior is based on experience and emotions. There has to be a reason why he is the way he is. Hopefully, you find the answer someday."

Talking about my parents was making me depressed. "Tell me something happy."

"You want to hear a joke?"

"Yes, please."

"You're a brunette so I can tell you this one."

"Oh, this should be good…"

"An old, blind cowboy wanders into an all-girl biker bar by mistake. He finds his way to the bar and orders a shot of whiskey. After sitting there for a while, he yells to the bartender, '"Hey, do you wanna hear a blonde joke?"' The bar immediately falls absolutely silent. In a very deep, husky voice, the woman next to him says, '"Before you tell that joke, I think it's only fair you should know five things since you're blind. One, the bartender is a blonde girl with a baseball bat. Two, the bouncer is a blonde girl with a Billy Club. Three, I'm a six-foot, one hundred seventy pound blonde woman with a black belt in karate. Four, the woman to your right is a blonde professional wrestler. And five, the person to my right is a blonde weight lifter. Now think seriously, cowboy...do you still want to tell that blonde joke?"' The cowboy thinks for a second then shakes his head and says, '"No, not if I'm gonna have to explain it five times..."'"

It took me a second to absorb the punch line, and then I busted up laughing. Tears came out of my eyes and I wiped away the moisture with a napkin. "Wow, that was good. Did you make that up?"

"No," he said with an amused laugh. "If I did, I'd be a comedian. I read it somewhere online. It stuck with me for some reason."

"Well, it was good. Thank you for cheering me up."

"No problem. You needed a pick-me-up."

Having saved my cherry for last, I picked it up and ate it off the stem.

He pushed his cup forward. "You can have mine."

"You gave me yours last time."

"I'm not a big fan anyway."

"Alright then...I'm going to scarf it down."

His eyes brightened in affection, like he was amused by my addiction to cherries. "Any day now…"

I snapped it off the stem then devoured it. "Yum."

He stacked our cups on top of each other just as I did last time. "Now what?"

"Well, golfing is out of the way so you're a free man."

"What happened to getting the most bang for your buck?" he asked.

"This date wasn't scheduled so I'm not going to take up all of your free time."

"I don't have plans," he said. "How about Battleship? I think I might beat you this time."

I laughed like a villain, high, cold, and loud. "No one can beat me."

The corner of his lip upturned in a smile. "I've been practicing."

"You can't practice Battleship," I said. "It's just guesswork."

"You sound scared…" He crossed his arms over his chest and gave me a cocky look.

"Listen up, escort," I said. "I'm not scared of anyone or anything."

"You should be scared of me," he said seriously. "Because I'm about to steal your victory."

I shook my head while I narrowed my eyes at him. "You're going down."

"You're going downer."

I tilted my head and gave him a quizzical expression. "Good one."

He covered his face then laughed. "Too much pressure…I couldn't think of something better." Every time he laughed, his lips upturned in a smile. He had the most amazing grin I'd ever seen. It made me feel warm. And it was infectious. When he was happy, I was happy.

"Hopefully you can stand the pressure of Battleship better than shit-talking."

"Let's find out."

***

"Seriously, are you cheating?" he asked from across the couch.

"How would I cheat?" I demanded.

He looked over his shoulder. "Is there a mirror behind me?"

"I'm just good," I argued. "Give it a try sometime."

"Burn..."

We played five times so I was worn out. "Do you play cards?"

"Like poker?" he asked.

"Yeah."

"Do you?" he asked in surprise.

"Why are you always shocked about my capabilities?"

He put the game aside. "I've never met a girl who plays poker. And I've certainly never met a grown woman who still loves Battleship."

"Hey, it's a great game."

He held up his hands in surrender. "I never said it wasn't."

"Well, I'm very good at poker."

"Who taught you?"

"Harper, of course."

"I really need to meet this girl," he said seriously.

A sudden surge of jealousy rushed through me. Harper was a beautiful girl and Rhett would obviously realize it the moment he saw her. What if he wanted to date her? What if

115

they hooked up? It shouldn't bother me since he was just my escort, but truthfully, I didn't want to share him with anyone, at least knowingly. "So, you want to play?"

"I'm not playing for money," he said firmly.

"Why? You don't want to lose your cash to a girl?"

"No...I just don't want to take yours."

"I'm a big girl." I opened up a deck and grabbed some poker chips.

"Let's play for fun," he said. "No money."

"Where's the fun in that?" I asked. "Let's at least play for change."

He considered it for a moment. "Change, I can do."

We pulled out all our quarters, nickels and dimes. Then we started the game. Rhett was good like I expected him to be, but so was I. We were evenly matched. Every time he won a hand, I won the next one. Change moved back and forth and no one seemed to have the edge.

"Not as good as you thought, huh?" he teased.

"Maybe you're cheating," I noted.

"I'm good at math but I can't count cards."

"Like you would tell me if you could."

"Actually, I would," he said seriously. "You could take me to a casino and show me off to your father. The money would be rolling in."

I rolled my eyes because that actually sounded like something that would impress my dad.

"What else are you good at?" he asked.

"Um..." I pondered the question for a moment. "I'm a pretty good pitcher."

"Yeah?"

"I played softball in college."

"Cool," he said. "Anything else?"

"Nothing comes to mind. What about you?"

"I can hold my breath for four minutes. The average is two minutes."

"Wow," I said. "What did the president say when you met him?"

He chuckled then kicked me playfully. "Hey, you try it. It's hard."

"I didn't say it wasn't. Where do you box?"

"I have a trainer," he said. "Crunch Fitness."

"Why do you box?" I asked. "For protection or fun?"

"Both," he answered. "And I get bored jogging and lifting weights. At least this sport is applicable to real life. I can actually use it if I need to."

"Maybe I should take self-defense. It could be fun."

"You should," he said. "Then you can really mess up your brother."

"Man, I would love that..." I put my cards down. "Full house, punk."

"Punk?" he asked with a laugh.

I took all the change in the center and pulled it toward me. "I'm going to visit a gumball machine and go crazy."

"Make sure you go to the dentist afterwards," he teased.

I shuffled the cards and put them back in the box. "Well, that was fun."

"You're always fun." His eyes bored into mine, like he was searching for something. The look was intense and vulnerable.

Before he swept me off my feet, I looked down. Spending time with Rhett was enjoyable and I looked forward to it, despite the fact my father having to be around, but I had to be smart about it. If I wasn't careful, I could fall in love with

Rhett. I didn't think that was possible after John but I was starting to have doubts.

He looked at his watch. "It's midnight already? I spent eight hours with you and it feels like ten minutes."

"Time flies when you're playing Battleship and poker."

"I haven't done any of this since I was a kid. It's nice to revisit it."

"Harper and I act like children, I swear." I put everything back into the Battleship box and placed the lid on top.

"That's not a bad thing," he said. "Everyone is so serious in New York. It's nice to meet someone who's cool and fun."

"Cool and fun?" I asked. "Me?"

"Definitely." Sincerity was in his voice.

"Harper would be the first to tell you I need a chill pill."

"The people who love us most tease us," he said. "Troy makes jabs at me whenever possible."

"Maybe they just don't like us."

He shook his head. "There's a thin line between love and hate."

"That's true." I tossed the deck of cards on top of Battleship.

He didn't move from the couch or act like he was about to leave. I assumed since it was midnight, he would be on his way, not that I wanted him to go anywhere. Sometimes I forgot I was paying him to spend time with me. He seemed like a friend, someone who'd been in my life for so long that the past was blurry. "Can I ask you a personal question?"

He'd never asked me something like that before. I hoped he didn't ask about John. But he didn't know about him so he shouldn't. I was just being paranoid. "Sure."

"Are you seeing anyone?" He rested his knee on the opposite ankle and sat perfectly straight. His shoulders were broad and powerful.

Against my will, I imagined him naked in the same position. I gripped his shoulders while I lowered myself onto his shaft. Then in the heat of passion, we moved together, gripping each other tightly as sweat covered our bodies. I shook the thought away, realizing I was being a huge pervert. "No." Why did he want to know? Hope surged through me then extinguished just as quickly. While I was attracted to Rhett, it was unlikely he was attracted to me. He did this for a living and he was always professional. I doubt he'd make it complicated over one girl, unless she was extremely special. "Why?"

"I was just curious," he said quietly. "If you had a boyfriend, I doubt he'd appreciate me spending all this time with you."

"I'm not dating right now." *Or ever, probably.*

"I remember you mentioning that."

"Then why did you ask if I was seeing someone?" I countered.

"Just because someone says something doesn't mean it can't change. Maybe you met someone on the subway and you really hit off. He asked you out and you couldn't say no. Life happens."

"No, I haven't had any romantic subway encounters."

He stared at me with an unreadable gaze.

"Are you seeing anyone?" Did I really just ask him that? I blurted it out without even thinking.

"No, I'm not," he said. "I went on a date with this girl a few weeks ago but it didn't go anywhere."

I felt bad for the girl. When he didn't call, she was probably devastated. I knew I would be. I'd only known Rhett for a few weeks and I was hooked. If he asked me out on a date, I'd be ecstatic. "It takes a while to find the right person." I didn't know what else to say.

"Actually, she walked out on me. We just finished dinner when she left without saying a word."

Did I miss something? "Why?"

"I told her what I did for a living, and she gave me a disgusted look then walked out."

Was she a psychopath? "The girl was obviously off her rocker so you probably saved yourself some headaches."

He smiled but the look didn't reach his eyes. "Stuff like that actually happens a lot. Girls don't like my profession, even though it's just friendly. They can't look past it. The girls who do want me are more interested in my money, looks, and sex. They don't see me as boyfriend material."

My mind was blank, but I was thinking a million things. A gorgeous guy like him probably got laid every night without trying. I was stupid to ever assume otherwise. If he wanted a girlfriend, he would quit his profession. But he obviously liked the lifestyle of a bachelor. I couldn't blame him. Any handsome man would do the same thing. Why settle down when he can have endless one-night stands with beautiful women? Sadness tugged at my heart and I hated myself for caring. There was no possibility he and I could even share a kiss so it was stupid to be disappointed. He was my friend as long as I continued to pay him.

"Can I ask you something else?" he asked.

I didn't want to discuss the topic anymore but I didn't want to be rude. "I guess."

"Why aren't you dating right now?"

I didn't want to talk about my relationship baggage. Telling a guy I was attracted to that my old boyfriend left me because I was terrible in bed didn't sound tempting at all. "I'm just not in the right place…" I couldn't think of a more vague response.

"Bad break up?" he asked.

"Something like that." I didn't make eye contact with him, hoping the conversation was over.

"When did this happen?" His voice was casual and gentle.

Heat was rising to my cheeks and I felt uncomfortable. My skin started to burn and I searched for an escape. "You know, I'm really tired. I should probably get to bed since I have to work in the morning…" I stood up and faked a yawn.

"Yeah, of course." He stood up then put his hands in his pockets. "It is almost one. Sometimes I forget that people work during the day."

"It must be nice not to wake up to the sound of an alarm clock."

"No complaints." He walked to the door then opened it. "Let me know when you need me next."

"I will."

"Don't be afraid to call me. You don't have to go through Danielle all the time."

"Okay."

Before he walked out, he did something he'd never done before. He pulled me into his arms and hugged me tightly. There was no one to impress, and this wasn't a performance. It was real.

He rested his chin on my head while he held me for a long time.

The touch felt wonderful. It was soothing and warm, comfortable and safe. His hard chest felt like concrete but it was inviting at the same time. His smell came into my nose, and

I was reminded of pine needles and a river. His shirt was soft on my cheek and I wish I were wearing it to bed. My hands moved around his waist, and not caring I was being ridiculous, I returned the embrace with more enthusiasm than normal. It was nice to feel someone hold me, especially Rhett. He was the most beautiful person I'd ever met, and to feel this connection with him was surreal. He was the friend I never had. Harper was always there for me but with Rhett...it was different. Did he feel it too? Or was it just me? It probably was just me. All his dates probably hugged him like a teddy bear and never wanted to let him go. I was just as obsessed, falling for a man I could never have. The fact he slept with random women and had meaningless sex didn't bother me. It was irrelevant. All I cared about was the man I knew, the man who showed more compassion and empathy than anyone else I'd ever encountered. Rhett was a beautiful person, on the inside as well as the outside.

He stayed still, letting the hug continue. He probably knew the embrace meant more to me than it did to him, so he let me soak it up. He had plenty of experience dealing with girls like me.

It took all my strength to pull away, but somehow I managed it. "Good night."

He stared at me for a long time, his eyes more blue than I'd ever seen. He didn't respond. Instead, he just stared at me.

I'd give anything to know what he was thinking. Absolutely anything. All the money in my savings, my apartment, even one of my kidneys.

Finally, he released a breath he was holding then stepped away. "Good night."

I watched him go. When the door was shut and the bolt was locked, I felt lost, like I lost a piece of myself the moment he was gone.

Rhett

Troy, Cato, and I were having Thai for lunch. There was a place in Manhattan that Troy insisted was the best Thai food in the world.

"The best Thai food in the world?" Cato asked with a voice full of sarcasm and annoyance. "Better than in Thailand?"

"Actually, yeah," Troy said before he stuffed fried noodles into his mouth with chopsticks.

"That makes no sense, bro." Cato shot him a glare before he continued eating.

It was nice not to deal with Troy's oddness for once. Cato could deal with it.

"Real Thai food is probably greasy and full of weird shit. Americanized Thai food is better. It's like it's made for Americans. You get it?" Troy kept eating like the matter was settled.

Cato opened his mouth to argue but I held up my hand. "Trust me, let it go."

Cato seemed to debate it for a moment before he decided my advice was wise. He turned his attention back to his pot stickers.

"How did your escort go?" I asked.

"It was okay until the end of the night," Cato said.

"What happened?" Troy asked.

"The girl was expecting me to sleep with her. I'm not sure why because Danielle made it clear that's not the type of business we run," Cato said.

"What did she do?" I asked.

"Something cliché," Cato said. "A trench coat with slutty lingerie underneath."

"Was she cute?" I asked.

"Very cute," Cato said. "But I hightailed it out of there quick. I really don't want to sleep with a girl who needs to pay for it. Can you imagine what she probably has...in terms of diseases?"

The thought had crossed my mind too.

"That gets so old," Troy said. "We make it clear what business we're running but every woman thinks we'll make an exception. Like, we'll fall in love with them or something." He rolled his eyes. "It's hella annoying."

"Yeah," I agreed.

"How's it going with Battleship?" Troy asked.

Cato turned to me. "Battleship?"

"One of my clients likes to play Battleship at the end of the night," I said. "She's pretty cool. Really gorgeous."

"Did you get a picture?" Troy demanded.

"No." Even if I had one, I wouldn't show it to him. Aspen had become a good friend and I didn't want men to objectify her. And I didn't want to share her with anyone either.

"Damn," Troy said as he snapped his fingers. "You need to get on that."

"Don't they have her picture on file at the office?" Cato asked. "Her driver's license?"

"Oh yeah!" Troy smacked his forehead in realization. "Let's head over there after dinner."

"No." I stared him down with that expression that said, "Drop it."

"No?" Cato asked. "We all got keys, man."

"I mean it." I didn't raise my voice but I threatened them with my tone.

Troy knew I wasn't messing around. He understood when I was being serious, partially serious, and straight up serious. Right now, he knew which one it was. "Let it go, Cato."

Cato cocked an eyebrow. "You got a thing for this broad?"

"No," I said. "I just don't want to head down to the office so you guys can rate her on a scale. She's my friend and I don't want you to disrespect her."

"You're the one who said she was a ten," Troy countered.

"A ten?" Cato asked in surprise. "The highest I've seen is a nine point five. A ten? Damn, that never happens."

Now I wish I hadn't said that to Troy. "Drop it, alright?"

"Battleship is off limits, apparently," Troy said as he gave Cato a meaningful look.

"That's not fair," Cato argued. "Just because you can't fuck her doesn't mean we can't."

"No one is going to fuck her," I snapped. "Even look at her wrong and I'll snap your neck."

Troy's face broke out in a stupid grin. "You so have a thing for this girl."

"No, I don't," I said. "She's been through a lot and doesn't need two fuckheads harassing her."

Cato watched me with squinted eyes, like he didn't believe me. "You're fucking her, aren't you?"

"I'm not," I said through clenched teeth.

"Dude, you can't do that," Troy said. "We could get in serious legal trouble if you did."

"I'm aware of that," I hissed. "Which is why I haven't slept with her."

"So you do want to sleep with her!" Troy fist-pumped the air like he solved a cold case.

"No, I don't," I said calmly. "She's a friend, like all my clients are."

"I'm not buying that," Cato said. "If you think she's a ten, then you're attracted to her."

"I never said I wasn't," I replied in a bored voice.

"Therefore, you want to stick it to her," Troy said.

"So, you're saying if she weren't your client, you wouldn't tap that?" Cato asked.

"I wouldn't say that..." I shrugged in omission. "If I met her on the street, maybe. But she doesn't strike me as the kind of girl who just sleeps with any pretty boy. I'm sure she gets hit on left and right. She probably gets tired of it just like we do."

Troy shook his head. "Rhett has always been a little sensitive..."

I ignored the jab. "Let's change the subject, alright?"

"You never answered my question," Troy said.

"What?" I asked.

"How's it going with Battleship?" Troy asked.

"Oh," I said. "Fine. Her dad is a total dick to her. I don't understand how this chick doesn't kill him in his sleep."

"She has daddy issues," Troy whispered to Cato.

"Those are the best," Cato whispered back.

I glared at them. "I'm not going to answer your question if you aren't going to listen."

"Pull your thong out of your ass, man." Troy sipped his soda then returned to eating his noodles.

"Her dad has taken a liking to me," I said. "I hope he'll give her the company soon. She deserves it. We went golfing last week and Battleship made a hole in one on her first try."

"Seriously?" Troy asked.

"Go, Battleship," Cato said in an impressed voice.

"She beat both of us," I said with pride in my voice. "And she's pretty good at poker."

"Does she have six brothers or something?" Troy asked.

"Just one," I said. "And he's a total dickhead. I hate the guy."

"This chick must have some serious issues," Troy said as he ate his rice.

"She handles it pretty well, actually." I smiled when I remembered how much ice cream she ate when she was upset. She was lucky she had a fast metabolism.

"At least she's not one of those emo girls," Troy said. "You know, the kind that cry all the time."

I couldn't picture Aspen crying. She seemed too tough for that.

"Really annoying," Cato said.

"Her dad expected me to golf with him at the drop of a hat. When she called me, I had to ditch my workout early," I said.

Troy knocked over his soda and it dripped off the table onto the seat. Cato was getting wet but he was too shocked to react. They both eyed me like I was crazy, oblivious to the mess they just made.

What did I say?

Cato finally snapped out of it then absorbed the liquid with his napkin. Troy helped and diverted most of the soda onto the floor. When the disaster was averted, they turned to me.

"What the fuck did you just say?" Troy demanded.

"I honestly don't know."

"She called you?" Cato asked. "As in, on your phone?"

Now I understood. "She's not a weirdo like some of the others. You guys can chill out."

"Are you crazy?" Troy's eyes were about to fall out of his head. His blue eyes looked black in his panic. "That's against the rules."

"Seriously, it's not a big deal," I said. "She's cool."

"She acts like she's cool until she turns into a stalker and tries to kill you while you sleep," Cato barked. "What the hell are you thinking?"

"It's my decision," I said. "And I think it's fine."

"Why would you even want her to have your number?" Troy asked. "If you don't want to screw her?"

"Just in case she needs me for a last minute meeting or event," I said. "This girl needs help and I'm going to get her through it. She wouldn't abuse my number."

"Until she starts texting you in the middle of the night, telling you she loves you and some shit," Troy said.

"Then I'll change my number," I said. "Problem solved."

"You're either really into her or you're an idiot," Troy said seriously.

"Then I'm just an idiot," I replied.

"Fine, it's your funeral," Cato said. "When she turns into a psychopath, we'll be there to spit on your grave."

I picked up my chopsticks and returned to eating. "Don't forget to piss on it too."

***

Aspen called me when I was at home watching TV. I stared at her name on the screen and felt warmth spark in my veins. It traveled through my body and lit me on fire. Then it disappeared just as quickly. "A1."

"Miss," she said with a laugh. "I would never pick A1."

"Why not?" I asked.

"Too easy," she said. "Now think of a spot and I'll try to guess."

"Okay." *B4.*

"You got it?" she asked.

"Yep."

"Hmm…" She thought about it for a long time. "B4?"

My jaw dropped. "Seriously, how do you do that?"

She laughed into the phone. "I guess I can read your mind."

"I knew you were cheating."

"Mind reading is not cheating," she argued.

"Well, it's definitely not fair."

"Who said life was fair?" she countered.

I shook my head even though she couldn't see me. A grin stretched my face and made my muscles sore. I tried to stop but my mouth wouldn't respond. "Good point."

"Okay, I'm thinking of one. Care to guess?"

"You're a cheater," I said. "If I guess right, you'll change your answer."

"I'm a cheater, not a liar. They're totally different."

"Actually, they aren't," I said with a laugh.

"Well, I promise I won't."

"Okay, fine." I pondered what she was thinking. Then I picked one. "D5."

"Nope."

I growled then slapped my thigh. "What was it?"

"A1."

"But you said you would never pick that one!"

"Why do you think I chose it?" She laughed into the phone.

I laughed even though I wished I wouldn't. "Aspen, I can't compete with you."

"Well, duh. You can't beat a cheater."

My cheeks hurt from smiling like an idiot.

"What are you doing?" she asked.

"Watching Criminal Minds."

"What?" she asked. "That show gives me the creeps."

"That's why I only watch it before the sun goes down."

"Even then…" She shivered over the phone.

"Don't care for horror?" I asked as I lay on the couch and propped my feet up.

"No," she said immediately. "I'm a drama, comedy kind of girl."

"Dramas have violence."

"I don't have a problem with violence, language, blood, or sex. I just don't like horror films. A movie created only to make me pee my pants in fright is not a movie I want to see."

"Well, Criminal Minds isn't horror. "

"It's still too scary."

"Do you watch Dexter?"

"I love that show," she said. "Well, the first four seasons. After that, it went down the drain."

"Hey, I say the same thing."

"I know," she said with a chuckle. "I read your mind."

I chuckled. "What am I thinking right now?" I focused on A1. She would never figure it out.

"Hmm…" She thought for a moment. "A1?"

"Okay, this is freaking me out." I ran my fingers through my hair anxiously, blown away by how well she could read me.

She laughed. "Did I actually get it?"

"Are you a mind reader?" I asked. "Seriously? Because now I'm convinced you are."

Her hearty laugh came into the phone. "I just know you really well."

I met Aspen three weeks ago, but she did know me really well. And I knew her. "What are you doing?"

"Painting my nails."

"What color?"

"I still have to decide that," she said. "I've narrowed it down to either pink, purple, or blue."

"Hmm..."

"What do you recommend, Rhett?"

I liked the way she said my name. Her voice had maturity to it but also a hint of playfulness. "Pink."

"Yeah?"

"Pink looks good on your skin tone."

"When have you seen me wear pink?" she asked.

"I can just tell," I said vaguely. "Purple would look good too."

"Make sure you get it right, Rhett. My nails are on the line here."

"Go with pink," I said firmly.

"Alright...I'm going for it." She adjusted the phone as she freed up her hands.

"Are you doing your fingers or toes?"

"Toes." I heard her blow over the phone.

An image of her blowing into my ear came into my mind. Arousal coursed through me suddenly and violently.

When I realized I was hard, I felt guilty. Then it went away. "Going out with Harper?"

"No. I got a date with my TV tonight."

"Steamy," I said.

"When nude scenes come on, it gets hot and heavy."

"Make sure you put the Do Not Disturb sign outside."

"Oh, I will. Wouldn't want to be interrupted." Her playfulness came out in full swing.

"What are you doing for dinner?"

"Probably eating a bowl of cereal," she said. "I'm too lazy to head to the store."

"What kind of cereal?" I asked.

"Lucky Charms."

"Excellent choice," I said in an awed voice.

"I prefer Captain Crunch but I ran out of that."

"Even better," I said.

"What are you doing for dinner?"

"I'll probably make some chicken, veggies, and potatoes."

"Yum," she said. "I can cook but choose not to."

"Come over." The words were out of my mouth before I realized it. The sentence hadn't even formed in my brain before I blurted it out. Now it was too late to take it back. And I didn't want to.

"Uh...tonight?" Hesitation was in her voice.

I couldn't pull out now. It would make things awkward. "Yeah. I'll turn off Criminal Minds so you won't be scared."

She still seemed on the fence. "I don't have anything to bring..."

"I got everything. Just come over. I want to see your nails anyway."

Aspen was quiet for a long time. "I'll be there in half an hour. Is that okay?"

I smiled against my will. "Yeah. I'll get cooking."

"Where do you live?"

I was going to break two rules—already. I'd never struggled to keep my confidentiality before. "You got a pen?" I gave it to her without hesitation. If she did become a crazy stalker, I was screwed. It was easy to change a number but more difficult to change an address. "I'll see you soon."

***

I had a nice apartment that overlooked the park. It had floor-to-ceiling windows, dark leather furniture, and the hardwood floors were new. When the money started coming in, I bought it at the first chance I had. It was spacious with a nice living room and an extra bedroom I used as an office. I felt at home, and the view was the best part.

She knocked on the door lightly, like she feared I was sleeping.

I never had a client at my place before. This was new territory for me. Aspen made me feel comfortable although I couldn't explain how. She was just easy to be around. Time couldn't be measured accurately. It was like I'd known her forever even though I really knew nothing about her. Her movements always caught my attention. I studied the way she ate with a spoon, noting how she slid it in and out of her mouth. While I cared about all my clients, I cared about Aspen in a unique way.

I answered the door and the anxiety I felt about my hasty choice evaporated. She wore jeans and a t-shirt. It was the first time I'd seen her wearing something casual. And she looked really cute. She held up a box of margaritas in a can.

"Okay...I know they're girly and cheap but it's all I had."

A grin stretched my lips involuntarily. "I like these."

Her eyes smiled but her lips didn't. "You're such a liar."

"Okay, you caught me. I've never had them before. But I'll give them a shot."

"I guess bringing nothing was better than bringing something in this case."

"Knock it off." My hand moved to her waist and I pulled her into the apartment. "Thank you for bringing them. Honestly."

She moved into my side naturally. "At least you aren't a jerk about it."

"When am I ever a jerk?" I looked down into her face.

"Never." She grabbed the canned margaritas and moved to the kitchen, leaving my embrace.

I hadn't even realized I was touching her until she moved away.

"It smells good in here."

I came behind her then stirred the vegetables. "Everything is almost ready."

"How can I help?"

"You can't," I said. "Actually, you can set the table."

"Good. I need to do something other than bring cheap booze." She opened the cabinets and pulled out the plates and silverware.

I removed everything from the oven and stove. The chicken came out perfectly, juicy and moist, and the potatoes were thoroughly cooked. I carried the dishes to the kitchen table then returned to grab the box of margaritas.

Aspen smirked when she spotted them. "Are we seriously going to drink those?"

I looked at the box. "They're mango flavored."

She laughed then sat across from me. The table faced the window so there was a view of the skyline. "Your apartment is beautiful."

"Thank you." I served the food for both of us then began to eat.

"How long have you lived here?"

"For a few years."

"It would be hard to leave this place."

"I bought it, actually."

"Oh cool," she said. "It's hard to find good apartments for sale. They're usually sold within minutes after they go on the market."

"I got lucky."

She ate elegantly, like someone trained to eat with grace at diplomatic work parties. "Everything tastes really good. I didn't realize you were a chef."

"Thank you. I know how to throw together a few things. Beyond that, I'm pretty clueless."

"Well, you're off to a good start." She ate most of her plate then grabbed a can. "I want to see just how bad these things are." She opened it then took a sip. Her face contorted into different expressions until she nodded. "Not bad."

I opened one and took a sip. "I'm actually impressed."

She held her can up to mine. "Cheers."

"Cheers." I clanked my can against hers then took a long drink.

She set hers down on the table then took a deep breath. "Whoa, those are strong."

I eyed the can. "It's eight percent..."

Her cheeks reddened in embarrassment. "I'm a lightweight."

"At least it's cheaper for you to get drunk." I finished one can then moved onto the next.

"Good thing I have no pride." She finished her plate until there wasn't a crumb left. "That was awesome."

I was glad she liked my cooking. "Thank you." She complimented me three times and I couldn't think of another response.

She stayed in her seat then opened another can. "How many of these do you think you can down?"

"Until you get drunk?" I asked.

"Yeah."

"All of them," I said bluntly. "And not even then."

She chuckled. "My max is four." She held the can to her lips and took a drink.

I eyed her nails. "Your nails look nice."

"Thanks." She held up both hands, and one set of nails was colorless. "Didn't get a chance to finish both."

I tried not to laugh. "It looks...cool."

She eyed them. "I'm starting a fashion trend."

"Teenagers all over the country will be following in your steps soon enough."

"What an accomplishment," she said sarcastically.

When I finished my sixth can, I pushed the box away. "I can't drink anymore of that." I laughed even though it wasn't funny. The eight percent alcohol was getting to me.

She pushed hers away too. "That's enough mango for one night. Good thing we had dinner first."

"Okay...they are pretty bad."

Her eyes sparkled in amusement, obviously not offended the drinks weren't a hit. "Harper brought them over one night and I was too lazy to throw them away."

"Harper brought them...sure." There was a teasing tone to my voice.

She kicked me playfully under the table. "Classy girls like me don't drink margaritas from a can."

"And what do they drink?" I asked.

She shrugged. "Beer?"

I laughed for the zillionth time that night. "If your father saw you drink beer, he would call you a dyke again."

She covered her face and laughed. "Ohmygod, he would."

"Do you need some water to wash down all the mango?"

"No, I'm okay," she said. "But thank you."

"So...Criminal Minds?" I asked.

"The sun is gone," she said. "We can't watch it now."

"But there're two of us. So it's okay."

"I'll never be able to walk home in the dark after watching that..."

"I'll walk you home," I said immediately. I was going to offer anyway.

"I don't know..."

"I have a bat under the couch," I said. "Does that help?"

She took a deep breath. "Okay, I think I can handle it."

We left the kitchen table then moved to the leather sofas. We sat beside each other as I turned on the TV. Her knees were pulled to her chest like that would give her extra protection. "I hope the victim is a dude," she whispered.

"Then I'll be scared," I said.

"Well, it can't be a girl."

"Maybe they can have the victim be an alien," I said. "Then no one would be scared."

"Did you know some of these are based off of true cases?"

I swallowed the pretend lump in my throat. "No..."

"See? It's terrifying."

"We'll be fine, Aspen." I patted her thigh absentmindedly then returned my hand to my lap.

We watched the show in silence, and Aspen only flinched once. When the credits rolled and the show ended, she relaxed.

"That wasn't so bad," I said.

"No, it wasn't," she agreed. "But I probably would have been terrified if you weren't here."

"Remember, I box. You don't want to mess with me."

"True." She was quiet for a moment before she checked her watch. "I should probably go. I didn't realize how late it was."

I was sad to see her go but I didn't say it. "Yeah, you're probably right."

"Are you a night owl or a morning person?" she asked.

"Night owl," I said immediately. "It's when I come alive."

"I'm the opposite," she said. "Like an old woman, if I don't go to bed by a reasonable time, I'm grouchy."

"Well, we're usually out until midnight."

"Midnight is usually when I go to bed."

"You're the only old woman I know who has a bedtime that late," I teased.

She grabbed her purse and stopped when she reached the kitchen. "Should we just toss those?"

"That's a good idea," I said. "My boys would tease me mercilessly if they saw those in my refrigerator."

"Wouldn't blame them."

On the way out, I dumped them in the trash shoot and walked back to her apartment. She walked close to me, peering into the shadows.

I watched her, amused. "No one is going to kill us, Aspen."

"You don't know that. It's best to be on alert."

"You got me for protection," I said. "So, you're safe."

She moved closer into my side.

When we reached her apartment, I walked her to the door. "Thanks for coming over for dinner."

"Thank you for inviting me." She tucked a strand of brown hair behind her ear, and her eyes flashed in an emerald color. They were captivating and alluring. Sometimes I couldn't stop staring at them. "You're a great cook."

"Thanks. You're a great guest...the margaritas aside."

She chuckled, and like always, it sounded beautiful. "I'll bring something better next time."

I was glad she assumed there would be a next time. "Bringing yourself is enough."

Her eyes softened while she regarded me. They looked into mine, like they were searching for something. She tensed under my stare then unlocked the door. "Well, good night."

"Good night, Aspen." I wanted to hug her but I held myself back. Last time I did that, I hugged her for five minutes. I'd never done that before either. All of this was old but it was new at the same time.

She gave me a final smile before she closed the door.

I stood there for a long time before I finally walked away. I released the breath I was holding then stopped before I reached the stairs.

Aspen opened the door and yelled. "Rhett!"

I walked down the hall again. "Yeah?"

"I forgot to tell you about dinner this weekend. My dad wants to go out. That's why I called. I just...forgot I guess."

I hadn't even noticed that she didn't tell me why she called. Our conversation just took off naturally, and after talking on the phone for an hour, I invited her over for dinner where we had a great time. She never explained her purpose and I never asked for it. It just happened, like a fire naturally combusting from nothing, like the moon appearing in the sky without attracting notice, like the clouds passing overhead without further thought.

Like it was meant to happen, it did.

***

When she opened the door, I held up the bottle of maraschino cherries with a red bow on top. "Way better than flowers, right?"

She took the bottle then held it up to the light. She grinned broadly, showing all her perfect teeth. Then she brought it to her chest and hugged it like a teddy bear. "This is the best date ever."

Her enthusiasm always made me smile. She was naturally playful, and she let that side out when she was around me. It was abundantly different than the serious side she showed when she was around her father. I wondered how many people got to see that smile and glowing eyes. "I'm glad you like them. I struggled to hand them over."

"You always give me your cherries."

"Somehow, I found the strength."

She set the bottle on the counter. "As soon as this stupid dinner is over with, I'm breaking into that bottle."

"I won't judge you."

"Good. Otherwise, I'd have to fire you."

The realization that she could made me smile. "You are my boss, technically."

"And don't forget it." She grabbed her clutch off the counter. She wore a pink strapless dress that stopped just above her knees. Nude pumps were on her feet, and a silver bracelet adorned her wrist. Her hair was pulled in an updo, revealing her slender neck and petite shoulders. I stared at her hard, unable to stop.

After she locked the door, she turned to me. "Ready?"

I was shattered from my gawking. "Yes." I looked down then grinned when I noticed something interesting about her hands.

"What?" She looked down then touched her dress. "Did I spill hot sauce on my dress?"

"Hot sauce?" I asked. "Why would you spill hot sauce?"

"Well, I was eating chicken wings not that long ago…"

"Wearing that?" I asked incredulously. The image of her dressed to perfection while gnawing at a greasy chicken bone made my chest tighten in preparation for a loud laugh.

"I put on my dress first then had to do my hair. But it was wet so I had to let it dry. And I was hungry…" She pointed her finger at me. "What happened to not judging?"

"I wasn't," I said immediately. "I just…nevermind."

"What?" she pressed.

I couldn't process my thoughts into words because I didn't really understand what I was thinking or feeling. It was more of a sensation, an awareness of how I felt. I went with the best explanation I could find. "You're the coolest chick ever."

"Oh." She looked at the ground then tucked her hair behind her ear, clearly embarrassed by my words. Then she adjusted her clutch. "You're pretty cool too…"

"Not like you," I said. "I'm stiff and boring."

"Are you fishing for compliments right now?" she asked. "Because it's really annoying when people do that."

I chuckled. "No..."

She pressed me with her look.

"Okay, maybe."

She hit my arm playfully. "You're the funnest person I've ever met. Don't tell Harper I said that."

I'd never gotten a compliment like that before. I usually got comments about my appearance and my physique. It was the first time someone noticed something else, and it was a nice change. "Why, thank you."

"Are you done fishing?"

"I think I caught a pretty big one."

"Then let's go." She took a step forward. "Wait, why were you staring at me like that?"

Should I tell her? "Your other nails still aren't painted..."

She immediately looked at the nails on her right hand. "Goddammit."

I chuckled. "I doubt anyone will notice."

"You noticed," she countered.

"But I was intentionally looking for it."

"Oh well," she said with a sigh. "It's too late now." She turned to me and shrugged.

When I looked into her face, I noticed something in the corner of her mouth. It was an orange spot, almost unnoticeable.

"What now?" she asked.

I tried not to laugh. "You have hot sauce in the corner of your mouth..."

She rolled her eyes. "Of course I do." She wiped the left side of her lip.

"Other side," I said, holding back my laugh.

She used the back of her hand to wipe the area but she missed.

Without thinking, I moved my hand to her cheek and wiped away the sauce with the pad of my thumb. When I felt her skin, warmth washed through me. Quickly, it burned and radiated everywhere. I'd never touched her this way before, and I was suddenly aware of how close we were. Her breathing was quiet a moment ago but now it was amplified, loud in my ears. Her eyes sparkled like the lights on a Christmas tree, and I was aware of the scent of peppermint on her breath. I was close, closer than I'd ever been, and like a moth to a flame, I felt like I was going to get sucked into her light even though I knew it would kill me. But I still wanted to get close.

I pulled my hand away and looked at the skin of my thumb. "There," I said. "I got it." I cleared my throat, suddenly feeling the buildup of unsaid words deep in my mouth.

"I'm such a slob," she said. "Whatever."

"Whatever?" I asked, amused.

"You know how you have flaws that you constantly try to change, but no matter what you do, you can't get rid of them?"

"I don't have any flaws." I gave her a cocky grin.

She gave me a glare but the look was full of amusement. "Actually, you do. You're a cocky son-of-a-bitch."

"Oh." I pretended to be surprised. "I guess there's a first for everyone."

She shook her head then walked away. "Let's go and get this dinner over with. I'm starving."

"Didn't you just eat chicken wings?" I asked incredulously.

"Not judging, remember?"

I smiled then walked beside her, trying not to laugh.

But with her that was always difficult to manage.

***

We were a block from the restaurant when Chase called me.

"Goddammit," I said when I looked at the screen. He could be calling me because he needed me to pick up a bag of chips or dishwasher soap, or he could be calling me because he was having a panic attack somewhere. If it was the latter, his call couldn't come at a worse time. I wanted to ignore the call but I couldn't.

Aspen turned her head my way. "Everything okay?"

I stopped walking and moved out of the path of walkers toward the dry cleaner shop we were standing in front of. "I'm sorry. I need to take this."

"That's okay." Concern was in her eyes but she didn't say anything more. She joined me near the building but stayed a few feet away, trying to give me privacy.

I took the call, hoping he was just inviting me over to watch the game. "Chase?" I said when I answered.

"Come get me." His voice shook. "I'm stuck and I can't get out."

Now of all times? I wanted to scream and tell him I was sick of this idiotic phobia. It was controlling my life. I couldn't move anywhere because I had to be near him, not that I wanted to, but that wasn't the point. It was interfering with my life. I loved my brother but he didn't have a real illness. It was all in his head. "Chase, I'm working right now."

"I know. I'm sorry." His voice was shaking. "I was walking down an alley when a street light came on. Now I can't move. They're going to get me..." Fear was heavy in his voice.

I eyed Aspen, who was watching people pass on the sidewalk, and then turned my back on her and lowered my voice. "I can't just leave right now."

"I know...I'm sorry. But I can't move. I'm stuck, Rhett."

"No, you aren't," I hissed into the phone. "Get up and walk away."

"I can't…" It came out as a shaky whisper.

"Chase, you can do this," I said firmly. "Get up and start walking. Just go. Keep your eyes closed."

"Please come get me," he pleaded. "I'm sorry for calling. I wouldn't unless I had to…"

I pinched the bridge of my nose then rubbed the area between my eyebrows. A part of me wanted to desert him and force him to figure out the situation on his own, but the other part of me was terrified something would happen to my brother. He would be mugged or beaten. If he was in an alleyway, he wasn't safe. "Where are you?"

Relief came into his voice. "On the left side of the Chinese place we always go to."

"I'm on my way. Just stay calm." I hung up then turned to Aspen.

She looked at me with fear in her eyes. "Is everything alright?"

"No…" I couldn't believe I was going to screw her over like this. I hated myself. But I couldn't leave my brother. No matter what I decided, I abandoned someone I cared about. "I have to go. I'm sorry."

"Why?" Surprise filled her eyes.

"My brother needs help…it's a long story." I knew she would be mad and tell me it was wrong for me to walk away. She paid good money for my time, and I was turning my back on her. It would piss off anyone.

"Is he okay?"

I did a double take. Did she just ask that? "I have to get him. Then he'll be okay."

"Let's go." She grabbed my arm. "Where is he?"

Wait...what? "What about your dinner?"

"I'll call Dad and tell him I had an emergency. I'll put the blame on myself so he won't dislike you."

I couldn't believe she was being so understanding about this. What I was doing wasn't fair to her at all but she didn't seem to care. "Are you sure?"

"Yes," she said in an irritated voice. "Now let's go to your brother. He needs you."

She wanted to come with me? I didn't want her to know I had a crazy brother but I couldn't ditch her then tell her she couldn't come with me. "This way."

***

When we reached the Chinese restaurant, we turned the corner into the alleyway. Aspen looked around like she wasn't sure what we were doing there. It was dark except for one bright streetlamp. It flooded the area between the two buildings, shining right where Chase sat against the wall, curled in a fetal position.

"Ohmygod," Aspen said when she saw him. "Is he hurt?"

I ran over to Chase then touched his arm. "Chase, it's me."

He didn't remove his arms from covering his head. "Do you have the sword?"

Aspen stopped alongside us and watched our interaction.

"I got it," I said. "They won't hurt you. Let's go."

"Are you sure?" Chase whispered. "They're about to swarm in..."

"You're safe," I said. "Come on. Let's go."

Aspen kneeled down then rested her hand on his leg. "It's alright, Chase."

He flinched. "Who is that?"

"Aspen," I said. "She's my friend, not a shadow."

He relaxed. "Okay..."

"Now get up." I pulled his arm from his head. "You're sitting in an alleyway of New York City. There's probably pigeon vomit under you." I tried to lighten the mood by making him laugh.

Chase groaned like he was in pain.

"Come on, man." I pulled his arms down then started to pull him up.

Aspen stepped out of the way.

Chase slowly came to his feet then leaned against my shoulder like he was a wounded soldier. "Get me out of here."

I supported his weight with mine then walked him out of the alleyway.

Aspen came on the other side of him then put her arm around his waist.

"They're coming," Chase said to me.

"No, they aren't," I said firmly.

We made it around the corner and to the sidewalk. Neon lights were displayed over the buildings but there were no streetlights. There were no noticeable shadows anywhere.

"Chase, you can open your eyes now."

He popped one eye open then looked around. Then he relaxed and walked forward. He kept his arm around my shoulder like he still needed me. He was still shaken up over something he didn't actually see.

When we entered the building, I turned off the lights every time we reached a new floor so he wouldn't cower. We couldn't take the elevator since there was no way to dim the lights. We finally reached his apartment then walked inside.

Chase slammed the door and locked it. "Shit, that was close."

His apartment was illuminated with black light. All the counters were outlined with a road like marker, and the floors had lights that directed his way through the apartment. Various glow-in-the-dark orbs illuminated enough light to distinguish the inside of the apartment without casting shadows.

Aspen must think he's a freak.

Chase moved to his refrigerator then pulled out a beer. He downed it in a minute then left the bottle on the counter.

"What were you doing?" I asked.

"Just picking up dinner."

"Why did you go that way?" I asked.

"There were no lights."

I tried not to snap. "Chase, it's dangerous to go down alleyways. I've said this to you a million times. There are worse things than shadows. People will mug you and hurt you. Don't you understand that?"

"I'm always careful," he argued.

"By cowering like a child?" I snapped. "I could have pickpocketed you and you wouldn't have done anything."

"It's just money and a few credit cards," he said.

"My money. My credit cards." My voice grew louder than I meant to. "But nothing is more important than your life. This stupid fear needs to stop."

"Give me a break," Chase said. "It only happens once in a while."

"You only need to be in the wrong place at the wrong time once," I snapped.

He turned away and sighed.

"I'm not done talking to you."

He turned back to me with a resigned expression on his face.

"I'm working right now. You can't just call me and ask me to be at your beck and call like that. I'm supporting both of us, in case you forgot."

"You never let me forget," he said quietly.

I took a deep breath and let the anger wash away. Screaming and yelling wouldn't change anything. That wasn't the best way to go about it. I came closer to him. "I'm sorry...you just scare me sometimes. I'm afraid..." I couldn't even get the words out.

"I know." He stared at the ground for a moment before he looked at me again. "I'll be more careful."

"You know you can always call me, even if I'm working. But...Chase you need help."

He shook his head. "I'm not going to a hospital."

"Not a hospital," I said. "It's just a place where they help you."

"With shadows," he argued. "What's the point in them helping me when I'm dead?"

Chase was intelligent and highly logical, but when it came to this irrational phobia, he couldn't see straight. It was like I was talking to a completely different person. In any other scenario, he was fearless and brave. But when a bright light came on, he was terrified. "Shadows can't hurt you. They have no physical form. I've told you that."

He crossed his arms over his chest then shifted his weight.

"Take the Shadow Sword," I said. "It will protect you."

"No, you're meant to have that," he said. "I can't just take it."

"Yes, you can." It was something I made up but he thought it was real.

"No. It was given to you, not me. It doesn't work that way."

"What doesn't work that way?" I demanded.

"A shadow fighter can only be a shadow defeater if he's chosen. You were chosen, Rhett."

I rubbed my temple and sighed. Aspen definitely thought Chase and I were freaks. "Just be careful from now on."

"Okay," Chase said. "Want to watch TV?" He said it like everything was totally normal.

"No." I turned to Aspen. "I guess now is the time to make introductions… Aspen, this is my brother Chase. Chase, this is my friend Aspen."

"It's nice to meet you." Aspen shook his hand.

"You too," he said brightly. "Sorry I ruined your night. I didn't mean to."

"You didn't ruin our night," Aspen said. "We're just glad you're okay."

Any other girl would have stormed out and screamed in terror.

"You want a beer?" Chase asked.

"I'm okay," she said. "But thank you."

Chase leaned toward me. "She's really cute." He lowered his voice but I was certain Aspen heard him.

"I know," I said in a normal voice.

"Is she single?" he asked.

"No." I rolled my eyes and gave Aspen an apologetic look.

She smiled like she was amused.

"Damn," Chase said. "The pretty ones are always taken."

"Yeah…" I stepped closer to Aspen. "Unless you need something else, we're going to go."

"No, I'm okay," Chase said. "I hope you can pick up your night again."

"We'll be fine," Aspen said.

"Bye." I opened the door and let Aspen walk out.

Then Chase came to me and hugged me. "I'm sorry I'm such a pain in the ass. I hope one day I can be there for you like you are for me."

I took a deep breath then returned the hug. It was hard to stay mad at him when I loved him so much. "I know you will." I patted his back then stepped away.

He grabbed my shoulder before I walked out. "Dude, she's really cute. Go for it."

"She's my client."

"Whatever," he said with a shrug. "If you don't go for her, I will."

"Like you could compete with me," I said with a laugh. "You're scared of shadows."

"But that doesn't mean I'm not ridiculously charming."

"You can't even take her out to breakfast."

"Who said anything about breakfast?" he asked. "She'll only be here for the night." He wiggled his eyebrows in a cocky way then retreated inside his apartment.

I rolled my eyes then returned to Aspen, hoping this night could somehow return to normalcy.

Aspen eyed me but didn't say anything.

"Don't judge me." I was half joking, half serious.

"I'm not," she said. "But you look like you could use some ice cream." There was a playful tone to her voice.

"I definitely could use some ice cream."

She gave me a bright smile. "I'll even give you my cherry."

***

153

Aspen and I ate in silence. She hadn't asked me anything about Chase and it didn't seem like she was going to. I knew she must be curious with a million questions going through her mind. But she held her silence.

"I'm sorry about tonight," I finally said.

"There's no reason to apologize," she said. "Things happen."

"Normal things, yes," I said with a sigh. "Not stuff like that."

She didn't laugh or make a joke. She continued to eat her ice cream like everything was okay.

"I'm sorry it happened tonight of all times."

She abandoned her ice cream then put her hand over mine. Her palm was warm despite the cold treat she was eating. The touch enveloped me and made me feel safe even though it was so innocent. There was a serious look in her eyes, but there was also sympathy. "My mom got Alzheimer's when she was thirty-five. It happened so suddenly I didn't even know how to process it. Within four months, she couldn't remember my face. Every day when I saw her, I had to introduce myself and regain her trust before she even let me read to her. It interrupted my life but I refused to leave my mother. I missed birthday parties, weddings, and everything fun so I could be with her. I understand that some things are out of our control. I'm not upset and I don't think less of you for attending to your brother. If anything, I would have been upset if you put work first." Her hand remained on top of mine, and her pulse was distant and faint.

I stared into her eyes and understood her at a whole new level. Her confession made me grow fonder of her. She'd experienced more pain than anyone should, and yet, she still found the strength to smile and laugh. I felt comfortable with her, no longer afraid of the secret I hoarded. She didn't judge me or think less of me. She understood me, completely and utterly. "Thank you…"

She pulled her hand away, leaving me cold.

"I'm sorry about your mom."

Aspen looked into her cup even though it was nearly empty. "It wasn't easy to go through. My mom was an amazing woman and to watch her lose her mind like that was…painful. I tried to hold onto her memory and let it be replaced by the terrified woman she'd become. When she died…I was actually glad she was gone. To live in a state of complete confusion is no way to live."

It made me realize I had no right to complain about Chase. He may have an unusual fear but it didn't affect any other part of him. He was still my brother, the same guy I'd known my entire life. We still played games together and had a good time together. He was still the same person he'd always been. "I'm sorry," I repeated. "I'm really am."

"I know." She gave me a sad smile. Then she grabbed her cherry by the stem and dropped it in my bowl. "A little something to lighten up your night."

"You already did," I said seriously. I ate the cherry then tossed the stem back in the cup.

She rested her elbows on the table and regarded me with an expression I couldn't identify. Was it pity? Was it sympathy? Was it affection? I wasn't sure. "You want to talk about it?"

Even if she didn't open up about her mom, I would have told her about Chase. "When I was seven and Chase was five, he and my parents took a camping trip in Connecticut. They'd planned the trip for a long time but I got sick, so they left me with my aunt and uncle. Naturally, I was upset about being left

155

behind, but as soon as my aunt made me Mickey Mouse pancakes and let me watch whatever I wanted on TV, I stopped complaining." I remembered that weekend vividly, like it just happened a few weeks ago. Just because I was young didn't mean my mind wasn't absolutely clear during that time. "Something happened, even to this day nobody knows what, and my parents drove off the road and down a cliff."

Her eyes were wide and a coat of moisture developed instantly.

"The car rolled a few times then stopped at the bottom. My parents died on impact, at least that's what the authorities say. Since Chase was in the backseat he survived without a scratch. But a pile of trees they'd smacked into crashed on top of the car. As a result, it was pitch black. Chase was trapped inside for almost three days before the authorities found him. I think that's where his phobia comes from. It was dark and he was stuck with my parents' corpses. That would scar anyone..."

She looked down then sniffed.

"I'm sorry. I didn't mean to make you sad."

"I'm fine," she lied, dabbing her eyes with a napkin.

"I've been understanding of Chase's fear because it was such a traumatic thing to experience. I hoped as he aged, it would go away. My aunt and uncle raised us, and they accommodated him as much as they could. But it never went away. He fears shadows because he claims they'll suck his soul out and kill him. Chase never talks about it, and every time I ask, he won't answer, but I think my parents were still alive after the crash. I think he watched them die and could do nothing about it. He watched the light leave their eyes and their bodies stiffen. As a child, he probably thought the darkness took them, not the collision itself.

"He doesn't go out during the day unless I'm with him. I made up a lie a long time ago about having a Shadow Sword. It's an undefeatable weapon that can pierce any shadow. It's the only way he'll go out under the sun. He goes out on his own when the sun is gone, but sometimes, like tonight, something happens to freak him out. Then I have to go get him.

"He's normal in every other way. He does computer programming from home and makes decent change from that but he can't support himself on his own. My aunt and uncle are poor, so we told them he moved on from his phobia and works a regular job. I know my aunt and uncle wouldn't let me support him. They would do everything they could to handle it themselves. They don't know I make good money because I don't want them to know I'm an escort, so we had to lie. Most days, everything is good. He and I hang out like normal brothers. But there are times like this when it gets difficult and he scares the shit out of me."

She listened to me passively with emotion in her eyes. Her thoughts were unknown to me, but I knew she was hurting for me. She stared at her hands on the table before she stood up then sat in my lap.

She'd never done that before. The most she'd ever done was hold my hand. But when she moved on top of me, I pulled her close. The proximity was against the rules. It wasn't handholding or an arm around the waist. But I'd broken so many other rules that I didn't care about breaking this one.

She wrapped her arms around my neck and rested her face on my shoulder. "I'm so sorry, Rhett."

People were in the ice cream parlor but they faded away. We were alone in the world, just she and I.

"You're a wonderful brother and an amazing person." Her voice came into my ear, quiet.

My face moved into the crook of her neck and I inhaled her scent. The aroma of vanilla soothed me. I took a deep breath as her embrace halted my emotion and made me feel safe. She was small in my arms, and my hand could easily span her back. She was light as a feather and fit perfectly against me. It was nice to be held and to hold someone in return. I couldn't remember the last time I shared the experience with someone, at least like this. It's not like that after sex cuddle that was forced so I wouldn't seem rude. This was genuine and true. I wanted to hold her forever. "Thank you."

"I complain about my father all the time but at least I have one parent..."

"He may be a parent but he's not your family. Harper is your family...I'm your family. We both have a lot to live for and be grateful for. My mom always used to say life was meant to be enjoyed. I try to live by those words every day...but sometimes it's hard."

"I know." She pulled away then looked into my face. Her eyes were still moist but the water was disappearing. Her fingers moved through my hair, and she touched me gently, like she'd done it a hundred times. "But we have to keep trying."

"We do." I'd never met anyone who understood me so well or who'd been through a similar experience. Aspen became a part of me the moment we met. She was a friend I'd known my whole life but I hadn't met until now.

She took a deep breath then wiped away the smeared makeup around her face. "Battleship?"

I forced a smile. "I'd love to."

Aspen

"You've been MIA for, like, ten years," Harper said. "How's it going?" She sipped her third cosmo while she sat across from me at the booth.

The bar was quiet on a Thursday night, and a few people lingered around the room. I didn't pay attention to anything other than Harper. "My dad really likes him. He loves him like a son, actually."

"Excellent," she said. "I think you should wait a little while longer then move in for the kill."

"What kill?" I asked.

"Encourage him to retire," she said like I was stupid for not figuring it out quicker. "He doesn't do anything anyway. The sooner he's out of there, the happier everyone will be."

"I don't want to make it obvious..."

"That's why I said wait a while longer." She snapped her fingers. "Then bam."

"Bam what?"

"He's gone."

"Why do you always have to talk like a serial killer?" I asked.

"Maybe I am a serial killer," she said with an attitude.

E.L. Todd

"Remember, we've been friends for a long time. You wouldn't be happy without me."

She smiled. "You're safe...for now." She sipped her drink again. "How's it going with Rhett?"

There wasn't enough time in the day to explain how it was going with Rhett. "Good."

She cocked an eyebrow. "Good? That's all you're going to give me? Seriously?"

"Fine," I said in an exasperated voice. "It's going great. He's the most amazing and handsome man I've ever met."

"That's better." She gave me a pointed look then sipped her drink. "What's he like?"

"I already summed it up. He's the most amazing and handsome man I've ever met."

She gave me that no-bullshit look. "What's your deal? Why won't you talk about him?"

I knew why I wouldn't talk about him. "My whole life, I assumed there's no such thing as a perfect man. They're all assholes to some degree and nobody is perfect. Disney princes are the fabrication of a lunatic and they don't exist in the real world. But then Rhett proved that theory totally wrong."

"So...what's the problem?"

"I'll never have him." The air left my lungs and made me feel faint. "It's like being close to a fire but never getting warm, or standing outside a candy store with your hand pressed to the glass. It's so close but so far away."

Harper sipped her drink while examining me like I was a specimen under the microscope. "Are you falling for this guy?"

I released a sarcastic laugh. "I fell for him a long time ago, the moment I laid eyes on him, actually."

"Are you being serious right now?"

"I wish I weren't."

She gave me a sympathetic look. "I assumed you would want to jump his bones but to actually have feelings for the guy…that's rough."

"I know it is." I was stupid for letting this happen.

"Girl, you're absolutely gorgeous and I can guarantee he thinks the same thing, but keep in mind, he does this for a living. He takes women on dates for a living. I'm sure it's really hard to impress him."

"I'm not insane," I said. "I know he's not interested in me. But sometimes I wish he were…"

"I just don't want you to get hurt and put yourself out there. I'm your best friend and I'll always be honest with you. I'm not saying you can't get a gorgeous man like that, because I know you can, but this is different. I'm sure this guy is bedding more women than a prostitute. He's not looking for something serious."

"I know." I was stupid but not ignorant.

"Just don't do something you can't take back. Because if you breach the contract and make Rhett bail, you'll be screwed with your father all over again. He'll say the same bullshit as he did before."

"I know. I need to keep my eyes on the prize."

"Just don't fall in love with him during the process. That'll make it so much more painful."

"Believe me, I'm trying." I snatched her drink then took a big gulp.

"What's the big deal about him anyway?" she asked. "This is New York. We see gorgeous men all the time."

"It's not that," I said. "His looks are what I value least, actually. He's just…" How could I explain his worth in words? There was nothing in the English language to describe him correctly. "He's drop-dead gorgeous but he doesn't seem to care at all. He's not cocky and full of himself like most guys. And he's so sweet and thoughtful. He's frighteningly intelligent and knowledgeable. And he's so much fun. Every time we're together, we have a great time. He's become...one of my closest friends."

Harper listened but she didn't seem impressed by my words. "Did you ever think that maybe he's this charming and perfect man because it's his job? He's being paid to act like Prince Charming so that's what he's doing? When he's off the clock, he's probably a jerk like everyone else."

"Maybe," I said with a shrug. "But I don't believe that. He's sensitive and deep. If he's that talented of an actor, then he's in the wrong business."

"Or the right one."

Her cynicism was wearing me down. "Why can't you just believe he's truly an amazing guy?"

She downed the rest of her drink and sighed. "John ripped you apart. Seeing you go through that was just as painful for me as it was for you. I couldn't stand it if you got hurt again, not this soon. I just want to protect you. I'm not saying what you want to hear, but as your best friend, I'm not supposed to say what you want to hear. I'm supposed to tell you the truth, no matter how painful it is to listen to. This guy is trained to make women feel important and beautiful. The innate foundation of his job is deceit. He pretends to be in love with hundreds of women and he's a pro at it. He tricks parents, siblings, and friends. Isn't there a slight possibility that he's tricking you just like he's done to hundreds before you?"

I knew she was right.

"This guy isn't what he seems, and there's nothing wrong with that. Just remember you're paying him to behave this way. That doesn't mean he really is that way."

I nodded and felt the pain in my chest. "You're right."

"So don't let these emotions grow. Because at the end of the day, he's only your friend because he's paid to be. When the money stops, he'll stop. The relationship isn't real. It's just an illusion."

Harper was gentle with me when I needed it but she also gave me tough love when it was necessary. "Thanks...I know it's hard to say the things your friend doesn't want to hear."

"You can hate me all you want, but I'd rather you hate me than get hurt."

"I don't hate you." I gave her a smile. "I could never hate you, no matter how much you annoy me and drive me crazy."

"Annoy you?" She flipped her hair over one shoulder dramatically. "Impossible. I'm the coolest chick in Soho."

"We live in Manhattan so that's irrelevant," I said with a laugh.

"Fine." She flipped her hair again. "I'm the coolest chick in Manhattan."

"Uh, hello?" I waved at her. "I'm pretty sure that's me."

"Can you flip your hair like this?" She did it again, being even more dramatic.

I copied her, snapping my neck and making my hair fly.

She shook her head. "You don't have what it takes."

"When did flipping our hair like prissy bitches make us cool?" I asked.

She shrugged. "I don't know. But it's still a lost art."

Harper was odd in her humor and personality but she never got boring. I couldn't imagine having anyone else as a best friend. The best thing about having a relationship like ours was being ourselves. Even on my darkest day, she still stood beside me. We fought sometimes, like all friends do, but we always found our way back to each other.

She lifted her empty glass and examined it. "I'm dry. I need a refill."

"You've already had three."

"Maybe you're a lightweight but I'm not."

Her sentence reminded me of the evening I had with Rhett. We had dinner then downed the canned margaritas and tried to pretend they weren't absolutely disgusting and cheap. The thought made me smile.

"Let's head to the bar. You're out too."

"One drink is fine by me," I said.

"Nope. If I'm going to have four drinks, you're going to have at least two."

I shook my head. "If I didn't know you better, I'd say you were an alcoholic."

"Maybe you don't know me better." She stood up from the booth. "Let's roll." She was clearly a little buzzed already.

She and I approached the bar then ordered our drinks. While we stood there, a few guys next to us cast discreet glances our way. After John broke my heart and humiliated me, I hadn't looked at another man. I felt no loyalty to John, but being with another guy didn't interest me at all. All it would lead to was heartbreak and regret. I wasn't ready to walk down that path again. Rhett was the only exception to that, but that was only because I couldn't resist him. If he wanted me, I'd have a really hard time saying no. Actually, it would be impossible.

One of the guys stood up then walked around until he stood on my left. He was close to me, and his gaze burned into my cheek. "I'd like to buy you a drink, if you'd let me."

At least he didn't open with a cheesy line. "That's very nice of you but I'm okay." I didn't want to lead him on and waste his time. He was cute, wearing slacks and a collared shirt, but I just wasn't interested.

Harper discreetly kicked me, clearly telling me to go for it.

I ignored the pain and tried to pretend like my best friend didn't just attack me.

"Who turns down a free drink?" His voice was gentle, not abrasive, and he had a slight smile on his lips.

"A woman who's not interested." I made myself sound playful, not rude. It took a lot of courage to strike up a conversation with a random person and I didn't want to discourage him from later pursuits.

"Well, why aren't you interested?" he asked. "I'm a nice guy. Just ask my parole officer."

I laughed because the cheesy line had been used countless times.

"I made you laugh," he said proudly. "Now I earned a few minutes of your time."

Harper nudged me closer to him. "He's cute. Go for it."

"He could be a serial killer," I whispered to her.

"Well, I'm here for backup if he is."

He watched our interaction. "I'm not a serial killer so you're good."

"That's exactly what a serial killer would say," I noted.

"True," he said. "But I'm not going to kill you here so you're safe for now. I'm Rich."

"No one likes a bragger..."

He laughed. "My name is Rich. I'm not that desperate."

"Oh." My cheeks blushed and I shook his hand. "Aspen."

He whistled. "Pretty name."

"Thanks."

"Have you been to Aspen?" he asked.

"I can't say I have."

"It's a beautiful place in the winter. You should go."

"You ski?" I asked.

"Snowboard. You?"

"I can barely walk straight, let alone balance on two pieces of sticks."

He chuckled. "You seem graceful to me."

This conversation was going to a dangerous place. "Rich, I'm going to be honest. I'm not dating right now and I don't want to waste your time. There are a dozen beautiful girls in this bar. I suggest you try your luck with them."

He sighed. "Some jerk broke your heart, huh?"

"Shattered it."

"That's a shame. You're so beautiful."

"Well...thanks." My cheeks blushed slightly.

"What the hell are you doing?" Harper hissed. "Give him a chance."

Rich eyed us with an upturned lip. "Your friend seems eager."

"She just wants me to get laid," I said as I rolled my eyes.

He grinned like an idiot "I can help with that."

I was terrible in the sack so he wouldn't want a rendezvous. "It was nice meeting you, Rich. Have a good night."

"You can't hate a guy for trying, right?"

"No, of course not." I waited for him to walk away.

He didn't move. "Now that you've thoroughly rejected me and I won't be getting laid tonight, can we just talk as friends? I could hit on one of the other girls, but honestly, I'd rather talk to you. You're much more interesting."

I didn't know what to say because his words were so unusual. I couldn't reject a guy if he just wanted a friendly conversation. "I guess." I anxiously tucked a strand of hair behind my ear.

"I won't ask you out again. I promise."

I relaxed a little more. "Okay."

Rich and I talked about life in New York and his job. He was a stockbroker working at a small firm in Manhattan. He was nice and attractive but I felt nothing on my end. We stood together at the bar for a long time, making small talk.

"Aspen?"

I'd recognize that voice anywhere. It came into my wonderful dreams and wrapped around me like a soft blanket. The visions were always blurred but his face and voice were always distinguishable.

I turned to see the blue eyes I couldn't get enough of. They were seductive, luring me in until I was too deep to pull away. Like an artic glacier, they were bright and shiny under the sunlight. His fair skin highlighted his eyes, and his strong jaw was irresistible. I wanted to trail the outline with my forefinger and feel the growth of hair after a few days without a shave. He towered over me in height and his shoulders caught my attention, like they always did. I wanted to grip them while I rocked into him from above. It was a fantasy I had the moment I laid eyes on him.

My body immediately tensed at the sight of him and the air left my lungs. Then I recovered, unable to contain my excitement at his unexpected presence. Perhaps everything between us was just an act. Maybe he wasn't the charming man he pretended to be. But somewhere, deep in my heart, I knew he was.

I immediately moved into his chest and hugged him, like I hadn't seen him in ten years. His strong chest was comfortable and familiar. The scent of pine needles came into my nose. Everything about him drew me in. I hated hugging him because I knew I'd have to let go eventually. If I had it my way, we would just stay like this—forever.

Rhett didn't seem to think my over-the-top affection was odd because he held me just as fiercely. His chin rested on my head and he gripped me tightly. His chest expanded against my face, and I could feel his heart flutter violently in his chest.

My arms were hooked around his neck and I was aware of how much time had passed. At least a minute had come and gone. I was still holding onto him, like we were dancing without moving. I'd give anything to have him the way I wanted him, to share a bed with him and cuddle until the sun rose the following morning. I'd give anything to make him stay.

Rhett still didn't move. His hand slid up my back then reached my hair. His fingers touched my neck lightly then rested there. The touch was amplified in my mind. Every movement registered on my skin. A fire ignited in every place his fingers grazed.

Knowing I'd been hugging him for far too long, I pulled away slightly, hoping not to see a look of confusion on his face from the inappropriate affection. I'd have to control my emotions better. Every time I steeled my resolve, he looked at me with those blue eyes and I was lost.

But that's not the reaction I got. He looked down at me with a slight grin on his face. His eyes flashed in brightness, like he was just as happy to see me as I was to see him. His hand remained on my neck and his face was close to mine, close enough for a kiss. "What a nice surprise." His voice came out a whisper, only loud enough for us to hear.

"It is." I couldn't think of something wittier to say. He caught me off guard with his unexpected appearance.

"I figured you would be home, sharpening your cheating skills."

I chuckled. "I don't cheat."

"You just read minds?"

"I guess."

"What am I thinking right now?" He glanced at my lips then looked at my eyes.

That he wants to kiss me. But that couldn't be right. "You want another margarita from a can."

His lips stretched into the grin I loved to see. "Hell no."

"I guess I can't read minds after all."

"Maybe we can actually have a fair game of Battleship for once."

"Maybe." I looked into his eyes and felt myself fall deeper than before. It was the moment I'd been fighting, the moment I'd been dreading. People say they don't know exactly when they fall in love. It just happens, and when they look back, they try to pinpoint the right moment but don't succeed. But my moment had come. It was then, in that moment, that I fell irrevocably and madly in love with Rhett. It was done.

"Can I buy you a drink?" he asked.

"As long as it's not a margarita and doesn't taste like mango."

"Okay," he said with a chuckle. "I can do that. But classy ladies drink beer, right? So that must be what you want."

"I like beer." I'd even drink slug juice because my head was so far in the clouds.

"Then that's what I'll order." His hand stayed around my waist and he guided me against the bar. One hand rested on the counter while the other remained around my waist.

Our faces were pressed close together, and I could detect the hint of alcohol on his breath. Maybe he was a little buzzed. But so was I.

"Two beers," he said to the bartender.

I forgot Rich and Harper. All I saw was Rhett, the man who'd become my best friend in just a month. I never had more fun than when I was with him. I'd spend every day with him if I could. But I simply couldn't afford it.

Rhett grabbed his beer and took a drink.

When I looked over his shoulder, I saw Harper.

"Who the hell is that?" she mouthed while she threw her arms around.

I couldn't respond without Rhett noticing.

Then Harper tilted her head sideways and stared at his ass. She gave me two thumbs up.

I rolled my eyes at her.

"Who was that guy you were talking to?" he asked quietly.

"Rich."

"You know him?" His voice was unreadable. I couldn't figure out why he was asking.

"He's just some guy I met."

"I see." His eyes were still bright blue but there was a tint of gray to him. "Did you score a date?" he asked casually.

"No. I'll never see him again."

"Yeah?" The gray faded from his eyes.

"Yeah. He's a nice guy but..."

"But what?" he asked.

"I'm not looking for anything right now." *Except you.*

He nodded then drank his beer again.

"Are you here with anyone?" I hoped his answer was no.

"Just my friends. Who are you here with?"

"Harper."

"The famous Harper?" he asked with a smile.

"The very one."

"I have to meet her." He put down his beer and his eyes were wide with excitement.

I was a little nervous. Harper was sexy and all the guys liked her. She was a petite woman that managed to take up the whole room. What if they hit it off? What if I watched her run off with the guy I'd fallen for? I knew my jealousy was unfair. Rhett wasn't mine and could do whatever he pleased. "She's right behind you."

He turned around and dropped his embrace from my waist.

Harper froze and pretended she wasn't just making rude gestures at me with her hands. "Top of the morning to you, lad." She tipped a fake hat.

He smiled then extended his hand. "It's nice to finally meet the woman Aspen worships."

"Worships?" She shook his hand but looked at me. "I always knew you were into me."

"I can't hide it anymore," I said with a bored voice.

She dropped her hand then sized him up. "What's your name, pretty boy?"

"Rhett," he said. "I'm a friend of Aspen's."

Her eyes almost fell out of her head because she recognized his name. "It's you?"

"I told you he was gorgeous!" I mouthed over Rhett's shoulder.

"Shut up!" she mouthed back even though Rhett could see her.

He chuckled. "Yeah...I hope she's said good things."

She crossed her arms over her chest and shrugged. "Maybe...maybe not."

"You're a loyal friend," he said with a nod. "I like that."

"You got that right," Harper said with attitude. "I'll pop any guy in the jaw for messing with my girl."

"I don't think you need to worry about me," he said.

"Better not," she snapped. She acted like a hard ass, appearing taller than her five feet of height.

"In all seriousness, I'm really glad Aspen has you. You're always there for her, and Aspen deserves someone like that. When she told me she had a friend who would do anything for her, I was really happy."

Harper dropped her guard slightly but kept her eyes narrowed.

"So, thanks. If you ever need anything, let me know."

Harper clearly didn't know what to make of this sweet and sensitive man. She was falling under his spell too, just in a different way. She shot a glance at me then turned back to him. "A drink would be nice."

He chuckled. "I'm more than happy to oblige."

A tall guy appeared behind her, wearing dark jeans and a t-shirt that highlighted his arms. Like Rhett, he was gorgeous, but in his own way. He moved behind Harper, clearly checking out her ass. Then he turned to Rhett and mouthed. "Who the fuck is that?"

Rhett rubbed the back of his neck nervously, knowing I just saw what his friend did.

I smiled but kept it to myself.

He came up behind her and acted like he was humping her, though he never touched her. "Hook me up, bro," he mouthed again.

I tried not to laugh.

Harper was oblivious to all of this.

"Harper, there's someone I want to introduce you to," he said quickly, no longer calm and smooth like before.

"Yeah?" she said.

The guy walked away then rounded again, pretending like he hadn't come from behind her. "What's up?" He put his hands in his pockets and acted like he wasn't just humping her a second ago.

Rhett gave him an irritated look but didn't say anything. "Troy, this is my new friend Harper."

"Harper?" Troy asked, coming closer to her. "Wow, that's a beautiful name."

Her eyes turned playful once she took him in. He had a strong jaw, he was tall, and he had the definition of an athlete. I knew what kind of guys Harper liked and he definitely fit the bill. "You like that?" she asked. "You should hear my phone number."

Her boldness stopped surprising me a long time ago.

He nodded his head in enthusiasm. "I'd love to hear your phone number."

"Well, I'll think about giving it to you." She shifted her weight and kept her stance.

Troy didn't seem offended. In fact, he seemed more interested. "Yeah? Well, I'll think about taking it."

Rhett watched them then cleared his throat. "Troy, this is Aspen."

I liked the fact he just said my name. He didn't say friend and he didn't say a girl from work. I was just Aspen.

"Battleship?" he asked in surprise.

"What?" I asked.

Rhett rubbed the back of his neck again, clearly flustered.

Troy approached me then fist-pounded me. "Rhett says you're the best Battleship player ever."

"Well, I do okay..." So he talked about me to his friends? Did he say good things? His best friend already had a nickname for me. What did that mean? When I was in Rhett's apartment, I noticed the picture frames on the counter. Now I recognized Troy's face. "You played baseball with Troy in high school, right?"

"How did you know that?" he asked.

"I saw the picture of you guys together in his apartment," I answered. "You guys looked so cute."

Troy's neck snapped in Rhett's direction and his jaw was on the floor.

What did I say?

Rhett sighed but didn't say anything else.

The vein in Troy's neck was throbbing. "A word, Rhett?" He nodded to the left.

Rhett turned to me, an annoyed look in his eyes. "I'll be right back. Don't go anywhere."

I never want to go anywhere without you. "Okay."

He walked away with Troy until they were back at their table. I couldn't hear what Troy was saying but it was pretty clear he was yelling at Rhett. And Rhett just took it.

"I can't believe this!" Harper dropped her indifferent attitude and practically jumped on her heels.

"Troy is hot, huh?" I was just glad she wasn't into Rhett and he wasn't into her.

"No." She waved away my words like they stunk. "Rhett is so into you!"

My heart slammed into overdrive. "What?"

"He's all over you! When he started talking to you, I thought he was some guy you were sleeping with that you never told me about. But that's Rhett? Your escort?"

"Yeah..."

"That guy is over-the-moon into you. Shit, I thought he was going to kiss you."

"He didn't."

"But it looked like he wanted to."

For just an instant, I had the same thought. "But you even said he's just acting that way because I'm paying him to."

Harper spun in a circle and indicated to the room. "Is your dad here? Because I don't see him. Are you paying him for tonight's performance?"

"No..."

"And why were you at his apartment?"

"He invited me over for dinner."

"And your father wasn't there?" she asked.

"No..."

"Did you pay him for that?" she asked.

"No..."

She clapped her hands and jumped on her heels. "He's soooo into you!"

The idea of Rhett wanting to be with me, to be more than friends, was exactly what I wanted. Just entertaining the idea was thrilling. I'd fantasized about kissing him too many times to count. "You think...?"

"Trust me, he is!" She gave me that wide-eyed look that made her look like a freak.

"But...that's against the rules."

"Men will break the rules for the right woman," she said. "And Rhett is breaking his. You should go for it."

"Go for it how?"

"Kiss him."

"I don't know…"

She gave me an irritated look. "When have you ever been scared to kiss a guy?"

"When I risk losing him altogether. In the contract I signed, it said if I tell him I have romantic feelings for him, he'll never speak to me again. So, if I'm wrong, I could lose Rhett from my life and as my escort. Dad would hate me even more and I'd have to start all over. I can't risk it unless I'm absolutely right."

"Girl, I'm pretty sure…"

"But you don't know what he's thinking," I said. "Maybe he's tipsy right now. Maybe he's just a playboy." I didn't think that last part was true. Rhett might sleep around but he wouldn't treat me like that.

"I have a strong feeling about this, Aspen."

"An hour ago, you were telling me I couldn't trust him."

"But then I saw you guys together," she argued. "And there's something there."

"I don't want to get my hopes up." It would crush me if he rejected me.

She clapped her hands like a light bulb went off in her head. "Wait for him to kiss you. Be sexy so he can't resist."

I gave her a look that clearly said, "You're kidding me, right?"

"You can be sexy!" Harper said. "You're a natural at it."

"Am not! I don't walk a runway half naked then look over my shoulder."

"There are other ways to be sexy," she said.

"Like how?" I demanded.

She scratched her head. "Just...it's hard to explain."

"Well, that really helped," I said sarcastically.

Harper glanced over to the guys. "They're coming."

"Okay." I tried to be cool. "You like Troy?"

"He's an escort, isn't he?" she asked.

"Yeah."

She shook her head. "Then no."

"What's wrong with that?"

"It's just weird."

The guys arrived and halted our conversation.

"Sorry about that," Rhett said as he came to my side. "I didn't mean to be rude."

"It's okay." Butterflies the size of skyscrapers were in my stomach.

His arm moved around my waist, immediately making my heart swell in size. "Let's get back to our beer, shall we?"

"Sure."

***

The four of us sat together in a booth, Rhett and I on one side while the other two faced us. His arm was around my shoulders and he sat close to me, our bodies touching.

I was in heaven, entertaining the idea that Rhett wanted something more with me. I knew I did. I never connected with someone the way I did with him. It was like we were two sides of the same coin. He was the earth to my moon. He was the shore to my sea.

Troy was sitting close to Harper but looked at me. "Battleship, how did you get so good at the game?"

I shrugged. "Practice?"

"She cheats." Rhett winked at me. "This girl can read my mind."

177

"Just yours?" Troy asked fearfully. "Or everyone's?"

I gave him a serious look. "Everyone."

His face paled. "Well, I'm sorry about…you know…what I was thinking earlier…"

I tried not to laugh.

"We're joking, you idiot," Rhett said.

"Oh." Troy loosened up. "Yeah, me too." He added a fake laugh at the end.

Harper eyed him with a raised eyebrow. "Good thing you're pretty."

He grinned from ear-to-ear. "Yeah?" He put his arm around her shoulders.

"I guess," she said with a shrug.

"Whatever," he said. "You've been making eyes at me all night. It's time you give me that number."

"You haven't earned it," Harper said.

"How many drinks do I have to buy?" Troy asked.

"Not enough drinks in the world," Rhett teased.

"Shut the hell up, lover boy," Troy teased back.

Rhett moved his lips toward my ear. "He's sensitive."

His lips brushed my skin and my entire body broke out in goose bumps. The touch sent shivers up my spine. I hoped he didn't notice.

"Battleship," Troy said. "I heard your dad is a dick."

"You heard correctly," I said, regaining my voice.

"Sorry to hear that," he said seriously. "Rhett talks about you all the time. Actually, he never stops talking about you."

I tried not to smile. "I hope he says good things."

"Oh yeah," Troy said. "He told me—"

Rhett kicked him under the table. "That you're an amazing golfer."

Troy groaned then rubbed his knee under the table.

I wondered what he was going to say. "Did he tell you I'm obsessed with sundaes?"

"He said he's shocked you have such a sexy bod after inhaling so much ice cream," Troy said seriously.

Rhett tensed beside me but didn't say anything.

Did Rhett really say that? He thinks I have a sexy bod?

"He's joking..." Rhett's voice didn't sound normal at all.

"Hey, if you're going to give this girl your phone number and share your address with her, you may as well be honest," Troy said. He turned to me. "And he said you were a perfect ten."

Rhett kicked him under the table again.

"The kneecap..." Troy groaned again.

Rhett opened his wallet and threw a few twenties on the table. "I'm going to walk Aspen home."

I wanted to stay but he clearly wanted to get out of there. "Good night." I shot Harper a meaningful look.

She winked at me. "I hope you score," she mouthed.

"It was nice meeting you, Troy," I said.

His face was resting on the table and he was rubbing his knee. "You too..."

Rhett put his arm around my waist and walked me outside. Once we were out of the building, he relaxed slightly. His warm arm kept me close, and together, we walked. "Troy is a bit irritating sometimes. I apologize."

"I like him."

"You do?" he asked in surprise.

"He's funny."

"Yeah, hilarious," he said sarcastically. "He seemed to like Harper."

"Well, everyone likes Harper. I'm surprised you didn't."

"Why would I?" he asked. "The most beautiful woman in there was you by a landslide."

Did he just say that?

Rhett seemed to realize his mistake. "You know...yeah." He couldn't figure out something to cover his tracks.

I looked away, grinning like a teenager.

We walked to my apartment then reached my door. Rhett wore a blue t-shirt with dark jeans. His chest was highlighted in the fabric, and he looked scrumptious. More fantasies came to my mind, of us doing things that I never did with John.

Rhett put his hands in his pockets and stared at me.

I couldn't tell if he wanted to come in or drop me off like he said. I looked into his eyes, wondering what he was thinking. I'd give anything to know how he felt. I'd give anything to feel him kiss me. "Rhett?"

"Hmm?"

"Did you really say those things?" I had no idea where my bravery came from. Perhaps Harper rubbed off on me tonight.

He shifted his weight then rubbed the back of his neck, his signature move. "Would you be offended if I said yes?"

"No."

"Then yes, I said it."

I forced myself not to smile, not to dance around in joy. He thought I was hot? He thought I was a perfect ten? "I think you're a perfect ten too."

His eyes narrowed on my face and he dropped his hand to his side. The look was different than any other he'd given me. I didn't know what to make of it. He stepped closer to me, his face dangerously close to mine.

Please. Kiss. Me.

His eyes were still glued to mine. "I also think you're the most beautiful person I've ever met, and I don't just mean physically. Your past doesn't darken your skies, and you shine on. You inspire me, make me want to be a better person. You're the coolest chick I've ever met, and I've never had a relationship with a girl like this, one that was based on friendship and not sex. And....it's given me more pleasure than I've ever known."

Kiss me.

He continued to look at me, his face close to mine. "I...just want you to know that."

"I think your physical attributes pale in comparison to the goodness in your heart."

His eyes softened and the emotion shined through. "And you're the best Battleship player I've ever met."

His words were meant to make me chuckle but they didn't. I stared at him, waiting for the kiss I desperately wanted. I wanted him to change the relationship, to make it clear it was okay for me to confess my deepest and darkest feelings.

Kiss me.

He stayed where he was, his thoughts unknown.

I wanted to close the distance myself. Courage had formed in my bones and now it was pushing me forward. I decided to go for it, not afraid to see what might happen. Just as I decided to lean in, he pulled back.

"I...I should go." He stepped back and looked away, like something just gripped him by the throat and squeezed. I hadn't leaned in so I knew my intent hadn't pushed him away. It was something else, something I couldn't figure out. "Good night, Aspen." Without waiting for me to enter my apartment, he walked away.

And I missed him.

***

Jane spoke over the intercom on my desk phone. Her voice was low. "Ms. Lane, Isabella is in the building. I just thought I should warn you."

Just hearing that witch's name made me angry. "Thank you, Jane." I decided to stay in my office so there was no possibility of running into her. She was my mother's sister's daughter so I wasn't sure why she was here. My father wasn't particularly close with anyone, especially her.

I tried not to think about it, and instead thought of the man who consumed my thoughts on an hourly basis. Rhett and I had journeyed into dangerous territory the other night. I was beginning to believe there was something between us, that we could have everything I wanted.

But something held him back. I didn't know what it was and I doubt he would tell me. I hadn't called or sought him out since then. If he needed space to figure it out, I would give it to him. Perhaps his hesitance came from his work situation. Being romantically involved with me was breaking one of his own rules, and I'm sure he made those rules for a reason. And I couldn't fire him as my escort because losing Rhett would sabotage my plan for the company.

"You can't go in there!" Jane's voice shattered my thoughts. "Ma'am?"

"Do I look old to you?" a woman hissed outside my door. It sounded just like Isabella.

Did she come all the way down here just to taunt me? That's how pathetic she was.

"I'll call security," Jane threatened.

"Go ahead," Isabella said. "See what happens to your job when you do." She opened the door then stepped inside with the stiffness of a queen. An evil sneer was on her lips, and whatever she wanted to say would obviously bring her immense satisfaction.

I stared at her blankly like her presence didn't affect me whatsoever.

"Hey, Aspen." She put her hand on her hip then flipped her hair over one shoulder. "I just got my hair done. You like?"

"Is troll the new look?"

She gave me a disgusted sneer. "I'm sure you're wondering why I'm here…"

"No, but I am wondering when you'll be leaving."

"Ha," she said sarcastically. "So funny. Aspen was always the smart one…"

"What do you want?" I asked with a bored voice.

"Oh, I don't want anything," she said. "I just came by to share a bit of news."

"That face transplant has been approved?" I asked. "Good. You won't be hideous forever."

"How hideous can I be when John wants to fuck me instead of you?"

That was low and she knew it. But I acted like the words meant nothing to me, like they didn't hurt me and rip me to pieces. I was over John, but I would never be over what happened.

"Your father just gave his approval to have the wedding at his mansion in Connecticut." She gloated openly, not bothering to have any grace about it. "Isn't that wonderful? It's the same venue you and John had in mind. It's interesting how things work out, huh?"

I kept a blank expression but I was livid. Isabella didn't matter to me, but the fact my father would host a wedding to a man who was supposed to marry me was a slap in the face. He was obviously doing it to improve his public image. But he cared more about that than his daughter. Why did his heinous acts still surprise me?

Isabella smiled, knowing she got me right where it hurt. "Well, have a wonderful day." She gave me the fakest smile I'd ever seen then waved like a princess. "I'll be seeing you." She walked out then laughed when she closed the door.

I rested my head on my desk for a few minutes before I pressed the intercom to speak to Jane. "Cancel all my meetings for the rest of the day and don't bother me for any reason."

Her voice came out sad. "Yes, Ms. Lane."

Rhett

The stars in her eyes glittered like they were winking at me, enticing me to move in and seal my mouth against hers. The soft strands of hair framed her face, inviting me to touch them with my fingers during a heated embrace. Everything about her drew me in, from her looks to her heart, and even her smell.

I almost ruined everything.

If I leaned in, it would have changed the relationship irrevocably. It could have been damaged to the point where it was unfixable. It was becoming undeniably clear that my feelings toward Aspen weren't friendly in nature at all. They were strong, passionate, and powerful.

But she told me, on several occasions, she wasn't dating right now. Whatever happened in her past changed her future. She wasn't looking for a boyfriend or anything serious. If I overstepped my boundary, I could lose her altogether.

But sometimes, I imagined that her feelings were the same. She smiled at me in a way she didn't smile for anyone else. Her eyes were brighter than normal, and she laughed more with me than she did with Harper. Did we have a great time together because we were so similar? Or was it because of another reason?

Overall, all I knew was I'd never had a relationship like this with another woman. They were usually physical and superficial. I met tons of women I was immensely attracted to, and that steered the course of the relationship. But I never felt this way for a woman, where I wanted to hear her speak more than see her naked.

Aspen had become my best friend.

And I almost ruined that by kissing her like an idiot. When we stood in front of her door, there was tension in the air. She asked if I really said those superficial things about her being sexy with a perfect body.

I didn't deny it.

It was pointless to deny an attraction to her. She wasn't oblivious to her looks, so if I said her appearance didn't do anything for me, we would both know I was full of shit.

I lay in bed and stared at the ceiling. My conversation with Troy came back to me.

"You're so in love with this girl," he said. "First, her number, now your address. You better be in love with her otherwise she's going to murder you."

"I'm not in love with her." I eyed Aspen out of the corner of my eye, seeing her talk to Harper.

"Let's cut the shit, alright?" he said. "The second you saw her it was like a scene from *Romeo and Juliet.* Who hugs a friend for five damn minutes?"

I didn't have an excuse for that. When she moved into my chest and hugged me, I didn't want to let go. The only reason I did was because she pulled away first. "We're just...really good friends."

Troy looked like he was going to smash a beer bottle over my head. "Nobody in this room believes that so don't bother. If you're into this girl, you need to terminate her as your client. You can't keep this up."

"She needs me. I can't do that."

"You're going to get us into a lawsuit for prostitution," he snapped. "Sleeping with her and accepting cash is prostitution."

"I haven't slept with her."

"Yet," he corrected.

"I won't," I said firmly.

He sighed. "Seriously, why don't you just drop her as a client then ask her out? It's what you want. And I admit, she is a perfect ten."

"One, I need to finish what I promised her I would do. Two, she said, several times, that she's not dating right now."

"Then be fuck buddies with her." Troy said it like it was the most obvious thing in the world.

"She's not like that and that's not what I want."

"Just tell her how you feel. She clearly feels the same way."

"I'm really not sure..." Sometimes I thought she did and sometimes I thought she didn't.

"Then you're blind," he said simply. "Stop being a pussy and just tell her how you feel. Who cares if she rejects you? When have you ever been afraid?"

"Never," I said. "But I've never felt this way about anyone before..."

"At least you admit it," he said as he rolled his eyes.

"It's too risky," I said. "If she doesn't feel the same way, I lose her altogether. If I make her uncomfortable, not only will she want nothing to do with me, but I'll ruin her chance of getting the company. I can't be selfish just to get what I want."

"Then what?" he asked. "What are you going to do?"

I rubbed the back of my neck while I considered the possibilities. "When our professional relationship is over, I'll go for it."

"At least we're getting somewhere," he said.

I continued to stare at the ceiling while the clock on my nightstand clicked distantly. Aspen's face came into my mind, and her image lulled me to sleep. When my thoughts drifted and became blurred, I knew I was asleep.

Then my dreams became livid and intense. Blinding emotions ripped through me, and the visions felt real. They were the kind of dreams I never wanted to end, the kind that made me want to remain asleep forever just to cherish.

In my dream, I lay on the bed with my back resting against the headboard. I was naked, and Aspen straddled my lap, her naked skin visible for me to enjoy. Her voluptuous tits were in my face and they shook every time she moved. Aspen gripped my shoulders while she rode me, taking in my shaft over and over. Every time I stretched her, she moaned dramatically, like sex had never felt so good in her life. My hands moved to her waist and I guided her up and down quicker, feeling the intense pleasure start at the tip of my cock and radiate everywhere. I breathed hard, and then suddenly, the vision ended and I was awoken.

I tried to catch the dream again by keeping my eyes closed but it never returned. I was suddenly aware of how warm I was. Sweat was on my chest and forehead. I kicked the blankets back and realized my cock was rock hard.

I took a deep breath, irritated my dream had faded. I still remembered the way Aspen looked while she rode me. I'd never seen something so beautiful in my life. Now my cock was throbbing and I was horny as hell. I wanted release but I wanted Aspen more. I wish she were here. I wish I could make love to her.

But she wasn't.

I peeled off my boxers then pulled out the lotion from my nightstand. My fingers wrapped around my shaft and I gave myself long even strokes, the kind I imagined I would give Aspen. The dream was gone but I tried to replicate it in my mind. I imagined her moans as she felt me inside her. Her pace matched the movement of my hand and I pretended my palm was the inside of her. Her tits bounced with every thrust she made. Her hands gripped my shoulders as she used them to move up and down.

I felt the burn deep in my groin then the tip of my cock. I tensed everywhere as I prepared for the climax that would make me groan. Aspen moved into me harder, giving me that extra push. Her green eyes brightened to emeralds as she gave me the pleasure I wanted. That playful look was on her lips, sexy and tantalizing.

I took a deep breath then felt the greatest pleasure I'd ever known. A moan escaped my lips involuntarily. My body tensed as I released then relaxed and I filled my hand.

I lay there for minutes, feeling satisfied but guilty at the same time. Aspen was my friend and someone I really cared about. Jerking off and thinking about her made me a perverted asshole. But I couldn't help it. She was what I wanted.

Obviously, my feelings for her were stronger than I realized. It snuck up on me, happening quickly and suddenly. The first time I saw her, she was wearing a green dress and her eyes immediately caught my notice. I wondered why a gorgeous woman like her needed to pay a man like me. I think, even then, I was falling for her.

***

E.L. Todd

The game was on in the background and the lasagna was in the oven. Aspen and I hadn't spoken in almost a week. She was on my mind constantly, and there were times when I found myself dialing her number just to talk to her. I missed playing Battleship with her. I missed looking at her.

Just as the thoughts entered my mind, my phone rang.

It was Aspen.

I cleared my throat and tried to sound cool and natural before I answered. "C3."

"Why do you bother?"

I chuckled. "One of these days, I'll best you."

"You're allowed to dream."

I smiled even though she couldn't see me. She always put me in a good mood. Our last interaction was awkward. I was going to kiss her but stopped myself. I hoped she didn't know what I was thinking. If she was a mind reader, she would know how much I wanted her. And that would be bad. "How are you?"

"I'm okay." Her voice immediately changed. It sounded different. It wasn't upbeat like it was a moment ago. It contained a hint of sadness.

"Are you okay?"

"I just had a bad day. I'm sorry to call you…I hope I'm not bothering you."

"You never bother me," I said immediately. She could call me whenever she wanted. "Do you want to talk about it?"

"Actually, no," she said quietly. "It just gets me worked up all over again."

I suspected it was about her father. No wonder she didn't want to mention it. "I'm making lasagna. Want to come over for dinner?" I didn't think when I spoke anymore. Being around her in the privacy of my home was probably a bad idea.

190

But I couldn't find the strength to remain professional. I wanted to be with her all the time. When I saw her talking to that guy in the bar, I admit I was jealous. I didn't know how to handle the emotion since I'd never felt it before.

"Uh, sure." She sounded hesitant.

Was it because of our last meeting? "We don't have to watch Criminal Minds."

She chuckled into the phone, and her voice sounded beautiful. "That's a relief."

"Come over," I said. "We'll have a good time."

"Okay." She sounded more enthused than before.

"I'll come get you."

"No, it's okay," she said immediately. "I can manage the walk alone. I haven't watched anything scary lately."

"Okay. I'll see you soon."

"Bye."

Once I was off the phone, I tidied up my apartment and prepared the table. Half an hour later, she knocked on the door, announcing her presence. I opened it and felt my mouth stretch into a smile at the sight of her. "Hey."

"Hey." She lifted up a bottle of wine. "I got something good this time."

I laughed then examined it. "It looks good."

"And it doesn't taste like mango," she teased. She had another bag in her hand but she didn't tell me what it was.

Every time I looked at her, I felt myself fall further. Her joy was refreshing, and even on a bad day, she found a reason to laugh. Without thinking, I pulled her into my chest and hugged her with one arm. Her scent came into my nose and her body felt right against mine. "I'm sorry you had a bad day."

"It's better now," she said as she returned the embrace.

I reluctantly pulled away, knowing the hug would linger indefinitely if I didn't move. "Dinner is ready."

"A home-cooked meal? Yum."

I put the lasagna on the kitchen table and we ate quietly.

"Is this vegetable lasagna?" she asked.

"I have to sneak vegetables into my food otherwise I won't eat them." I poured two glasses of wine then returned to eating.

Her lips stretched into a grin. "Pretty smart. The last time I ate lasagna, I told the waiter I wanted it extra greasy. And then I ate all of it." She shrugged at the end and didn't seem embarrassed.

"That's hot," I blurted.

"What?" she asked with a laugh. "A woman eating like a fatass?"

"Actually, yeah," I said. "Most of the time, girls order salad with no dressing and just squeeze lemon on top. It's lame."

"I think it sounds healthy."

I shrugged. "Do you go out to eat healthy?"

"I don't think I've ever ordered a salad in my life."

"I knew I liked you for a reason."

Her lips pressed tightly together in a smile then she sipped her wine. "Can I ask you something?"

"You can ask me anything, Aspen." Only she had that privilege

"Do you work out every day?"

"I box every morning except Sundays. I do weight training as well."

"That's dedication," she said.

I shrugged. "I can't be an escort unless I'm in great shape."

"I could never do what you do. I haven't stepped foot inside a gym since..." She thought for a moment. "I can't even remember."

"I would never suspect that by looking at you." She already knew I thought she had a nice body so I didn't see the point in hiding it.

"I jog. That saves me."

I finished my plate then ate a piece of garlic bread.

"Can I ask you something else?"

I nodded.

"Why don't you live with your brother? Wouldn't that be easier?"

I shook my head immediately. "I refuse to live in the dark like he does—literally. When I go to his apartment, I can only hang around for a few hours because my eyes start to hurt. Plus, I need my own space. This phobia of his is something he makes up so I refuse to sacrifice my life to wait on him hand and foot. He needs to be independent and understand I'm not always around to help him."

She nodded. "That's understandable."

"I love my brother but I couldn't live with him."

"He doesn't work?"

"He does but doesn't make enough to support himself."

"You're a good brother," she said quietly.

"At the end of the day, we always have each other," I said.

"Yeah," she agreed. She cleared her throat and chose her next words carefully. "Have you ever...sought professional help?"

I would never forget the attempt. "It was a disaster."

She stopped eating and gave me her full attention.

"I admitted him into a therapy ward for psychoanalysis. The doctors were supposed to help him overcome his fears until they disappeared altogether but...Chase didn't make any progress. He cowered into a ball and screamed indefinitely. He didn't eat or sleep for seven days straight because he was so scared. Doctors feared he would die if he went a few more days without food. So I took him home."

"Why didn't they give him a sedative?"

"I told them they couldn't give him drugs. He just needed someone to talk to. It was painful to watch him go through that and I haven't taken him back since. His illness reduces his quality of life but...it's better than going through that again."

She nodded. "I can imagine..."

"I don't think he'll ever get over it, unfortunately." I tried not to let Chase's situation weigh me down. But sometimes it made me sad. "But he seems happy. He gets laid whenever he wants, he has friends, and he does what he wants—for the most part."

"He gets laid?" she asked in surprise.

"Oh yeah," I said with a laugh. "The girls like him. They think he's eccentric." I shrugged.

She smiled. "Go, Chase."

"He has more game than I do."

"I find that hard to believe," she blurted. She seemed to realize her mistake because she didn't look at me. "I got something that might help. I hope it doesn't offend you."

"You could never offend me, Aspen."

She picked up a bag that had the Target logo on it. Then she pulled out a plastic sword. The blade was yellow, and the rest of the pieces were black. "I think the best thing for Chase is to eradicate the problem altogether so he can live a normal life. But since you've already tried that...this might help."

"What are you thinking?" I asked.

"He thinks he's safe with your invisible Shadow Sword but he won't take it from you. So, what if we left this on his doorstep? Like someone put it there? Then we'll tell him it's another Shadow Sword. He can wear it when he goes out, in the daylight or at night, and he won't be afraid. It doesn't remove the phobia altogether but at least he can live a normal life. It glows in the dark too."

I eyed the sword on the table then picked it up. I examined it and felt its lightness in my hand. "I've never thought of that..."

She shrugged. "It might work. It's worth a shot, right?"

"Yeah." I turned it over and saw the engraving on the side. *Shadow Sword.* "This is a great idea."

She smiled. "People might think it's weird if he carries a plastic sword everywhere he goes but it's the lesser evil."

"It is." I felt the sword in my hand then placed it on the table. "Want to head over there now?"

Her eyes lit up. "Okay."

***

We set the sword on his doorstep with the *Shadow Sword* engraving on the surface. I knocked then we quickly ran down the hall and hid behind the corner. We listened as we heard the door crack.

I knew Chase would look through the peephole first then spot the sword on the ground. He would be too intrigued not to open the door. Wearing his blanket made of foil, he emerged then grabbed the sword.

Aspen and I peered around the corner and watched him.

He held the sword by the hilt then touched the yellow blade. His fingers rubbed against the engraving then he spun it around his wrist. His body relaxed and the foil blanket fell away slightly.

"I think it's working," I whispered.

Chase spun it in his fingers again then walked back into his apartment.

I turned to Aspen. "He took it. That's a good sign."

"He let the blanket fall," she said. "I think he feels safe with it."

My phone rang. When I pulled it out of my pocket, I saw Chase's name on the screen. "It's him."

"Answer it," she said quickly. She moved next to the phone so she could listen to him on the other line.

"Hey, Chase," I said casually.

"Dude, you'll never guess what happened."

"You finally learned how to not pee all over the toilet seat?" I teased.

"No." He didn't bother insulting me back. "Someone left a Shadow Sword on my doorstep."

Chase was incredibly intelligent and quick witted. The fact he reverted to childhood mentality when it came to this subject was difficult for me to understand. Perhaps the trauma of my parents' death affected him so deeply this was the only way he could cope. I refused to judge him for that. "Really?"

"Yeah," he said. "It's even engraved. And it glows in the dark."

"Wow," I said. "Now the shadows can't hurt you either. That's great."

"Yeah..." He was quiet for a while. "This is incredible."

"Now you can go out in the daylight freely," I said.

"Well, I haven't tried it out..."

"Then take it for a spin."

"I'm not going to do that by myself," he said immediately. "Can you come over?"

"Sure. Aspen and I just left that Chinese place we like. We'll be there in five minutes."

"Okay," he said. "She's cute so bring her. She's single, right?"

I rolled my eyes. "I don't think she's into guys who are afraid of the dark."

"It's shadows," he said. "And I may not be anymore."

"We'll be there in a few minutes." I hung up.

Aspen smiled in excitement. "This might actually work."

"I know." It was hard to believe. My brother was so close to having a normal life. And that was because of Aspen.

After we waited ten minutes, we knocked on his door.

It cracked like he'd been expecting us.

"Turn off the lights," he said.

"You have the sword. You'll be fine," I said.

"Okay," he said. "I'm coming out without my blanket."

"Okay." I tried not to laugh because this fear was so ridiculous.

He stepped out with the sword tied to his belt. He looked around like something might get him any second. His eyes were wide and his body was rigid.

"The sword works," I said in excitement. "This is great."

"Wait," Chase said. "You have your sword. What if that's why they aren't attacking?"

"I'll take it off in your apartment," I said. "Then we'll see."

Chase looked terrified. "Uh..."

"It'll be fine," I said. "Worse comes to worse, I'll run in and grab it."

He swallowed the lump in his throat. "Okay."

I walked into his apartment, pretended to remove a fake sword, and then walked back into the hallway. "It's gone."

Chase gripped the sword and looked around, waiting for something to happen.

I crossed my arms over my chest and tried not to laugh.

Aspen looked around, like she was searching for the shadows Chase swore existed. "That's a powerful sword," she said. "They won't even come near us."

"Yeah," I added. "That sword is stronger than mine."

Chase seemed to relax. "They aren't coming..."

"It's because of the sword," I said. "It's undefeatable."

"Yeah," Chase agreed. "I think so..." He walked down the hallway and looked around. Then he came back to me. "Now they're scared of me."

"They should be," I said seriously.

"Now I know how you feel," Chase said. "Nothing can hurt you."

"Exactly," he said.

He released the hilt then crossed his arms over his chest. "Wow...I need to redo my apartment."

I tried not to laugh. "Yeah...get some lights or something."

"I can't wait until the sun rises," Chase said. "I'm going to go to Starbucks and see what all the fuss is about."

His words made me sad. He missed out on such simple things because of this phobia. It just made me appreciate his change all the more. "Yeah..."

"And I'm going to jog in the park," he said excitedly. "I've always wanted to do that."

"Yeah." I took a deep breath and tried not to get emotional.

"Hey," Chase said with wide eyes. "You want to get breakfast tomorrow?"

I took a deep breath and tried not to cry. "I'd love to, man."

"Then we can walk through the park." He paced the hallway excitedly. "Then we have to go to Little Italy."

"Whatever you want." I tried to keep my emotion in check.

"Sweet," Chase said. "I can pick up girls in the daylight now."

"Yeah," I agreed.

"I'm going to go inside and start looking for a new job," he said. "Preferably something with a window."

"There's no rush," I said.

"I wonder who left the sword," he said.

I shrugged. "I have no idea."

"Well, I'll see you tomorrow." He spun his sword around like he was about to fight someone. Then he walked into his apartment and shut the door.

I closed my eyes and rubbed my temples, unable to believe that really just happened.

Aspen touched my shoulder gently. "You okay?"

My eyes burned with tears. "I...I never thought this would happen."

Her eyes matched mine. "I'm happy for you."

"Thank you so much." I lowered my hand and looked at her. "This is all because of you. You've given me my brother back."

She rubbed me for a moment before dropping her hand. "It's because of both of us."

The door opened again and Chase look panicked. "Dude, you forgot your sword."

I forgot that I left the imaginary weapon in his apartment.

"You need it otherwise they'll get you."

"No, they won't," I said quietly. I looked at my brother, finally seeing him in a different way. I imagined us walking together in the park, acting like normal people on our day off. We'd get breakfast together then discuss sports and music. The world offered endless possibilities and we could experience all of them. "Because I have you."

***

Aspen and I sat on my couch and watched SpongeBob SquarePants.

"You like this show?" I asked.

"Yeah. It's funny." She sat beside me with her knees pulled to her chest. I noticed she always sat that way when we were alone together. It was like she was restraining herself.

"I've never met a girl who likes cartoons."

"I love cartoons," she said. "Sometimes you just need something mindless to recharge your brain."

"I guess that makes sense."

"My job can be really stressful, and if I make a mistake, it affects thousands of people. When I get home, it's nice to be entertained by something that doesn't require any thought."

"I don't think it's mindless," I said with a grin. "I think it's inspirational, intelligent, and engaging."

"Oh yeah?" she asked playfully.

"Yep. This guy lives in a pineapple under the sea. The symbolism of that is astounding. It represents the middle class of the American people, having houses so perishable while they drown under the weight of the high cost of living, taxes, and healthcare they can't afford."

She turned to me, a slight smirk on her lips. "That got dark real quick..."

I laughed then sank back into the couch. "It did, huh?"

"Let's just enjoy the show superficially and let it be mindless."

"That does sound better." Feeling buoyant from my brother's new life, and sharing endless laughs with Aspen, I put my arm around her shoulders. The courage stemmed from deep within, and I didn't think about my actions until they were completed.

She didn't react to the touch. It was like she expected it to happen—or even wanted it to happen.

We watched a few episodes, laughing at the ridiculous parts until it grew late. I was tired and I suspected she was too. But I didn't want her to leave. I hoped she didn't either.

Her head moved to my shoulder, and her hair scattered down my shirt. One strand touched my neck, and its softness reminded me of the dirty dream I had about her. And the daydream I had afterward while I jerked off. My cheeks blushed and my cock hardened.

I moved my head to the armrest of the couch and lay down, pulling Aspen with me. She didn't hesitate. In a fluid motion, she moved with me. Her head rested on my shoulder and her hair sprawled out across my chest. She moved her hand around my waist. One leg tucked between mine.

I was in heaven.

I'd never laid on the couch and watched TV with a girl. Any time a girl came to my apartment, we got down to business in my bedroom. I fucked her on my sheets then called a cab the next morning. We didn't cuddle during the night. She stayed on her side of the bed and I stayed on mine.

But I broke all my habits and rules for Aspen.

She was light while she lay on top of me. My hand wrapped around her waist then rested on her hip. The curve of her body was noticeable to me. She had an hourglass figure, a slim waist with noticeable hips that led to tone thighs. She had long legs, and I often imagined them wrapped around my waist. The scent of vanilla came to my nose, and I breathed it in and felt my body relax. Instead of watching the TV, I watched her. Her hand rested on my stomach while she held me. We were wrapped around one another like we fit perfectly together. I'd crossed so many lines already that I decided to cross more. My left hand moved to hers, and I intertwined our fingers together.

Her hand immediately reciprocated, and she released a quiet sigh, like she was ready to fall asleep.

I continued to stare at her, forgetting the show, until my eyes grew heavy and I fell asleep.

***

When I woke up, the TV was off. The time on the DVR said it was two in the morning. Aspen was in the same place she was before she fell asleep. Our hands were still linked together.

The armrest was uncomfortable for my neck and my bed called my name. I'd rather sleep in there. I doubted Aspen would mind. Careful not to wake her up, I moved from under her then lifted her from the couch. She was feather-light like I expected.

I laid her on the bed then pulled her shoes off. Then I tucked her into the sheets and removed my shirt and jeans. Just wearing my boxers, I got into bed beside her.

Aspen stirred then squinted her eyes. She looked at me, half-asleep, and then moved into me. Her arm curled around my waist and she inserted her leg between mine. Aggressive like never before, she cuddled with me like she needed me. I moved against her and held her tightly.

Then we fell asleep again.

***

When I woke up the next morning, I realized I'd broken another rule.

I slept with her.

We didn't have sex but she still slept with me in my bed. Now there was only one rule left unbroken.

Kissing.

I had to hold out and not make the move. I had to wait until Aspen no longer needed me to get her company. Then I'd move in and ask her to be mine. I'd kiss her like she's never been kissed before.

I just had to be patient.

I opened my eyes and stared at Aspen. She was wrapped around me tightly, sleeping peacefully. The sunlight drifted through the window and highlighted her fair skin. Her brown hair cascaded around her. If her lips were swollen, it would look like we'd had a rendezvous the night before. Just the thought alone made me hard. I only wore boxers so I hoped she didn't notice my morning wood.

Aspen sighed then her eyes fluttered open. She took me in for a moment then she closed her eyes again. "How do you get up in the morning?" Her words came out garbled and incoherent.

"Sorry?" I tried not to laugh.

"Your bed is so comfortable." Her words were sharper that time. "How do you get up in the morning?"

"I don't," I said. "Now you know why I'm a night owl."

"I understand perfectly." Her hand moved across my stomach to my chest. Then it rested there. She seemed to understand I was shirtless because her eyes popped open. She stared at my naked chest then abruptly closed her eyes.

A cocky grin stretched my lips. "Did you just check me out?"

"No..."

"I saw you."

"I don't know what you're talking about..."

"Just admit it." I leaned over her, pressuring her with my proximity.

Her eyes opened again and her leg shifted around my waist.

My hard cock was pressed against her thigh and I realized my mistake moving against her like this. But the damage was done.

Her breathing increased and she just stared at me, her eyes brighter than I'd ever seen them.

Fuck, this was dangerous.

I wanted to lean in and kiss her. I'd imagined feeling her lips against mine countless times. I was so close. She was under me, in my bed. I wanted to roll around on my sheets, sucking those lips and touching her in all the places I fantasized about.

Before I did something stupid, I moved to my back. "I'm meeting Chase soon... I should get ready."

She stayed in her spot. "Yeah...you guys will have a good time."

I got out of bed and pulled on a t-shirt. "I'll walk you home."

"I can manage." She got up then fixed her hair with her fingers. "It's not dark."

"Are you sure?" I asked. "I don't mind."

"It's fine, really." She rubbed the wrinkles from her dress then slipped on her shoes.

I pulled on my sweatpants to hide my obvious hard-on, not that it made a difference now. She felt it pressed against her thigh. She knew how hard it was and how much I wanted her.

I walked her to the door, feeling awkward for my stupidity. I came onto her while we were lying in bed. I pressed my cock against her like a jerk. I didn't want her to think I was trying to sleep with her. I wasn't. I mean, I *wanted* to. But I wanted a lot more than that. "Thanks for helping out with my brother. You have no idea how much it means to me." I thought it was best to change the subject. I may have made a stupid move but I also pulled away when I realized how badly she could interpret my actions.

"I'm glad I could help," she said. "And thanks for making me feel better."

"We go well together," I said without thinking.

"Yeah, I think we do..." She tucked a strand of hair behind her ear.

Why did I keep saying stupid shit like that? I wanted to smack my forehead.

"Have a good day." She stepped out with her purse over her shoulder.

"You too."

"Bye." She gave me a small wave before she walked away.

I shut the door then leaned against it, wishing she would stay with me—forever.

Aspen

I was faced with the truth of Harper's words. I think Rhett felt the way I did. My heart raced when he was near, and when his chest was pressed to mine, his heartbeat was like one with my own. His hand held mine even though there was no one to put on a show for. He slept with me in his bed, and he even.... My cheeks blushed when I thought about it.

But he hadn't kissed me. There were times when I thought he might but it never happened. I was growing impatient. Rhett was the first man that made me melt. He was the first guy I fell for without sharing a single kiss. He'd become someone I trusted more than anyone else. After what John did to me, how was that even possible?

Maybe I should just tell him how I felt and get it over with. Maybe I should just kiss him and see if he returned the embrace. I should just roll the dice and take my chances. There was a good possibility I would lose everything I was working toward but it didn't seem to matter anymore.

For the next few days, all I thought about was him. Work suffered because I was distracted. I fantasized about kissing him, about him showing up at my office then taking me on my desk. I dreamed of a million things, and they were all inappropriate.

Isabella's visit was forgotten. Rhett made me forget about her taunts and evilness. It was hard to be upset when I was so happy with him. When Chase took the sword and finally dropped his fear, I felt warm inside. I was glad I could help him, but I was happier that I helped Rhett. Emotion was in his eyes and I thought he might cry. That look of gratitude was one I'd never forget. He deserved to have his brother back. Other than his aunt and uncle, Chase was all he had left.

I sat at my desk and went through a report on my computer when Jane's voice came over the intercom. "Mr. Lane wants to see you, Ms. Lane."

I couldn't wait until I changed my last name. Being a Lane was a disgrace. I hated sharing something so intimate with my father. "Thank you, Jane." I didn't want to speak to him. I hadn't seen him since Isabella came into my office and squished me like a bug. My anger was difficult to handle and sometimes I struggled with it. I wanted to smack my father in the face with a golf club. When it gave me satisfaction, I realized how evil of a person I was.

I entered his office and retained my coolness, pretending I didn't despise him, that I didn't loathe him. "You needed me, sir?"

He was hitting a ball across the small green in his office. "How's Rhett feeling?"

When we ditched dinner a few weeks ago because of Chase's breakdown, I lied and said Rhett got a severe case of food poisoning that put him in the hospital due to dehydration. "He's well. He had a long recovery but he made it through."

"Glad to hear it. What did he eat, if you don't mind me asking?"

"Lasagna from Santiago's," I lied. That was my favorite restaurant and I never wanted to run into my father there.

"I'll stay clear of that place." He hit the ball then sunk it into the hole. He hadn't looked at me once.

"Is that all, sir?" I wanted to get out of there as quickly as possible.

"No, actually." He hung his club on the wall then leaned against the front of his desk. "Your cousin, Marie, is having an engagement party this weekend. I want you to bring Rhett."

Why did I have to go at all? Marie was Isabella's sister. I kept my cool. "Do you think that's wise? Don't you think it's a conflict of interest?" Isabella would be there, and so would John. I didn't want to see either one of them.

"You need to save face, Aspen. If you show up with your head held high and a man on your arm, people will stop talking about you."

"Or they'll talk more..."

"The matter is settled," he said dismissively.

I hated it when he bossed me around like I was a dog. He may be my boss but he couldn't control my personal life. "I'm not going and you can't make me."

He turned those cold eyes on me. "What did you say to me?"

"I'm not going," I said firmly. "All I'll be is a talking point, something everyone will gossip about. I have no business being there. It'll just start drama."

"You will go," he said sternly. "You will act like everything is completely fine. This is important to me."

"Well, it's not important to me," I hissed.

"I'll fire you if I have to," he threatened.

I narrowed my eyes at him. "This has nothing to do with work."

"It has everything to do with work! You will show up and smile. You will introduce Rhett to everyone and say how wealthy he is. You will act like you don't have a care in the world. You will act like John meant nothing to you and his marriage to Isabella is something beneath you. You can't be weak, Aspen."

"And I'm supposed to show up at the wedding too? The one you're hosting?" My eyes burned into his. My hands shook. I was so close to storming out and telling him how much I despised him.

He lowered his voice. "It's all about image. What could be more powerful than making a gesture like that? Isabella can have John because you have someone else."

"You know how much I wanted to get married there! Now I can't because Isabella is."

"Nonsense," he said. "You can get married there too."

"No, I can't!" I tried not to scream but I was struggling. "I will not get married at the same place that horrible woman married my ex-fiancé. How could you agree to that without even asking me?"

"It's not your decision. That's why." His voice was ice cold.

I took a deep breath and stilled my tears. They didn't emerge from sadness or pain. They came from overwhelming stress. I felt trapped and unable to break free. I was stuck under his thumb until I could get rid of him.

"You better not cry."

I steadied my resolve. "Does it look like I'm crying?"

He watched me for a moment before he adjusted his watch. "Be there and bring Rhett with you. Otherwise, you can find yourself another job."

I couldn't let him dangle me like this anymore. "Will you give me the company now? I have a serious boyfriend and I've repaired my image. I've done as you asked."

He crossed his arms over his chest. "You're definitely on the right track." He walked to the window then looked out, silently dismissing me.

I stormed out of his office then shut the door. I leaned against it, feeling the tears leak from the corners of my eyes. My heart ached in pain and I felt weak. "I wish you would die already."

***

When Rhett knocked on the door, I was in my bedroom at my vanity, finishing my makeup. "Come in," I called.

The door opened and I heard his footsteps. "It's me."

"I'm just finishing," I said. "I'll be out in a moment."

"Take your time."

My bedroom door was open but he didn't approach it. He probably sat on the couch and waited.

I wore more makeup than usual and made sure it looked absolutely perfect. My eyes were dark with smoky eye shadow and the black eyeliner made my eyes look bright and noticeable. My foundation was blended to perfection and my lips were highlighted with a bright sheer color. My hair was pulled back in a fine arrangement. I wore a purple strapless dress that was simple but elegant at the same time. A platinum bracelet was on my wrist and I had my nails done.

I was ready to go but I still hated my appearance. It wasn't me at all. I never wore this much makeup or put this much effort into how I looked. The idea of going to this party and pretending what John did to me was perfectly okay was despicable. And what Isabella did was worse. Why was I the pathetic one? Why did the family see me as the weak one?

Isabella was the slut who stole her own cousin's boyfriend. Why didn't anyone see it that way?

I leaned over my vanity and closed my eyes. Tears were constantly bubbling and I worked hard to control them. The last thing I wanted to do was go to this stupid party. I didn't want to pretend I was okay because I wasn't. Why couldn't I have a normal father who stood by my side when no one else did? Why couldn't he take me out to ice cream when I had a bad day instead of telling me I was weak? Why did he scream at me and tell me not to cry? Why couldn't he just hold me instead?

Keep it together, Aspen. It's just a few hours. Rhett will be there. You aren't alone.

I took a deep breath and tried to clear my thoughts.

Large hands moved to my shoulders then gently squeezed. "You okay?"

I opened my eyes and looked at him in the reflection of my vanity. "I'm fine."

He stared at me with sad eyes. The blue color of his eyes was absent. Now they were just gray. "Talk to me." He rubbed the muscles of my shoulders, trying to relax me.

"I really don't want to go to this party..."

"Why?"

"I just...don't like my family much."

"Then why are you going?"

The same reason I did anything. "My dad is making me. He wants me to introduce you to everyone...and tell them how rich you are." Disdain was heavy in my voice.

"Then that's what we'll do. I'll take care of it, okay? Just stand there and look pretty."

Easier said than done.

His hands stopped rubbing me. "You're more stressed out than normal." It wasn't a question.

"I'd rather spend the day scrubbing toilets."

He kneeled beside my chair then leaned close to me, his face just inches from mine. "Aspen." His voice moved down my spine then radiated everywhere. There was so much comfort in his words. He made me feel whole. "We're in this together. I'll get you through it. I promise."

A sad smile moved into my lips. "Yeah?"

"Yeah." One hand moved to my neck and he pressed his forehead to mine. He'd never done that before. We were so close, closer than ever. A kiss was what I needed, what I wanted.

But I didn't get it.

"We'll get monster sundaes afterward. And of course, some canned margaritas—your favorite."

That made me smile. "That doesn't sound so bad."

"Not at all. Now let's get this over with."

***

Rhett pulled up to the country house in his charcoal gray Jaguar. It was pristine and shiny, fitting in with the line of luxurious cars parked along the side of the driveway.

A valet took the car then Rhett put his arm around my waist and escorted me inside. "Beautiful house."

"House?" I asked. "You mean mansion. And only two people live here. So stupid."

He leaned close to me. "I'm glad you aren't a snooty brat like the rest of your family."

"If I were, you'd have my permission to shoot me."

He chuckled. "Duly noted."

We reached the garden path then walked to the rear of the house. A large patio with green hedges and stone statues

213

highlighted the backyard. Large tables were set up everywhere, and lines of white lights hung overhead. Waiters moved around with trays of flutes. It was as pretentious as every other party I'd been to.

"What do your aunt and uncle do?" Rhett asked.

"My uncle used to work with my dad at the company. He left a few years ago and cashed in his stock. Now he's retired."

One side of Rhett's lip upturned in a gentle smile. "I'm sure he's a lot happier now."

Yeah...having a skanky daughter who steals her cousin's man must make him really happy.

Once the crowd noticed us, dirty looks were shot my way. Sometimes, I got looks of sympathy and pity. Other times, I just got glares. Overall, no one was pleased to see me even though I did nothing wrong.

So it begins.

Rhett seemed to pick up on the tension because he pulled me closer to him. "You look beautiful tonight. I forgot to say that earlier."

His compliment fell on deaf ears. "Thank you." No matter how hard I worked to make myself look beautiful, would I ever actually feel beautiful? "You look nice too." Rhett wore a black Armani suit like it was made just for him.

"You outshine me, easily."

Whatever you say.

"Drink?"

"Please," I said. "And keep them coming."

He grabbed two glasses from a passing waiter then handed me a flute. He clanked his glass against mine. "Hope it doesn't taste like mango." He smiled then took a sip.

I returned the smile but it didn't reach my eyes. I drank almost the entire thing with a single gulp.

Rhett escorted me through the crowd. "Anyone you want to talk to?"

"Not even a little bit."

"There you are." My father's voice was heard over the quiet sounds of conversation.

I growled quietly enough that no one heard me.

"Rhett, I want to introduce you to someone," Dad said.

Seriously? He forced me to come but he wasn't even going to acknowledge me? Now I didn't feel bad for wishing he were dead.

Rhett pulled me with him until we reached my father. "Good evening, sir. How are you?"

"Well." He clapped Rhett on the shoulder and gave him a smile.

He never smiled at me.

As soon as Rhett shook his hand, his arm returned to my waist.

"Bill, this is Aspen's boyfriend, Rhett," Dad said. "He's a fine young man."

"How do you do?" Bill shook his hand.

"It's a pleasure to make your acquaintance," Rhett said politely.

Bill was my uncle but he pretended like I didn't exist, just like my father did.

Fucking asshole.

Rhett engaged them in conversation, still holding me close. He discussed working for GMC, which was a lie, and discussed stocks, politics, and wealth like he was holding a cigar and drinking brandy. Like everyone, Dad and Bill were fond of him.

215

And I just stood there.

Bill waved my aunt over. "Dear, come meet Rhett."

Aunt Nancy came to his side. She looked at me with absolutely no warmth in her eyes then turned to Rhett. "It's a pleasure to meet you. We've already heard so much about you."

"The pleasure is mine," Rhett said politely. "You have a beautiful home. It reminds me of my family's estate in Vermont."

"That's wonderful," she said. "What do they do?"

"We have a few wineries here and in Australia," Rhett answered.

How did he lie on his feet like that? He really was a trained master.

"I'm fine, by the way." The words slipped out before I could stop them. I just blurted what I was thinking.

"I was just going to ask, dear." Aunt Nancy gave me a fake smile. "So...how did you two meet?"

"A coffee shop," I said.

Rhett gave me a fond look. "I saw her and knew right then and there."

"Knew what?" Aunt Nancy asked.

"That she was the one." He turned back to Aunt Nancy and gave her a serious look.

I'd faint if Rhett said that to me and meant it.

Aunt Nancy had a skeptical look on her face. Her lips were pressed tightly together, almost in disapproval, and when she sipped her champagne, she barely drank it. She eyed Rhett like he wasn't real then shifted her questioning gaze to me.

I knew what she was thinking. *How could she land a guy like him?*

Rhett leaned in and rubbed his nose against mine, affection he'd never given me before. "She turned me down a few times but I wore her down. I wasn't going to give up."

Aunt Nancy coughed into her glass and almost choked. "Excuse me."

I forced myself not to roll my eyes. Was it that shocking someone like Rhett could like me? I hated John for how he ruined my life. My family used to respect me but now they viewed me as some stupid and pathetic girl that no man wanted. If I saw him here tonight, I'd struggle not to kick him right in the danglers.

"You okay, dear?" Uncle Bill asked.

"I'm fine." She dabbed her mouth with a napkin.

Uncle Bill patted her back gently.

Could we go now?

"We're so excited to have our two daughters married off," Aunt Nancy said, giving me a particular look. "Isabella will be married in just a few months and now Marie."

"How wonderful," Dad said. "Isn't it?" He turned to me, silently commanding me to be polite and act like I was okay even though I was drowning inside.

"Truly wonderful," I forced myself to say.

"Hopefully we'll be next," Rhett said, moving his head against mine.

This party would break my soul if Rhett weren't here to protect me. I'd be there all alone, and people would gossip more. At least it was better to have them question how I got Rhett than to rip me apart for being alone. "Yeah." I flashed him a fake smile.

"I'd love to have you as a son-in-law," Dad said. "You're a wonderful young man."

"Thank you, sir," Rhett said gracefully.

Dad was clearly pleased how the night was going. Rhett was a hit and everyone liked him. Of course, no one understood how a gorgeous man like him could end up with a troll like me, but it was still going well.

"Excuse us," Aunt Nancy said. "We need to mingle."

Please do. I yanked on Rhett's arm, telling him I needed a drink.

Rhett guided me away and grabbed me another glass. "Why does your family treat you like that? It's appalling."

I took a long drink and didn't answer. I looked across the crowd and spotted a circle of girls with short dresses and styled hair. Heels were on their feet, and they were all looking at me, either dogging me or laughing at me. When I recognized Isabella, I wanted to hightail it out of there.

Rhett caught my look and followed my gaze. "Who are they?"

"Let's go somewhere else." I pulled him into the crowd with me.

We migrated to a nearby table then sat down, blocked from view by the crowd. If Isabella were there, John wasn't far behind. I could be fake to anyone, but being fake to him would be impossible.

Rhett was quiet, his eyes distant.

Maybe he was angry. Maybe he wanted to leave as much as I did.

I wouldn't blame him if he did. I sipped my drink, thankful I felt a small burn in my stomach from the alcohol.

"I know her from somewhere..." Rhett's voice came out quiet.

"Sorry?"

"That girl," he said. "I know her."

You've got to be kidding me. If he slept with Isabella, I'd throw myself over a cliff. I could never get past that even if Rhett did want something from me. "The blonde girl in the middle?"

"No, the brunette on the right." He rubbed his chin while he thought for a long time. Then he snapped his fingers. "She hired me a few months ago. That's where I know her from. I knew I recognized her."

My eyes widened and my heart fell into my stomach. "Are you sure?"

"Definitely. She wanted to make her ex jealous."

I covered my face and almost broke down. "Ohmygod..."

"What?" he asked with concern. "What's wrong?"

Rhett always exhibited his intelligence but right now it was lacking. "Don't you get it? Since she hired you, she'll know I hired you. Then everyone will know this is all a scam. My father will find out and...god, this is humiliating."

His eyes widened in realization then he rubbed the back of his neck. "Wait, hold on."

"What?" I said in a defeated voice.

"She won't say anything."

"Why the hell wouldn't she? She would love another reason to humiliate me."

"If she says I hired you, she'd have to admit she hired me." He said it with a smile. "She wouldn't confess that secret just to expose you. It would be too embarrassing."

I relaxed a little. "But she still might..."

"I doubt she will," he said. "From what I remember, she cared about image more than anything else. It's unlikely she would risk public shame like that. It'll be okay, Aspen."

I was still anxious.

He pulled me close to him. "Just relax."

E.L. Todd

"Easier said than done."

"I'm here. Remember that." He squeezed my hand. "And I'm not going anywhere."

How did he make me fall for him at a time like this?

"Just think about that monster sundae," he said. "And I'll give you my cherry—like always."

An involuntary smile formed on my lips.

Marie approached our table wearing a white dress. Her hair was curly and her engagement ring flashed in the light. "You actually came?" She put her hands on her hips and gave me a fake, high school smile. "It looks like I owe Janet twenty bucks."

Why did my life suck so much? "Hello, Marie," I said coldly. "It's nice to see you."

"Yeah, you too," she said quickly.

"And congratulations." Disdain was in my voice even though I smiled while I spoke.

Marie turned her eyes on Rhett. "When people told me you brought a hot boyfriend, I couldn't believe it. I still don't."

Rhett pulled me closer to him. "And when Aspen agreed to be mine, I almost didn't believe it. I still don't." He intertwined our fingers together and acted like he absolutely adored me.

Marie eyed my dress. "JCPenny's?" Disapproval was in her voice.

"Target," I said without shame. Everyone wore designer gowns but I was happy wearing something I loved, whether it was cheap or expensive.

"You already give people enough reason to make fun of you. Don't give them more ammo." She laughed loudly, like what she said was hilarious.

I was close to exploding. I wanted to stand on the table and tell every single person there to go fuck themselves. What happened with John wasn't my fault. I was a good person and didn't deserve to be treated like shit. I wanted to slap that smug look off her face.

"John is here," she said with an evil smile. "Make sure you stop by and say hi." Then she turned on her heel and strutted away.

That was it. I couldn't take it anymore. This treatment had finally broken me. I just needed to get out. I needed somewhere to hide. I needed somewhere I could scream. Why did she have to mention John, especially in front of Rhett? I jumped from my seat then took off, heading into the house where I could find the nearest bathroom so I could cry behind a closed door. I couldn't make it to the car and I couldn't drive anyway.

"Aspen." Rhett's voice came behind me.

I ignored him and kept going. I made it inside the house and moved past waiters on my way to the bathroom. When I reached it, I turned the knob. But it was locked.

Fuck.

"Someone's in here," a snooty voice said.

I headed down the hall then entered the first room I could find. I walked inside then began to shut the door.

Rhett squeezed in before I could close it. He shut the door behind him. He stared at me with sad eyes, like he was about to cry as much as I was.

"Don't look at me." I turned around and faced the other way, feeling the tears break free. I felt even worse for crying since my father forbade me from doing it. It felt like I was doing something innately wrong. My chest heaved with pain and I couldn't stop it.

Rhett grabbed me then forced me into his chest. He pulled me close and held me, letting me cry on his shoulder. His hand moved through my hair and held me while I released every drop I had. "You're a wonderful person and you don't deserve this—at all."

I held him tightly, taking advantage of the comfort he was giving me.

"You're the most amazing person I've ever met. How they don't see that is beyond me." He continued to rub me gently. "Don't let them hurt you like this. There's no reason you should feel this terrible."

I closed my eyes and breathed hard, trying to control my reckless emotions. I needed to gather myself and pretend everything was okay. All I had to do was get through this. Then I would go to my father and force him to step down so I didn't have to jump through hoops anymore. I could finally be free.

I pulled away from him then wiped my tears away. I fixed my makeup then steadied my breathing.

"Guess." Rhett cupped my face while he looked into my eyes.

I knew what he meant. "D2."

A smile upturned his lips. "No."

"E5."

He shook his head.

Then I realized what it was. "A1."

"You've sunk my battleship."

I chuckled lightly then fixed the rest of my makeup.

"There's my girl," he whispered.

"I feel better now." I blinked my eyes several times. "Does it look like I've been crying?"

"A little." He used the pad of his thumb to touch up my makeup. Then he used the edge of his sleeve to dab away the extra moisture. "No one will be able to tell."

"Thanks…"

"Let's just sit by ourselves and have a good time together. We'll take off as soon as dinner is over."

"Sounds like a plan." I moved to the door when I heard voices outside. It sounded like there was a line for the bathroom.

Isabella's voice was heard. "Aspen is a walking disaster. Mom said she looks sick."

"Purple is not her color," another girl said, one I didn't recognize.

"I can't believe she even showed up," Isabella said. "I'd be humiliated if my fiancé up and left me because I was terrible in bed then hooked up with my cousin. She's such a loser."

I closed my eyes and cringed. If I heard it, so did Rhett. I didn't want him to know. His opinion was the only one I really cared about, and now he would look down on me like everyone else. He would never want to be with me, not when he knew another man left me because sex with me was so boring. God, this night couldn't get any worse.

"Rumor has it," another girl said. "That her boyfriend isn't really her boyfriend. He's an escort."

"Shut. Your. Mouth." Isabella's high-pitched voice sounded through the door. She sounded utterly delighted that I had to pay someone to be my date. "I knew he was too hot for her! This is priceless."

Kill me now. Just kill me now.

"I bet she has to pay to have sex with him," a girl said. "Because John wouldn't even do it for free."

I couldn't look at Rhett. I could never look at him again. I was so ashamed and so humiliated. If my life ended right then and there, I wouldn't even fight it.

"They don't have sex with their clients. They don't even kiss them. They have very specific rules. If those rules are breached, they end the arrangement. They just stand there and hold your hand or put their arm around your waist," the girl said.

"How do you know that?" Isabella asked.

"Oh…" She faltered. "I heard about it from a friend. And I think I recognize him from the website."

Fucking liar.

"No wonder why he hasn't kissed her," Isabella said like she just solved a case. "That is so pathetic. John actually told me he almost fell asleep while having sex with her. That's how bad she is."

Why couldn't they stop talking? Hadn't they destroyed me enough? Why did I have to stand in this room with Rhett beside me and have him listen to every word of that? I'd never been so humiliated in my life. Whatever chance I had with Rhett was gone.

"Let's go find her and make her life miserable," Isabella said. Their heels echoed against the floor as they waked away.

I stood there, absolutely still.

Rhett didn't move.

I didn't look at him, not wanting to see his reaction. My biggest secret was out, and now there wasn't the slightest possibility that Rhett would want me. My family scandal had finally reached his ears, and no amount of humor could get him to smile at me ever again. I turned to the door and opened it.

"Aspen." Rhett grabbed me. "Hold on."

I twisted out of his grasp without looking at him. "Don't touch me." I stormed out and headed down the hallway. I just had to get my purse from the table then I could get out of there. After I reached the main road, I would call a cab. I didn't want to be at this party, surrounded by people who only wanted to see me drown, and I couldn't look at the man I loved and see him stare back at me with pity and disgust. I couldn't handle it if Rhett looked at me that way. He was the one person who actually made me feel good about myself.

I was near the table when I heard Isabella.

"There she is! Let's get her, girls."

If she came near me, I'd deck her. She wouldn't get any mercy from me. I wouldn't take the high road again and just walk away. Now I would punch her right in the nose and break it.

I reached my purse and snatched it. They were closing in on me. I just had to get out of there and make it to the main road. In my haste, I knocked over a glass but I didn't have time to clean it up. I turned and prepared to take off.

Rhett appeared out of nowhere and blocked my path.

"Move—"

Rhett cupped my face then gave me a hard kiss on the mouth. His lips were soft despite his aggression. The hold he had on me was unbreakable. I couldn't run even if I wanted to. His lips slowly moved against mine, and when I realized what was happening, my mouth reciprocated. The music faded and the sound of Isabella's voice became muted. All I heard was the sound of Rhett breathing. All I felt was his kiss. One hand remained on my face and the other moved around my waist. He held me close to him, having no intention of letting go.

This was not how I imagined our first kiss, but it's exactly how I hoped it would feel. It was explosive and hot, scorching me with every purposeful kiss he gave me. He kissed me like he loved me and couldn't live without me. I'd never been kissed that way before. I'd never been held like that.

Rhett parted my lips with his tongue then lightly touched mine. The feel of our tongues dancing was enough to make my knees give out. It was electrifying and wonderful. I breathed hard because I couldn't get enough air. He knocked the wind right out of me.

I gripped his shoulders just the way I wanted to, and gave into the desire I felt for him. My lips devoured his like I'd wanted to. His lips were soft and felt perfect against my mouth. I could kiss him all day. I could do this forever.

Rhett reluctantly broke the kiss, keeping his face against mine. He breathed hard and his eyes shined in desire. It seemed like I was the only one in the room who mattered.

"I guess you were wrong, Jessica," Isabella said in a disappointed sigh. Her heels trailed away as she and her posse walked off.

Rhett continued to stare at me. "I quit."

I searched his eyes, unsure of his meaning. "What?"

"I quit. I will no longer be escorting you."

What did I do...? He was the one who kissed me. Was he that embarrassed of me? I tried to hide my hurt.

"I would rather be your boyfriend—if you'll have me." His thumb stroked my cheek as he held me close. It trailed my face then moved to my lips. He looked at them for a moment before his gaze shifted back to mine. "Will you?"

All the pain I felt from that night faded away. The drama and hurt seemed irrelevant. The only person who mattered in the world was standing in front of me, looking at me the way I should be looked at. Tears burned in my eyes but not from sadness. For the first time, they were from joy. "Yes."

Rhett

"Why are you grinning like a dumbass?" Troy demanded.

"No reason." I shrugged then relaxed against the booth.

Troy could see right through my act. He narrowed his eyes like he didn't believe a word I said. "You fucked Battleship."

"No."

"Battleship gave you head?"

I shook my head. "Nope."

"Did she jerk you off with her feet?" he asked. "That shit is pretty hot, actually."

I rolled my eyes in response.

"Then what the hell happened?" His beer was untouched, his entire focus on me.

"She's my girlfriend." I kept grinning from ear-to-ear.

"That's it?" he asked sadly.

"We kissed."

"Dude, you know this is a lawsuit waiting to happen. She could turn on us and sue."

"Battleship would never do that. Besides, I quit."

"You did?" he asked in surprise.

"She's no longer my client. I still escort her but now I do it for free." I drank my beer, feeling happier than I had in a long time. I had an amazing girl all to myself. I'd never felt anything like this for a girl before. Normally, I just wanted sex. But Aspen made me want a lot more. A night of playing cards and eating ice cream was more than enough. Just being with her satisfied me.

He shook his head in disapproval. "It's your funeral."

"Hey, you're the one who told me to go for her."

"Yeah, I meant get laid, not commit to her," he said. "Relationships are stupid. They don't work and they never will."

I could tell he was still bitter about his break up even though it happened years ago. I never mentioned it because it put him in a sour mood. "Aspen and I will make it work."

He shook his head. "I'm just glad you dropped her. That was the smart thing to do."

"Yeah."

"Make her sign a termination contract, just in case."

"You're being paranoid."

"Hey," he snapped. "We were sued once before. Battleship seems like a nice girl but don't screw over the rest of us by being careless."

"I won't," I said. "I'll take care of it."

"So, when are you going to sleep with her?"

I shrugged. "It'll happen when it's meant to happen. I just kissed her for the first time. There's no rush."

"How long have you known this girl?"

"About three months."

"Have you gotten laid in that time frame?"

"No," I said. "I haven't even gone out with another girl. I was kinda with Aspen...but not technically."

"So, you haven't gotten any for three months?" Troy asked. "That's a long ass time…"

"I'll manage." My sex dreams of Aspen had become more vivid and occurred more often. As a result, I was jerking off more often. It was holding me over until I could get the real thing.

"Fuck that, man," he said. "If I held out that long for a girl, she better give me something. Even a hand job."

I chuckled but didn't say anything.

"Are you in love with her?" he asked bluntly.

I dodged the question. "What is this? Gossip hour?"

"You are, aren't you?" He shook his head in disapproval. "Well, if you're happy, I'm happy for you."

"Thanks for getting on board…and for being a jerk about it at the same time."

He laughed then clanked his glass against mine. "To Rhett, for finally settling down."

My glass hit his then I took a drink. "To Troy, for being next."

***

Aspen and I sat down in front of Danielle's desk.

"What do you need me to sign?" she asked.

"A termination agreement."

She looked at me blankly.

"It just covers me legally."

"Okay."

Danielle slid the paper toward her. "By signing here, you state you and Rhett have not slept together by this date. You also state that Rhett did not breach the contract during his time working for you."

I did breach the contract, several times.

Aspen didn't say otherwise and signed it.

229

"Initial here and here," Danielle said as she pointed to the paper.

Aspen filled them in.

"Excellent." Danielle took the paper and made a copy of it. "For your records..."

Aspen folded it and placed it in her purse.

"Congratulations, love birds." Danielle gave us a smile then returned to her desk.

I turned to Aspen. "Lunch?"

"Okay," she said with a smile.

We left the office hand-in-hand then walked inside a deli. After we ordered our food, we took a seat outside on the patio. It was a beautiful day and we wanted to soak up the sun.

"Why did you want me to sign that?" she asked.

I knew what she was really asking. "A few years ago, one of the guys slept with his client. She took it to court and said it was prostitution, since she technically paid him for the evening. We were almost shut down."

"Now I understand." She took a small bite of her sandwich. "That's unfortunate."

"She was upset he didn't want more. She wanted revenge."

"I'm glad your business didn't close."

"That makes two of us." I nudged her knee playfully with mine.

She smiled then took another bite of her sandwich.

"So, me being an escort doesn't bother you, right?"

"I trust you, Rhett."

Those words filled me with warmth. "Your trust isn't misplaced."

"But, I'll get into a catfight if any of those girls tries for something more."

I chuckled. "I can't picture you hurting anyone."

"If you get me angry enough…"

"Even then." I gave her a fond look. "But that's not a bad thing."

After we finished lunch, we walked back to her apartment. There was one thing on my mind. I wanted to go inside and make out with her until the following morning. I'd wanted to kiss her without any interruption.

When we reached her door, she turned to me. "Want to come inside?"

"Definitely." My hand was still on her waist.

She unlocked the door then we entered her apartment. She set her purse on the kitchen table and ignored the pile of mail sitting there. "So?"

"So." I came close to her then moved my hands to her hips. "What do you want to do?"

She looked at my lips. "I don't know. What do you want to do?"

"Battleship?"

She shook her head.

"Poker?"

"Nah."

"Margaritas?"

"Yuck." She made a disgusted face.

"Make out on your bed?"

Her eyes lit up like the New York skyline. "I've wanted to do that since the moment you walked inside that coffee shop."

"Good," I said. "Because I've wanted to do the same thing." My hands guided her to her bedroom then to the mattress. I lay her down then moved on top of her. Her arms hooked around my neck, ready for me to lean in. I grabbed her leg and wrapped it around my waist. "Have I ever told you I love your legs?"

"No."

"Well, I do." I fisted her hair then kissed her. Energy flowed through my body, and blood immediately headed south. My cock hardened the moment our mouths sealed together and I knew she felt it against her hips. But now I wasn't ashamed.

Aspen was an amazing kisser. Her lips teased me, giving me a small amount sometimes then giving me more passion than I could take. Her small tongue moved against mine, sending chills down my spine. I could do this all day.

Aspen pulled my shirt off then felt my hard chest with her palms. Her other leg wrapped around me and held me close. Every fantasy I had about her came to the front of my mind. I wanted to be inside her, to make love to her, but I didn't want to rush it. I already knew everything about her, and had been dating her, in a way, for three months already. But I would take this as slow as she wanted.

But judging the way she kissed and touched me, she wanted me the same way I wanted her. She wanted all of me, right then and there. Her mouth devoured mine like she couldn't get enough. Her lips were swollen from all the kissing but that made her mouth feel better against mine.

Hours passed and neither one of us came up for air. Aspen gave me a final slow kiss before she pulled away and looked into my eyes. The sun had set and now it was dark. Time had passed without our knowledge.

"I love kissing you," I whispered.

"I love kissing you." Her forefinger outlined my lips then moved to my jaw. "But I have to pee."

I released a reluctant laugh. "We have been kissing for…" I glanced at the clock on her nightstand. "Three hours."

She chuckled, and when she did so, her eyes lit up.

I leaned in and kissed her neck. "Pee and then let's eat."

"What do you want to eat?"

"I don't know," I said. "What do you got?"

"A drawer of takeout menus."

I chuckled then kissed her shoulder. "I'll order a pizza then."

"I love pizza." She left the bed then went into the bathroom.

I sat up and felt dizzy as the blood started to move back to my head. I forced myself to stop thinking about kissing Aspen. Otherwise, I'd have a permanent boner and would need to head to the ER. When I felt calm, I made the call and ordered.

She came out of the bathroom. "What did you order?"

"Half moose meat and half raccoon."

She cringed. "Looks like I'm not eating tonight…"

I pulled her to the couch beside me then put my arm around her. "Kidding. Pepperoni."

"Can't go wrong there."

"Now what?" I moved into her, my face pressed close to hers.

"You tell me." Her green eyes challenged me.

"There's something I want to tell you," I said. "Get it off my chest."

"Okay." She patiently waited for me to speak.

"In the bar, I asked you what I was thinking. You said I was thinking about a canned margarita. Do you remember it?"

"Yes," she said. "It was the one time I couldn't read your mind."

"Want to know what I was thinking about?"

233

"What?" she whispered.

"Kissing you. Actually, I've thought about it at least a dozen times. But I was thinking about it then, in particular. I didn't like seeing you talk to that guy. It was then that I realized just how much you meant to me."

Her eyes softened as she stared at my face. "I've had a thing for you...for a really long time."

"I wish you told me." I grabbed her hand and kissed her wrist. "Because I've been into you for a long time."

"I was afraid you would stop seeing me...for breaching the contract."

I nodded. "I was afraid you would stop seeing me because I made you uncomfortable."

"You never make me uncomfortable." Her eyes flashed as she said it.

I kissed her wrist again. "You're the sexiest, coolest chick I've ever met. I want you for as long as you'll have me."

"Then expect to be around for a long time."

"I look forward to it." I rubbed my nose against hers.

"Can I ask you something?"

"Anything."

"Have you...ever had a relationship with another client?"

"Never," I said bluntly. "I've escorted more women than I can count but nothing ever happened. I never felt anything for any of them. You're the first. I broke every rule and didn't feel any guilt as I did it."

Aspen's cheeks reddened slightly. "I feel special."

"You are special—extremely." I kissed the corner of her mouth then pulled away.

"Can I ask you something else?"

"I'm an open book."

"Have you ever had a relationship before?"

"Not a serious one," I said. "The longest I've seen the same girl is about two weeks. And most of those relationships were just physical until the lust grew stale." I refused to lie to Aspen and try to hide my past. That wasn't fair to her. But I didn't think it would bother her anyway.

"How many women have you slept with?"

I hated this question. It was the worst. "A lot."

"Can I have a number?"

I looked her in the eye. "Does it really matter?"

"It does." She pressed me with her eyes.

"A little less than a hundred."

She took a deep breath. "Wow…"

I cringed. "I wish I could give you a different answer."

"No," she said immediately. "I'm not mad or disappointed. I knew the number would be high but…that's a lot of girls."

"I liked to sleep around because no girl ever caught my attention long enough to keep me around, not like you."

Aspen's eyes lost their light and she quickly looked away. Something got under her skin. Was it the number? Was it the fact I used women for sex? Did it change anything? "Aspen?"

"Hmm?" She wouldn't look at me.

"Tell me what you're thinking."

She was quiet for so long, I didn't think she would respond. "I don't care about the number…or what you used to do before we met. You're the most handsome man I've ever seen. It doesn't surprise me that you went from woman to woman, and I certainly don't judge you for it."

"Then what is it?" I whispered.

"It's just…" She shook her head. "Nothing. Forget I said anything."

"No, tell me," I said firmly. I grabbed her chin and directed her gaze on me.

"If you've had that many partners, that means you have a lot of experience."

"So?" I asked.

She tried to look away again.

"Look at me when you talk to me." I turned her face back to me. "What is it, Aspen?" She'd never struggled to tell me something before. She was always open with me, vulnerable. "I'm your best friend. You can tell me anything."

"It's embarrassing."

"Nothing you say will ever make me think less of you. Just tell me."

"You heard what Isabella said…about John. About why he left." She down casted her eyes.

I remembered the conversation on the other side of the door. I remembered all the horrible and mean things they said about Aspen, the sweetest girl on the planet. Now I understood her embarrassment. "You think I'm going to leave you too, since I'm so experienced." It wasn't a question.

"Not in those words…"

"Aspen, you don't have to worry about that." My hand left her chin then moved through her hair. She never admitted weakness. She was always so strong all the time. "You never told me you used to be engaged."

"Because he humiliated me," she whispered. "I didn't want you to know."

"There's no reason to be embarrassed. He's the one who should be embarrassed. The guy is a fucking idiot. If any man can't see how incredible you are, then he's blind—literally." I kissed her cheek. "You're an incredible woman. You stole my heart the moment we met. No girl has ever made me look twice. But you...I didn't stand a chance."

She smiled slightly. "There's something I need to tell you."

"What?"

"The reason why I hired you was because...my father told me I disgraced him when John left. I humiliated him to the public and destroyed his image. Because of that, he said I could never be the face of the company. I thought if I hired you as my boyfriend, he would change his mind."

Anger like I've never known washed through me. I tensed then felt my hands ball into fists. Aspen noticed but didn't flinch. "Let me get this straight. This guy leaves you for another woman after asking for your hand in marriage, and all your dad cares about is his image? All he cares about is how it affects him?" I stopped myself from punching a hole through the table. "Then he made you go to that engagement party? What the hell is wrong with him? He's the coldest and cruelest man I've ever heard of."

"I know." She said it simply, like she accepted it.

"It's unacceptable, Aspen." I stared at her with angry eyes.

"I know," she repeated. "Every time I'm around him I...it doesn't matter. I just need to hold on a little longer. Then the company will be mine and I won't have to deal with him anymore. I just need to get through it."

I rubbed my temples. "Aspen, I really hate him." I didn't feel bad for saying something so ugly. "I *really* hate him."

"I hate him too," she said calmly.

"You shouldn't have to put up with that."

"I know."

I leaned back in the chair and controlled my anger. Snapping wouldn't make Aspen feel better. I needed to remain calm. "You're such an amazing girl. It's a waste he doesn't see or appreciate it."

"Life isn't always fair." She said it with a hollow voice, like all the emotion left her like a drain. "But I have people who do care about me." She looked at me. "Who are there for me. And it just makes me appreciate them even more."

Only she could see the bright side to a dark situation. "You're right about that." My arm moved around her shoulders and I pulled her close. "But I can run him over with my Jaguar if you want. Just wait for him to cross the street..." I gave her a playful look that told her I was kidding.

"And ruin that beautiful car?" she asked. "Absolutely not."

"Yeah, his fat ass would break the windshield pretty quick."

She laughed then intertwined our fingers together.

The silence stretched but it was nice to listen to. Aspen and I didn't always have to speak to each other. We were comfortable enough to not say anything at all. Just feeling her beside me made me forget everything else in the world. "You don't have to talk about it if you don't want to, but what happened with John, exactly?"

She tensed noticeably. "His father is the owner of a successful computer company, so one day he'll inherit it. John and I met through my father. I liked him, and of course, my father loved him because of his status and wealth. A marriage to me would be ideal."

"Is this the medieval times?" I said sarcastically.

"I told you my dad was old-fashioned," she said. "Anyway, I liked him. I thought he liked me. We dated for a few months, and then he proposed. I said yes because I loved him, not just because he was a good match my father would approve of. But I couldn't deny the convenience. He had his own wealth to look after, leaving me to take care of my father's company when Dad retired. It was the perfect arrangement." She paused and looked away. "At some point, he started sleeping with Isabella. Then he called it off between us because he said it was the right thing. He and I haven't spoken since."

The betrayal was painful. Why would a man want anyone but Aspen? You couldn't find someone better. "I'm sorry that happened," I said honestly. "But I'm also not sorry."

She turned to me with absorbing eyes.

"Now I have you."

A slight smile upturned her lips. "I was bitter about it for a long time, mainly because I've taken so much heat for it. But now I'm grateful it happened. My relationship with John was nothing like what I have with you. You and I, we have something special. We're playful and fun, but there's trust and friendship. You're the dream guy I never thought I would have."

"We're perfect together." There wasn't a doubt in my mind. It just felt right with her. With other girls, there was always a hint of awkwardness and obligation. With Aspen, the conversation just unfolded naturally. It wasn't forced, and I never had to exert any effort to make her laugh or smile. It was like I was made for her. And she was made for me.

"That's pretty cheesy, but I admit, I agree." She gave me a teasing look.

"It's only cheesy when it's not true."

She leaned in and kissed my cheek.

I felt warm everywhere. The touch was innocent but it still sent waves of pleasure throughout my body. "Any man who says a girl isn't good in bed says that because he can't get her to come. That's a little secret I'll share with you."

She shrugged and looked away.

"Don't let his words bother you. The fact he would badmouth you in such a way is disgraceful and pitiful. I can already tell he has a small dick."

She released a loud laugh then choked for a second. "Ohmygod…"

"He does, doesn't he?"

She shook her head like she couldn't believe my question. "I wouldn't know. John is the only guy I've been with."

I suspected that was true. "I'll show you by comparison then." I winked at her.

Her cheeks blushed slightly. "I look forward to it."

***

Aspen took the bat wearing jean shorts and a Yankee jersey. A navy blue baseball cap was on her head, and her hair was in a tight ponytail. She spun it in her wrist. "You ready for this?" she shouted to Chase.

"Bring it." He moved twenty feet closer to the mound.

She shook her head but there was a slight smile on her lips. "You're way too close…"

"I know what I'm doing," Chase said. "Just do your best, Battleship."

Now everyone was calling her that. She didn't mind so I didn't mind. I actually thought the nickname was cute. I stood on the pitcher's mound. "Ready?"

She took a stance then tapped the bat against the mound a few times before she held it at the ready. "Bring it."

"I'll show you my famous curve ball."

"If you're holding it like that, you aren't going to throw a curveball."

I forgot she used to play in college. "Maybe I'm trying to trick you."

"You aren't doing a very good job."

I narrowed my eyes at her, even more attracted to her because the lip she just gave me.

"Are we going to play or just banter back and forth?" Chase shouted.

I wound up the pitch then threw it hard.

Aspen hit the ball right in the middle of the bat and sent it flying. It flew past Chase's head and toward the very end of the field where the fence stood. She tossed the bat aside then moved like a snail to first base. "I got the time..."

Chase sprinted to get the ball but I knew he would never make it back in time. His sword hung at his side, looking like a cheap toy children played with.

Aspen looked at her watch as she walked. "Making good time." She rounded second base.

I watched her with my hands on my hips, grinning even though I wish I wouldn't.

"Some curveball, by the way." She walked around third base with her head held high and her shoulders straight. "Totally threw me off." She walked to home plate.

I blocked her path and stood in her way. "Cocky, are we?"

"It's not my fault your teammate underestimated my abilities." She tried to get around me.

I blocked her path each time. "Maybe you shouldn't underestimate mine."

"Your behavior is a foul." She tried to push me away but I didn't budge.

"I don't see a ref anywhere." I turned to Chase. "Hurry up and run to home plate!"

She darted to the right and tried to reach the plate.

I grabbed her and held her back. "Maybe if you'd run around the plates instead of being an arrogant jerk, this wouldn't have happened."

"I'm a jerk?" She tried to push me again. "You're a jerk."

I laughed then I picked her up with one arm and threw her over my shoulders.

"Put me down!" She kicked and smacked me in the back.

"Nope." I stood there and waited for Chase.

"This isn't fair!" She kept flailing in my arms.

I smacked her ass. "Life isn't fair, baby."

Chase ran up then reached home plate. "Out!"

She stopped fighting and growled. "Rhett! I'm going to kill you."

I put her down and faced her. "Me? Your best friend? You don't have it in you." I looked down into her face and challenged her. But I smiled as I did it, not making it very convincing.

"You guys are both cheaters and I'm never going to play with you again," Aspen said. She poked us both in the chest.

"Maybe you should be a graceful winner," I said.

She turned to Chase. "Maybe you should back up when I tell you to. Just because I look like a girl doesn't mean I hit like one."

"I'll remember that for next time," Chase said with a laugh.

Aspen turned her glare on me. "I'll get you back for that."

"I'm so scared…" I rolled my eyes.

Her eyes smoldered in rage.

I pecked her on the lips then walked away. "I'm up."

She growled then took the pitcher's mound. Chase ran to the outfield.

I swung the bat a few times for practice then stepped into the box. "Give me your best, Battleship."

"I'm going to sink your ship alright," she said.

"Bring it."

She wound up the pitch then threw it hard.

I hit the ball hard, sending it into the outfield. Chase took off but it would take him a while to return. I dropped the bat and started to walk. "Who am I—"

Aspen tackled me to the ground and moved on top of me.

My body hit the dirt and the wind was knocked out of me. Like a tiger, she pounced on me when I least expected it. "You aren't going to be able to keep me here." I was amused she tried even though I was almost a hundred pounds heavier than she was.

"I beg to differ," she said with a confident look.

"Oh really?" I sat up and was about to lift her off the ground.

She cupped my face then gave me a scorching kiss.

Her touch froze me. Her lips moved against mine, massaging my mouth with hers. The taste of honey came onto my lips. She moved me back to the ground and slid over me, still kissing me and making my body burn in longing. I released a growl as I kissed her. "Goddammit, Battleship."

***

We had breakfast at a diner after the game. Aspen and I sat on one side of the booth while Chase sat on the other. We were all a little dirty from the game, me especially since Aspen tackled me like a linebacker.

243

E.L. Todd

"What are you getting?" I asked her.

"French toast." She said it quickly, like she knew what she was going to order the moment we walked inside. "With lots of butter. Extra butter."

My heart burned in affection while I looked at her. "Good choice."

"What are you getting?" she asked.

"The same thing," I said. "With extra butter."

Chase watched us from across the table. "You guys will be fat in no time but at least you'll be happy."

"Very happy," Aspen said with pride.

Chase sipped his coffee then looked out the window. He was relaxed as he watched the people pass on the sidewalk. It was a cloudless day and shadows were cast everywhere. The stretches of darkness didn't seem to bother him at all. It was like the phobia was gone entirely. Just having a plastic sword on his hip was enough to make him feel safe. He looked ridiculous wearing it, but it was a small price to pay to have my brother back. "You're the first girl Rhett has introduced me to," he said. "I mean, I've met some of his girls but not like this."

"Oh." Aspen clearly didn't know what else to say.

"And I really like you for my brother," he said. "Thanks for making him happy."

Chase said really sweet things without thinking. It didn't seem like he meant to be sentimental. He just said what was on his mind without further thought.

Aspen's cheeks reddened. "He makes me happy too."

"And I like that you aren't slutty like all those other—"

"Chase." I silenced him. "She gets it."

Aspen laughed. "It's okay, Rhett. It doesn't bother me."

"It doesn't?" I asked. "It's one thing to know about my past but another to keep bringing it up." I shot Chase another glare, telling him to cool his jets.

She shook her head. "You liked those girls because they were pretty. You like me because you think I'm pretty in places you can't see. It's a compliment, really."

Aspen was different than all the other girls I met. She didn't understand jealousy or entitlement like the others did. She was confident in herself, not conceited, and that allowed her to trust me. After what John did to her, I assumed she would struggle to trust me. But that didn't seem to be the case at all. "You're exactly right." I kissed her cheek then rubbed my nose against hers.

Chase watched us then sighed. "I need to get a girl."

I looked around the diner. "There's a cute redhead over there." It was actually an old lady. She had to be at least seventy.

Chase eyed her then rolled his eyes. "Go to hell."

"That brunette over there is really pretty." Aspen nodded to a table on the other side of the diner.

The girl looked our age, and she was sitting alone. A stack of newspapers was in front of her, and she was reading one while sipping her coffee. She was cute and small, but she had nothing on Aspen.

Chase turned and discreetly glanced her way. "You're right. Good eye, Battleship."

She shrugged in modesty. "I have a knack for this sort of thing."

Chase downed the rest of his coffee. "I'm going for it."

"Leave your sword," I said, trying to help him out.

"Are you crazy?" he said. "It's a conversation starter. Chicks totally dig it."

They do?

"It's nice to hit on chicks during the day. Now I see what they really look like. In the darkness, it's hard to tell sometimes," Chase said. "And that chick is definitely a cutie."

"Then go for it," I said. "We'll order for you."

"Alright." Chase stood up. "Wish me luck." He walked away.

Aspen sipped her coffee then looked at me. "Does he find lady friends often?"

"Like you wouldn't believe," I said. "They must think he's joking when he talks about the shadows."

"But when they go to his apartment...they must think he's crazy," she said.

"He tells them his apartment is like the universe and he'll give them sex that's 'out of this world.'"

Aspen laughed and almost spit out her coffee. "And that works?"

"He gets laid more than I do," I said.

"Wow." She nodded her head in amazement. "That's impressive."

"I don't know how he does it," I said with a shrug.

We watched Chase interact with the girl reading the newspapers. When he patted the sword on his hip, we knew it came up in the conversation. When she laughed, we knew Chase said something charming. Then he slid into the booth across from her. Her newspaper and coffee were forgotten, and all her focus was on him.

"He's got game," Aspen said.

"You know where he gets it from, right?" I wiggled my eyebrows.

"Yeah...you spent three months with me before you made your move," she said sarcastically. "That's game..."

I tried not to laugh, and as a result, I smiled unwillingly. "I would have had you sooner if I knew you weren't off limits."

"Sure..." She sipped her coffee and tried to hide her smile.

I stared into her face. "You're lucky you're cute, you know that?"

"Or else?"

"I'd..." I couldn't think of anything to say.

"You're lucky you're cute too," she said. "Because you're aren't so bright upstairs."

"That's it," I said. "I'm eating your French toast."

She gasped like I just threatened to kill Harper. "You wouldn't..."

"Watch me," I said. "All that butter and syrup is mine."

"No!" She gave me a frightened look like she was in a horror film. "Don't you dare. I'd never forgive you."

I shrugged. "I can't let that comment slide. If I do, you won't learn your lesson. There has to be some sort of punishment."

"Then say something mean back," she said in exasperation. "Don't eat my breakfast."

"Nope," I said. "This is how it has to be. I'm sorry." I reminded myself of a parent telling their kid they were going to get spanked.

The waitress arrived with our plates. She set my breakfast in front of me then set Aspen's down. A tense moment passed between us as we looked at our food. She knew I was going to snatch it away, and I was wondering how I would get it without knocking anything over.

247

Once the waitress walked away, Aspen quickly snatched her food and inhaled it like she was in an eating contest. Syrup and butter got everywhere, across the table and all over her face. She ate so quickly she couldn't enjoy it, just trying to make sure I couldn't get it.

I stared at her, trying not to laugh and smile at the same time.

She kept eating, quicker than I could watch. Her path looked like a bombed trench in World War II. There was food everywhere. She eyed me carefully while she kept eating, making sure I wouldn't get any of it.

I just stared at her, feeling something form and burn in my chest. Time seemed to stop and the world disappeared. "I love you."

She froze in mid-bite, her cheeks caked in syrup and butter.

"I love you so damn much." I cupped her cheeks, feeling the stickiness on my hands, and then kissed her. She tasted like syrup and butter, and I felt like I was kissing French toast more than Aspen.

She kissed me back but a chuckle escaped her lips. "I look like a pig right now."

"Maybe I like pigs," I whispered.

"That bodes well in my favor."

I stared into her face, unable to stop smiling. "So, how long are you going to leave me hanging?"

Her eyes flashed in an emerald light, and emotion was clear on her face. She looked at me like I was her whole world, the only thing that really mattered. Words didn't need to be said because I knew how she felt. But I wanted to hear it anyway. "I love you too."

***

As soon as we crossed the threshold to my apartment, our bodies were pressed together and our lips were attached like magnet to steel. My hands gripped her hips as I directed her toward my bedroom. I was devouring her, and she was consuming me with the same passion. We knocked over a lamp in our hasty movements and it shattered on the floor.

"Oh no," she said. "I'm so sorry—"

I silenced her with my kiss. "I don't give a damn." My hand fisted her hair and got a strong hold as I moved her to my bedroom. The curtains were closed so it was dark and cool in the room, hidden from the summer sun. I moved her to the bed then lay her down. I'd been thinking about this moment for a long time. I'd fantasized about her on this very bed, and that made me more turned on than I already was.

My hands moved to her shorts and I pulled them down her long legs. When I reached her ankles, I pulled off her shoes and socks. Then I moved back up and kissed her inner thighs.

Aspen immediately dug her fingers into my hair and arched her back.

Feeling her excitement egged me forward. I gripped her thong then pulled it off, feeling my heart beat harder than it ever had. Once I saw the area between her legs, my cock twitched. My mouth moved to the nub and I kissed the area, loving the way she tasted. My tongue circled her clitoris then plunged deep inside her.

Her hands moved to my shoulders and her nails dug into the skin, almost piercing it. Deep, musical sighs escaped her throat, and made my spine shiver the second they entered my ear.

I sucked the area a final time before I moved up and pulled her shirt off. She wore a pink bra underneath. The curve and swell of her breasts were just as I imagined them to look.

They were perfect and round, flawless skin that wasn't blemished with a single mark. Before I moved in, I kissed the skin of her chest then moved down to the valley. Then I unclasped the back and felt it come loose.

I peeled it off then stared at her naked chest, loving its perkiness. Her nipples were hard like the tip of a pencil, and they were red like someone had already sucked them until they were raw. My mouth moved over them and I took each one in my mouth, loving the way her skin felt. She moaned louder and harder, and her hands moved under my shirt as she prepared to pull it off.

I used one hand and helped her remove it. Once the fabric hit the floor, I looked down at her. Long, lean legs led to wide hips. Her petite waist had the definition of small muscles, and her rib cage spanned the length of my hand. I could crush her if I wanted to. Large breasts contrasted against the tightness of her stomach, and I thought I would blow my load right then and there. "You're perfect."

"I bet you are too." Her hands moved to my jeans and got them off. Then she pulled my boxers over my ass, letting my long cock out. She stared at it for a long moment then wrapped her fingers around the shaft.

I kicked off my jeans and boxers the rest of the way then pressed my naked body against hers. Her skin was scorching hot next to mine. We fit well together, like we were made for one another.

Her hands moved up my chest and to my shoulders. "Geez, you're hot."

I didn't smile but I was amused by her bluntness. "So are you." I spread her legs with mine then pressed my forehead to hers. "Are you on the pill?"

"Yes."

Good. I didn't want to wear a condom. I'd never had sex without one, but Aspen was the only woman I've ever loved. I never wanted to wear one with the one woman I gave my heart to. I wanted to feel my skin rub against hers. I didn't want us to be separated by cheap latex. And I wanted to come inside her, to claim her in a sensual way.

Once I was positioned over her and my face was pressed to hers, she tensed noticeably. It was like I hurt her or she was extremely uncomfortable. The arousal that was in her eyes a moment ago disappeared like a shooting star. It was like she didn't even want me anymore. "What's wrong?"

"Nothing..." She still remained rigid like she was closing off from me.

"We don't have to do this." I was extremely disappointed but I would never tell her that. "There's no rush."

She sighed, like she was irritated.

Then it hit me like a lightning bolt. I knew exactly what was wrong. "Aspen, relax."

She looked into my eyes with uncertainty.

"Relax," I repeated.

"I don't want you to be disappointed."

I cupped her face while I looked down at her. "First of all, you can never disappoint me. You're the woman I love. Even if you are terrible in bed, it doesn't mean we can't practice. And I would *love* to practice."

That still didn't loosen her up. I tried a different tactic. "There's a big factor that determines good sex, and it's not just one person. It's both. Sex is good when both partners have the right chemistry, the right feeling. It can't just be one person. So, it was stupid for him to blame you for its lack of goodness. It was both of you, because neither one of you really loved the other. Aspen, you and I are madly in love. It'll be amazing."

251

"Yeah?" She relaxed slightly.

"Yeah," I said with confidence. "And I would never leave you over something like that. You give me so much more than physical satisfaction. I already know you're going to be amazing. You want to know how?"

She nodded.

"You're the best kisser I've ever had. You make me want to explode just from pressing your mouth to mine. If you give that same kind of passion now, I won't be able to keep up with you."

She moved her fingers into my hair and felt the strands. "You always know the right thing to say."

"Because I know you—better than anyone." I kissed her gently before I pulled away. "Now, can I make love to you?"

She wrapped her arms around my neck and pulled me closer to her. "Yes, please."

I rubbed my nose against hers before my lips sought hers in a gentle embrace. The kiss was purposeful but slow. My hand felt her long brown hair and I breathed hard while I kissed her.

She tensed in the beginning but she loosened up within minutes. Her passion had returned, and she kissed me harder than I kissed her. Her nails stuck out like claws and she gripped the muscles of my back.

I directed my head to her entrance then gently pushed. The moisture moved against my tip, and I knew she was more than ready for me. She was soaked, desperate to feel me move inside her.

I paused because it felt so good. Aspen felt right, nothing like all the other girls. I pushed further inside her and listened to the quiet moans she made. It was turning me on even more. Once I was completely sheathed, I kissed her and gave her a moment to acclimate to my large size.

She cupped my face then breathed. She looked into my eyes as she allowed me to stretch her.

Then I moved inside her gently, keeping the pace slow. I wasn't in a hurry. I wanted to make it last as long as possible, for her as well as for me.

She rocked into me from below, matching my thrusts like they were synced together. She sucked my bottom lip then ran her hands down my back. Sometimes she would moan loudly then crush her mouth against mine just so she wouldn't scream. Then she would whisper my name over and over while she pulled me inside her.

I wasn't going to last if she kept this up.

I kissed her, concentrating on her lips. My cock moved inside her tightness. It felt unbelievably good, better than I've ever had. My dirty fantasies couldn't compete with reality.

Aspen tightened further, squeezing my cock while I moved in and out of her. Her breathing changed and became deep and raspy. Her nails dug into me harder, and she suddenly wanted more of me, wanted it harder.

I kissed the corner of her mouth while she exploded around me. She yelled my name. It sent ripples down my body, listening to her hit a climax that was powerful and blinding. I moved into her harder, wanting to make her pleasure last as long as possible. Her moans faded away as the moment passed. When she finished, her chest was red and her nipples were hard. Stars were in her eyes and she looked dazed.

I kissed her, feeling my tongue dance with hers.

She gripped my arm then pushed me gently. Then she turned me on my back.

I looked up at her and tried to hide my surprise. Since she was self-conscious about her performance, I assumed she would want me to be on top and lead the way.

She moved me back against the headboard and forced me to sit up. "I've always wanted to do this to you." She straddled my hips then balanced on the balls of her feet. Then she gripped my shoulders.

I breathed hard and felt my cock twitch when I realized what she was doing. I wasn't even inside her yet and I wanted to come.

"This is what I imagined when I touched myself." She directed me inside her then sheathed me.

I released a loud involuntary gasp. That was the hottest thing I've ever heard. I fulfilled my fantasy with her, and now she was fulfilling her fantasy with me. The idea of her touching herself and thinking of me was enough to make me explode then and there. "Aspen…"

She guided herself up and down, her tits shaking in my face. Her perfect body moved quickly, and her hair reached the top of her breasts. I grabbed her hips and directed her movement, giving her extra support as she slid up and down my cock over and over.

I breathed hard and felt myself prepare for an orgasm that would leave me breathless. I tried to hold on because I wanted to make this last forever.

Aspen moved one hand between her legs and rubbed her clitoris while she continued to ride me. Her eyes were brighter than I'd ever seen them, more vibrant than the moss on Oregon trees. Her head rolled back as she moved into me harder then she released a scream as she came around me again.

I couldn't hold on a moment longer, not after that performance. My fingers dug into her skin as I squeezed her and a tidal wave of immense pleasure rocked through me. My body tightened in preparation and I released. "Fuck, Aspen..." I filled her, having the most intense orgasm of my life.

She leaned forward and pressed her chest to mine. Her arms moved around my neck and she held me as she caught her breath.

My face moved into the valley of her breasts and I inhaled her scent. It smelled like vanilla mixed with sweat. It was intoxicating. I kissed the area gently, still catching my breath. "You're the best I've ever had." It wasn't a line to boost her ego or an attempt to mask a terrible performance. It was the truth, and only the truth.

Aspen knew I wouldn't lie to her. She looked at me with a relaxed expression. Her eyes searched mine, looking for something only she knew. "Because I'm in love with you."

E.L. Todd

Aspen

Rhett and I didn't leave the bedroom often. We were wrapped around one another, going at it like rabbits in winter. Our lovemaking was sensual and slow, and neither one of us wanted to reach the finish. He took me gently, and I seemed to want it harder than he did most of the time.

Sex with him was completely different than it was with John. In comparison, I wasn't even sure what John and I did. It was awkward and uncomfortable. It didn't even feel good most of the time. Rhett was different. I could never get enough of him. Despite how often we did it, I was never sore because he knew what he was doing.

As soon as he got off work in the evenings, he came to my place and we retreated to the bedroom until we needed food and water. I never asked about work or whom he was escorting. I trusted him and knew he would never betray me, but I didn't want to hear about him spending the evening with random women, even if he only touched their hand or their waist. Rhett was smart enough not to bring it up.

On Saturday morning, I woke up to him sleeping beside me. He spooned me from behind, his arm wrapped around my waist. His breathing fell on the back of my neck, and his chest was pressed to my back.

I wanted to lie there and never move but I had breakfast to make. I decided to make him French toast, eggs, and bacon to get the day started. He always cooked for me and I wanted to do something for him.

I slipped out of his embrace without waking him then threw on one of his t-shirts. Once I was in the kitchen, I began cooking and tried not to screw anything up. I wasn't completely clueless but I wasn't a chef either.

I was on cloud nine, making breakfast while my ridiculously hot and sweet boyfriend slept in my bed. My life was amazing, absolutely amazing. I'd never been so happy before. If I saw Isabella right now, I would hug her and thank her for taking John from me. She could have him. John was a minnow that escaped from my line and Rhett was the large swordfish I caught by accident. It worked out in the end.

I was singing under my breath when there was a knock on my door. I flipped the French toast in the pan before I walked to the peephole. It was probably Harper, wanting all the dirt about the size of Rhett's package and how he used it. But it wasn't her.

It was John.

What. The. Hell.

I froze, unable to believe I was looking at him through my peephole. We hadn't spoken since the night he dumped me. I didn't even see him at the engagement party. What could he possibly want?

I decided to stay absolutely still, hoping he would just go away.

"Aspen, are you home?" he said through the door. He wore a suit like he just got off work. That was unusually dressy for a Saturday morning.

I didn't even breathe so he would just give up and walk away. The last thing I wanted to do was have a conversation with him. What would we talk about? The weather? And I didn't want Rhett to see him. I wasn't sure how he would react, but I knew he wouldn't be happy that my ex-fiancé showed up on my doorstep this early on a Saturday. I patiently waited for him to leave.

The alarm on the oven went off, telling me the rolls were ready. It beeped loud and high.

Son of a bitch!

I ran over and quickly turned it off like that would erase the sound it already made.

"Aspen?" John said again.

Fuck. My. Life. "Stupid rolls," I mumbled. I turned off all the appliances so they wouldn't make any more noise.

"I just want a minute of your time," he said through the door.

I stood in the kitchen just wearing Rhett's shirt. I didn't know what to do. I needed to get rid of him before Rhett woke up. We'd spent the past two weeks in heavenly bliss and I didn't want to ruin that. Why did my past have to haunt me like this?

"Aspen?" John said.

I wanted to strangle this guy. He wouldn't go away unless I got rid of him. And I had to shoo him away before Rhett woke up. I put on my big girl panties and cracked the door open. Thankfully, Rhett's shirt trailed past my knees. I hoped the sight would make him uncomfortable. "What?" I snapped. "You didn't catch me at the best time." My meaning was clear, and I hoped he would be so discomfited that he would just walk away without saying a word.

He eyed my legs then dropped his jaw. "Uh..."

"Rhett and I are in the middle of something so can you just go away? Thanks." I shut the door and locked it. I looked through the peephole and waited for him to walk away.

He covered his face for a moment like he was embarrassed before he turned and disappeared.

"Crisis averted." I turned back to the kitchen and got back to work. A minute later, Rhett walked out of my room, just wearing his boxers. His chest was wide and expansive. It was hard like a slab of bricks and I loved feeling it against my back when he took me from behind. His stomach was outlined with muscle, an eight-pack that looked like rocks, and then a noticeable V led into his boxers. He had a thin happy trail that disappeared under the fabric. His legs were toned and thick, and they were long, like a soccer player. His hair was messy from rolling around the night before, but it still looked sexy. He stared at me for a moment. "What?"

"Huh?" Did he say something? I was too distracted to notice.

"Why are you looking at me like that?" He had a cocky grin on his face, like he knew exactly why I was staring at him like that.

I realized how ridiculous I looked. I stood there holding a spatula while my jaw hung to the floor. I eyed him like an underwear model just walked into my kitchen. "I just...you want breakfast?" I couldn't think of anything else to say.

He ran his fingers through his hair, still smiling. "I'd love breakfast." He came behind me then pulled me to his chest. "What a nice surprise."

"I wanted to make you breakfast in bed."

"Well, I'd rather have you in bed." He kissed my neck. "That would save you time. But I admit, seeing you wear that t-shirt and cook me food is pretty damn hot."

"I think it's the spatula that's got you so excited..."

He took it from my hand then spanked me playfully. "Hmm...let's use this later."

I chuckled then faced him, giving him a big peck on the lips.

His hands moved up my shirt to my stomach. "I could get used to this."

"So could I."

He rubbed his nose against mine. "Who was at the door?"

All my giddiness faded. "What door?" I blurted.

He cocked an eyebrow but seemed amused. "The bathroom door," he said sarcastically. "Because I'm sure you have guests come through there all the time."

How did I get out of this? I didn't want to tell him it was John. We were having such an amazing morning. I wasn't willing to sacrifice that for anything.

"So, who was it?"

Think, Aspen. "Girl scout cookies." That was believable, right?

He seemed more confused. "Don't they come in early spring?"

Was this guy a detective? Why did he have to be so smart? "Fine, it was Harper." She was my lifeline. "She had to drop off something."

"Oh." He seemed to believe that. "You should have invited her for breakfast."

"No, I want you all to myself."

He smacked my ass playfully again. "Well, I'm all yours."

I liked knowing that. It was the reason I woke up with a smile on my face.

"Do you need help?" he asked.

261

"No, I think I got it."

He looked into the pan. "Well, the French toast is burned and..." He opened the oven. "So are the rolls." He gave me a grin. "But I'm sure it'll taste great."

"Okay, I'm terrible at this. Please help."

"My pleasure." He grabbed the apron off the rack and put it on. It was pink and red.

I eyed him like he was crazy. "Um...what are you doing?"

"You're wearing my shirt," he said. "I don't want to get burned."

"Well, it looks good on you." I tried not to laugh.

"Only a man secure with his masculinity could wear a pink apron and pull it off."

"You definitely pull it off." I smiled while I eyed him.

He grabbed me then lifted me on the counter. Then he pulled my underwear off. "I'll show you."

"What about breakfast?"

"Forget breakfast," he said. "Let's go out—after we're done."

***

"You've been happy every single day for the past few weeks," Jane said when she handed me my coffee. "What's with the change?"

I couldn't stop smiling. "I'm in love." I sighed after I said it. I was higher than a cloud.

"With that new boyfriend of yours?" she asked with a smile. Jane was a few years older than me and she was a great assistant. We weren't necessarily friends, but we were friendly.

"Yep. He's dreamy."

She smiled. "I'm glad you found someone, Aspen. You deserve to be happy."

"Thank you, Jane." She was nicer to me than my own father, and I had a feeling it wasn't because I paid her. "Any messages?"

She shifted her weight, suddenly looking uncomfortable. "Actually, yes."

I eyed her, waiting for her to continue.

"Marshall from Canadian Oil called. He wants you to return his call."

That wasn't odd. "Okay."

"Then Scott from payroll needs to discuss the 401k packages for the employees."

"Okay." None of these were a cause of alarm.

"And John called…" She fidgeted with her hands. "He wants to have lunch. He wants you to give a call back with the details."

This could not be happening to me. "Did he say what he wanted?"

"I'm afraid not. When I asked, he said it was between you two."

What the hell did he want? He never called me when I was suffering, but the second I was happy, he butted back into my life. Did Isabella know he was calling? Was this another ploy to torture me? "If he calls again, tell him I don't have time to see him. And tell him not to call again."

She nodded. "You got it." She walked out and left me alone with my thoughts.

When he saw me in Rhett's t-shirt, I figured that would scare him off permanently. I doubted he'd come back and try to talk to me again. But now he was cornering me at work.

What the hell did he want?

***

Right before I took lunch, Jane's voice came over the intercom. "Ms. Lane, John is here."

I froze, feeling my heart increase to a dangerous level. A minute passed and I was unable to move or speak.

"Ms. Lane?"

Why was this happening to me? "Tell him to leave."

"Yes, ma'am."

I stayed in my office and decided to skip lunch. I was starving but I'd rather struggle with hunger than speak to that man. At least I would get more work done and get off work early. The earlier I got off work, the sooner I would see Rhett.

Jane's voice came over the intercom again. "He's gone, ma'am."

I breathed a sigh of relief. "Thank you, Jane. Do you mind running out and picking up a sandwich for me?" I didn't usually send her on runs like this but I didn't want to leave the office on the off chance I bumped into him.

"Of course. I'll be back soon."

***

After I finished lunch and responded to a few emails, Jane's voice came over the intercom. "Your father is coming down to see you."

Did I hear her right? He never came down to see me. "Did he say why?"

"No. But John is with him."

Fucking son of a bitch.

"I can't send them away," she said. "I'm sorry."

"I understand, Jane. Thank you." I covered my face with my hands and tried to remain calm. It was such a low blow to go to my father to talk to me. If we were two guys in a fight, he just kicked me in the nuts.

A minute later, Dad walked inside without even knocking. "Hey, Aspen. Hope you aren't busy."

Like it would matter if I were.

John came in behind him, wearing a similar suit to the one I last saw him in.

"How can I help you, gentlemen?" I kept my cool.

Dad put his hands in his pockets. "John told me he's been having a hard time getting a hold of you."

I looked at John, silently telling him I absolutely loathed him, and then looked at my father again. "I'm very busy. You know that, Dad."

"Well, you don't look busy now." He turned to John. "Take a seat."

"Thank you, sir." John shook his hand.

Dad took it then walked out.

A father shouldn't shake hands with the man who left his daughter and humiliated her. When would my father understand the meaning of family and loyalty? Never?

Dad shut the door, leaving us alone.

Palpable tension filled the air. I seriously considered picking up my keyboard and beating him with it. My anger didn't come from the betrayal he caused me. It was the fact he was in my office, ruining my happiness with Rhett. If he kept this up, I wouldn't be able to hide it from Rhett anymore. And that would ruin what we had.

He sat down in the chair facing my desk then adjusted his tie.

I stared at him, waiting for him to speak. If I spoke first, I would only scream.

He turned his blue eyes on me. "How are you?" he asked casually.

Was this a joke? "How do you think?" I said coldly.

He looked away for a moment before he turned to me. "I want to apologize—"

"John, I'm over it." I didn't want to hear the rest of his sentence. "I'm madly in love with the man of my dreams, and I'm grateful you left me for Isabella. I hope you two have a happy life together—truly. Now you can leave."

He adjusted his tie again, clearly nervous. "I hate the way she treats you. I can't stand it, actually."

"It shows," I said sarcastically.

"I never said you were bad in bed and...whatever else she said. She's just spinning that to get a rise out of you."

"Honestly, I don't care." I just wanted him to leave so I could go back to being happy. "Bad in bed or great in bed, I don't lose any sleep over it. I'm over our relationship and never think about it. If you came here to absolve your guilt, consider your endeavor successful. I'm okay. Are we done now?"

He played with his watch. "You hate me." His voice came out quiet.

"No, I'm indifferent."

"That's worse." He sat still and rested his arms on the chair.

I rested my hands on the desk and tried to think of a way to end this conversation as quickly as possible.

"What happened with Isabella and I...it was just lust. It happened once and then it happened again—"

"I couldn't care less, John. You don't need to explain anything." I kept my voice calm even though it was difficult.

"She and I…it's not like it used to be. Now I see the way she treats you and other people and I can't stand it." He shook his head. "I don't think I can go through with it."

Through with what? The wedding? I didn't ask.

"I know you said you're with this guy—"

"Rhett," I snapped. "He has a name."

"Rhett," he said. "But…I was hoping that we could try again." He pleaded with me with his eyes.

What the hell was going on? "Let me get this straight…" I felt my voice rise. "You cheat on me with her then leave me. And now you're trying to get back together with me, effectively cheating on her, and you want to leave her? You're the biggest piece of shit I've ever met, and remember who my father is. You still beat him by a landslide."

He looked down, almost ashamed.

"You're a terrible person." My eyes were cold and my voice was full of venom. "How can you do this to her? To me?"

He stared at his hands in his lap.

"Let me make this clear. I'm in love with Rhett and I'm going to marry him—someday. There's never a possibility of you and I. Leave my office and never show your face again." I stood up then opened the door. "Now."

He sighed then rose to his feet. He gave me a final look before he walked out. "I made a mistake and I won't make it again. I would never cheat on you again."

"Oh." I touched my chest in a gesture of emotion. "That's so sweet. You won't cheat on me again? Wow…I feel so special." I dropped my fake smile then grabbed him by the arm and shoved him out.

Then I slammed the door in his face.

Rhett

Losing my parents at such a young age was difficult. The worst part was I hardly remembered them. Some memories came into my mind but they were always vague. I recalled more than Chase but it still wasn't enough. But whether I remembered them or not, they left a void in my chest.

I never noticed it until now—because Aspen filled it.

She gave me the love I'd been missing, and she gave me joy no one else ever could. My life had become an image of pastel colors, all bright and mesmerizing. Every day was better than the last. She was mine and I was hers.

I didn't miss my bachelor life at all. Now that I'd experienced a loving relationship, I realized how lonely my old ways used to be. I wasn't sure why men enjoyed it so much. It really wasn't that great.

I walked to work with a skip in my step, thinking about seeing Aspen tonight. I wanted to take her to dinner then ice cream. I wanted to smear whipped cream all over her body then lick it off. I wanted to lick chocolate sauce from the valley between her breasts. I got hard thinking about it.

I entered the office then reached Danielle's desk. "It's a beautiful day, isn't it?"

She gave me a skeptical smile. "Not that you get out much...too busy with Aspen."

"I wish I were busy with her now," I said seriously. "So, you got a new client for me?"

"Yeah." She pushed the file toward me. "She wants to meet tomorrow at noon."

"Okay." I didn't even look inside the folder. "What's her story?"

"She said she wants to get revenge on a woman who stole her man." She shrugged.

"How would I help with that?"

"I haven't got a clue. But it's easy money."

"True."

"Anything else, Rhett?"

"Nope." I rose to my feet. "I'll see you later."

"Tell Aspen I said hi."

I winked. "I will."

***

"So, how's she in bed?" Troy asked over lunch.

I gave him an incredulous look.

"That bad?"

"No." I rolled my eyes.

"Just tell me," he said. "I'm your best friend. You tell me about all the other girls."

"Battleship is different and you know it."

He grinned stupidly. "Do you call her that in bed? Battleship?" He laughed. "That would be a funny thing to say in bed."

"Aspen," I answered. "It's much sexier than Battleship."

"I beg to differ." He drank his soda then belched loudly.

"That's hot," I said sarcastically.

"I'm surprised you aren't tapping her right now."

"She's at work," I said sadly. "And then I'm meeting a new client in an hour."

"She doesn't care about your profession at all?"

I shook my head. "She said she trusts me. But she never asks me about it. So I think it does bother her, in a way."

"She might disapprove it as you become more serious."

"No," I said. "She said she understood. Aspen would never make me quit my job. She knows I like it."

"Women can be controlling, dude."

"Not Aspen," I said immediately. "I work my own hours, I make a great salary, and I help people. I told her how miserable I was working for that credit card company. She would never make me do something I hated."

"Give it time..." He ate a few fries then drank his soda again. "You want to hear me burp the alphabet?

I gave him a serious look. "What do you think?"

"Is that a yes? Okay, here I go." He opened his mouth and burped, "A."

I raised my hand. "No, stop." I waved away the stench of soda.

"I can do other songs too," he said. "Like *Sexy Back* by Justin Timberlake."

"How do you get laid?" I blurted.

He pointed at his face. "Hello?"

"Looks can only get you so far..."

"I bet Battleship would like it."

Actually, she would. She would probably think it's hilarious. The thought of her laughing as Troy burped a Justin Timberlake song made me smile against my will. "She would."

"I'll do it for her next time I see her."

I shrugged. "Knock yourself out."

"Or I can teach you." He wiggled his eyebrows. "Maybe it'll get her in the mood."

"Listening to me belch isn't going to get her wet," I said. "I already know how to do that."

"Do you fart *Sexy Back*?" he asked seriously.

I looked at my watch. "I got to go. I can't handle any more of you for the day."

***

Before I walked into the coffee shop, I pulled out the folder from my bag then flipped it open. I forgot to do my homework because I was too busy doing Aspen. I skimmed through it and found her name.

Isabella.

That was a weird coincidence. I walked inside then looked for the copy of her driver's license. When I saw the face I recognized, I felt sick. It was her. It was the same Isabella.

What the fuck?

"Hello, Rhett."

I looked up to see Isabella staring at me, wearing jeans that were so low on her hips I thought her ass might pop out at any moment. Her low-cut shirt showed her cleavage but I didn't look. "Danielle will give you a full refund. Goodbye." There was no way in hell I was escorting Isabella, not when she treated my girl like shit.

"Whoa...hold on." She grabbed my arm.

I twisted out of her grasp violently. "Don't touch me."

She smiled and it just irritated me. "You shouldn't walk away. There's something I need to tell you, and it could ruin your career."

Ruin my career? "I love Aspen and nothing you say will change my mind." She probably wanted to seduce me so I

272

would cheat on Aspen. *Good luck with that.* I couldn't get it up if I tried.

She laughed. "You really should sit down and let me talk. Your life hangs in the balance."

I hated the fact her ploy was working. What was she talking about? What did she have hanging over my head?

She moved to the table and sat down. "Take a seat."

Glaring at her the entire time, I sat across from her.

"How's it going?" she asked.

"Cut to the chase. What do you want to say to me?"

Her lips upturned in a smile. "Stern man...I like that."

I've never had the urge to hit a woman before but I seriously wanted to bash her face into the table. I never loathed someone I didn't know, but I absolutely despised this woman.

"Fine, I'll get to the point since you're such terrible company."

I stared at her blankly.

"This is the deal." Her flirty attitude disappeared and a serious one emerged. "I know Aspen is paying you to pretend to be her boyfriend."

"No, she's not. I'm her boyfriend and I love her."

"Whatever," she said. "I know she's paying you, which is pathetic, by the way."

"And what are you doing now?" I said coldly.

She ignored the jab. "You're going to go to her father and tell him the truth, that she paid you to pretend to be seeing her. You will provide all the necessary documents and transactions to prove it's true."

"I'll never do that," I said firmly. "I can't be bought and I can't be manipulated."

"We'll see about that..."

There was nothing this girl could do to change my mind.

"It would be a shame if your business closed, putting six guys out of work." She gave me an evil smile.

Where was this going?

"What would you do, Rhett? Where would you work?"

Why was she drawing this out? I didn't rise.

"You will do this, Rhett. If you don't, I will shut your company down."

"With what authority?" I asked. "I'm not breaking any laws."

"Prostitution is against the law. And you've already been sued once. You can be sued again."

She did her homework.

"We haven't had another incident since. And I didn't sleep with Aspen until after I quit working for her. You have nothing on me."

"I don't?" she asked in mock surprise. "I'm not so sure..."

My heart started to palpitate.

"All I have to do is check into a hotel tonight and say you were with me. I've already paid for five dates, and with my father's money, I will run you into the ground. After a second offense, I doubt the court is going to be very sympathetic toward your plight."

I couldn't believe this was happening. How could someone be so cruel? How could someone want to cause another person so much pain? "Why do you hate Aspen so much? What did she do to you?"

"She never told you?"

"No."

"That company is supposed to be mine." Her eyes darkened in anger. "Aspen ran my father out because she said he was mentally unstable and making too many mistakes. She persuaded her father to cash him out of the company, ruining my chance of having it. That's what she did."

"I can assure you, she didn't intentionally try to hurt you. If you asked her father for a job, I'm sure he would give you one."

"A job, yes," she said. "Not the CEO position. He's going to give that to Aspen unless I intervene."

Everything was coming together. "You never wanted John. You just stole him to humiliate her."

"For a pretty boy, you're awfully smart," she said coldly. "And now I will destroy you. After that, her father will never look at her the same. And I can swoop in."

The weight of the situation crushed me. Isabella wanted revenge and she would do anything to get it. She was borderline crazy. I knew her threat wasn't idle. She would do everything she could to sabotage the company I built on my own. She could rip it apart and even get me jail time if she had a good lawyer. This was some serious shit.

"I suggest you head down to the office and tell him the truth. And your little business will be spared." She gave me a victory smile, like she won the battle and the war.

She obviously didn't have enough evidence to prove Aspen hired me as an escort, so she needed me to bring the truth about. I was the key to her plan. "No."

She cocked an eyebrow, like she was shocked. "Excuse me?"

"I'm not doing it."

"Do you think I'm bluffing?" she asked. "I will pull your feet from under you and I will not stop until I have every single piece of you. There will be no mercy. I will make it my purpose to destroy your life."

"I feel sorry for you," I blurted. I wasn't thinking when I spoke. It just came out. "I don't care what you do to me. Take away my company and put me in jail for a year. It doesn't matter. The only thing I care about is Aspen and you can't take her away from me. Everything else is irrelevant."

She stared at me with cold eyes. The frustration shook her limbs.

"Aspen deserves that company." I rose to my feet. "And she's going to get it."

***

I decided not to tell Aspen what happened with Isabella. If I did, I knew what Aspen would do. She would tell her father the truth and sacrifice everything she worked for to spare me. She would put me first.

But I couldn't let that happen.

Beautiful Entourage was important to me. I didn't just take girls on dates. I helped people. I formed friendships with people. What I did made a difference, no matter how odd it was. My friends and I loved our jobs, and I liked making a high salary. Who didn't?

But Aspen was more important. All she'd ever known was heartbreak. Her own family treated her like a nuisance. No one ever stood beside her and defended her. No one ever showed any loyalty. Well, I would stand beside her. They could do whatever they wanted to me. Aspen would remain untouched.

She was passionate about that company, and she wanted to make the world a better place. The money meant nothing to her. If she could, she would stop using oil altogether and use all her resources for research into alternative fuels. Her position was far more important than mine. And she was more important than I ever would be. I would never bring her pain or hurt her—ever. I'd gladly go to jail instead of throwing her under the bus. She would wait for me to get out and we would be happy again.

But it was difficult to pretend everything was fine when I was around her. For the next few days, she seemed to know something was on my mind. She was particularly quiet, like she was stressed about something.

I sat across from her on the couch with Battleship in my lap. "F7."

Aspen stared at her board.

I waited for her to say 'hit' or 'miss'.

Instead, she kept staring.

Maybe she didn't hear me. "F7."

A blank expression remained on her face.

"Aspen?"

She finally looked up. "Sorry, what?"

"Are you okay? You seem distracted."

"Oh…" She tucked her hair behind her ear. "Just work…a lot of stuff going on."

"Do you want to talk about it?" I asked.

"No, not really. What was your guess?"

"F7."

"Miss."

***

I lay in bed beside her and stared out the window. The lights from the city glowed like they were on fire. Days had passed and I waited to be served any moment. Isabella would come after me. It was only a matter of time. She was probably getting her legal case together.

"Rhett?" Aspen was wrapped around me, her head on my chest.

"Hmm?" I moved my fingers through her hair.

"Is everything okay?" she whispered. "You just seem off lately."

"I'm fine," I said immediately. "I just have a lot on my mind."

"Like what?" she asked.

"Just work and stuff."

"Do you want to talk about it?"

"Not really," I said honestly.

She rested her hand on my chest and didn't move. Then she spoke again. "Did I do something?"

I turned to her, seeing the fear in her eyes. "No, of course not."

"You just seem distant from me. I feel like I did something."

Now I felt terrible. My stress was affecting our relationship. I turned toward her and pulled her close. "You did nothing. It's all me. Don't worry about it. I love you more than I ever have."

"Promise?" she whispered.

I kissed her gently. "Cross my heart, hope to die, and stick a needle in my eye."

The corner of her lip upturned in a smile. "That's the weirdest promise I've ever heard."

I laughed. "It doesn't make much sense, does it?"

"No."

"How about this?" I hooked my pinky with hers. "Pinky promise?"

"That makes even less sense."

I chuckled. "You're right. How about just a promise then?"

"That works for me."

I rested my hand on her neck while I looked into her eyes. I stared at her silently until her eyes dropped with heaviness. Then I fell asleep.

***

"Don't panic!"

"Don't panic?" Troy asked incredulously. "You just told me I might be out of a job! I just bought a beach house. What do you mean don't panic?" He paced my living room with tense shoulders.

"It might not even go anywhere," I said. "Isabella hasn't even contacted me."

"That doesn't mean she isn't going to. She's probably planting evidence and building a case as we speak!" His eyes were about to pop out of his head.

"Stay calm."

"You stay calm!" He pointed at me.

"I am calm," I said quickly. "Look, we'll get through this. We just have to be smart."

"Let's kill her," he said seriously. "I have a few friends that know about this stuff."

"We aren't killing anybody," I said immediately.

"I'm not going to let this bitch ruin my life. The gig we have is incredible. I'm making half a million a year. I'm not giving that up!"

I grabbed his shoulders and steadied him. "Hey, we'll be okay."

He pushed me off. "I told you to be careful. You didn't listen to me."

"I am careful."

"Then why are we in this situation?" he demanded.

"It has nothing to do with me," I said. "Don't blame me. We're just unlucky."

"I'll say…"

"The only other option I have is betraying Aspen and I can't do that."

He put his hands on his hips and stood in the middle of the room.

"What?" I asked. "You want me to throw her under the bus?"

He was quiet for a long time.

"She's the victim in all of this."

"No," he whispered. "I don't want you to screw her over. She's a really nice person."

I breathed a sigh of relief, glad he was on my side. "I'm sorry this is happening. But there's a chance that it might not go anywhere. It's not like she can prove I had sex with her."

"She can just get another guy to do it and leave evidence."

"Well, unless the guy steals my cum, he's going to have a hard time pretending to be me."

"That's true," he said, sounding a little more optimistic.

"Don't worry the guys just yet," I said. "Let's handle this on our own before we bring them into it. No reason to cause a panic."

"You're right," he said.

I clapped him on the shoulder. "We'll get through it. We always do."

"I hope so, Rhett. I hope so."

Aspen

Rhett seemed off lately and I couldn't figure out why. He was extremely distracted and seemed to be thinking of other things when he was with me. He wouldn't tell me what was on his mind but he said I wasn't the cause of his distress. He promised me so I decided to stop worrying about it. Rhett was still with me all the time so I didn't think he was having doubts about our relationship.

Meanwhile, guilt was eating me alive. I felt like I should tell him about John. The incident was two weeks ago and nothing happened since but I still felt deceitful. I just loved what Rhett and I had and I didn't want to ruin that by bringing up John, someone I loathed. It didn't make sense to me.

I couldn't tell if Rhett was the jealous type but he might be. He said he didn't like it when I spoke to Rich at the bar. It might push him away, and he was already acting odd so I didn't want to give him another reason to be distant.

I decided to keep it to myself. If something else happened with John, then I would come clean. If not, I would let it go. Since John and I already said everything that needed to be said, I didn't think there was any reason for us to cross paths again. It was over—for good.

E.L. Todd

When I was in my office, Jane spoke over the intercom. "Mr. Lane would like to see you in his office."

"Thank you." I finished my email then headed for my father's office. Dad never called me, usually saying whatever he needed to say over the phone. But when he did, he made me walk all the way to the other side of the building like a show animal. It irritated me beyond reason but I held my tongue.

I knocked on his door then stepped inside. I froze when I saw someone I hoped I'd never see again. John was standing near the desk, his hands in his pockets. Dad was sitting in his chair, spinning a pen through his fingers.

When will this nightmare end?

I walked forward, keeping my composure. "You want to see me, sir?"

"Sit down," Dad commanded.

I hated being told what to do. I loathed it. But I did it anyway, acting like an obedient dog.

Dad rose then came around the desk. "John and I were just talking about you."

I eyed him, giving him an obvious look of hate. I didn't bother dimming it in front of my father. That's how pissed off I was. "Oh?"

"He told me he made a mistake by being with Isabella. He apologized to me for over an hour," Dad said.

"Over an hour?" I didn't mask my sarcasm.

Dad either ignored it or didn't pick up on it. "He seems really sincere."

"Well, I forgive him," I said quickly. "Can we move on now?"

"That's wonderful news," he said. "I always hoped you two would find your way back to each other."

"Whoa...what?" My eyes widened in confusion.

"John asked for my permission to marry you," Dad said. "Of course I gave it to him."

I rose to my feet, the anger consuming me like a lit firework. "What?" I couldn't process this. I couldn't handle it.

"I want you to marry John," he said. "Rhett is a fine young man but John has always been my pick."

I tried to keep my breathing calm but I was struggling. I'd been mad a lot during my life but I'd never been this blindingly angry. "Even though he cheated on me and humiliated us?"

"Him coming back to you restores that good faith," Dad said with a stupid smile.

"Or makes me look pathetic for going back to a cheater!"

"No one is going to think that," Dad said with a wave. "And John's company combined with yours will make us unstoppable."

I turned to John. "Did you even break up with Isabella before talking to my father?"

"Of course, I did." His eyes didn't contain his sincerity.

"Liar," I hissed. "I know you, John. I know when you bullshit."

He looked away and avoided my gaze like a coward.

"So you have her to go back to if I say no." I shook my head. "Despicable."

"If you say no?" Dad asked. "You're saying yes. This is the perfect arrangement."

I turned to my father. "Excuse me?"

"You heard me," he said. "This is what I want."

I almost screamed. "But it's not what *I* want. I'm in love with Rhett."

"He's a fine young man," Dad said. "But he's just not right. John can give us everything we want."

I shook my head and tried to stay calm.

Dad seemed to know I needed some privacy. "John, wait outside please."

"Of course, sir." John walked out and shut the door.

I fantasized about throwing my father off the balcony of his office. And watching his body break as it hit the street. Perhaps I'd become hateful and dark. But I was too far gone.

Dad continued when we were alone. "Aspen, this is the best move."

"I'm not marrying him." I wouldn't compromise on this. Never. No way.

"You will," he said coldly.

"Forget it," I said. "I won't change my mind."

He stiffened, like he'd been slapped.

Take that, asshole.

He stared me down with his conference room eyes. "Aspen, you want this company, don't you?"

This had to be a nightmare.

"If you don't marry John, I won't give it to you." He said it simply like he didn't really care about the conversation. "I won't compromise on this."

I breathed hard, feeling my heart slam into my chest like it might give out. My eyes burned from tears that emerged from anger. I'd never been so poorly treated in my life. My father was my biggest tormentor. He made Isabella look like a butterfly. He would forever hold the company over my head, and he would forever make my life miserable. I wanted him to die. I wanted him to disappear. I just wanted him gone. "I don't want the company." My voice came out surprisingly calm.

Dad's eyebrows raised, like he hadn't understood me. "Excuse me?"

"I don't want it." My voice came out stronger. "I wanted to run this company because I know I would do the best job. Maybe the only thing that's important to you is money, but that matters the least to me. Leaders care about the common good, not the self-interest of one selfish man. I absolutely hate it here. I hate seeing you every day. I hate having you as my boss. I've been biding my time because it's my duty to make the world a better place.

"But I'm done with your bullshit. You're the coldest and cruelest man I've ever known, and every time I look at you, I feel sick inside. Vomit forms in my throat and it never stops. You disgust me. Disgust me." I'd never been so cruel in my life. I'd never said such mean things. But I couldn't stop.

Dad stared at me blankly, his thoughts and emotions unknown to me.

"I am not a mare that you can pick a stud for. I am not a cow that you can pick a bull for. In case you forgot, I'm a human being with thoughts and feelings. And more importantly, I'm your own daughter. But you've never cared about me. When John broke my heart, I lost fifteen pounds and cried in the bathroom every day at lunch. You never noticed the weight loss or the redness in my eyes. Whenever you brought it up and I would cry, you commanded me to stop. I'm sorry I'm not a farm animal that can be as emotionless as you want. I have feelings as any normal person does, and if that's displeasing to you, I don't care." My eyes started to burn and the tears fell. "Tell me to stop. Tell me to knock it off. Dismiss me!" The warmth fell down my cheeks and into my mouth. I didn't wipe them away, not caring how I looked or how I sounded.

"You've been the worst father to me, and you're a terrible human being. Instead of standing beside me and being the crutch I needed, you made me feel pathetic for John leaving, like it was my fault. When he came in here and asked to speak to me, you were supposed to punch him in the face. That's what a real father is supposed to do, not shake his hand and give me to him. You're a monster."

Dad didn't move. He hardly breathed. He just stared, looking at me like I was a TV.

"No one has ever hurt me the way you have, and stupidly, I've tried to get your approval for more years than I can count. I took golf lessons so we had something to do together, but when I showed you how good I was, you called me a dyke." The memory burned painfully. "A dyke..."

Dad finally looked down.

"You wouldn't survive without me running this company. You just hit a golf ball around and schedule lunch dates with your buddies. You take lavish trips with your stupid bimbos but you've never even taken me out for ice cream. You raised a pathetic excuse for a son but you don't acknowledge a single good quality I possess. And when Mom was in the hospital..." My voice faltered. "You never came to see her. When she lost her mind, you never held her hand and made her feel safe. When she went senile, you didn't even check on her. The second she was sick, you abandoned her. I was the only one who took care of her. Maybe you paid the medical bills but that doesn't matter. What I did mattered. How do you sleep at night? How do you continue this existence of utter meaningless? If I died, would you care? If I were in the hospital, would you even send me flowers?" I knew the answer. "No, you wouldn't. I mean nothing to you. There's no one on the planet that means anything to you.

"I've put up with this treatment for too long. I'm not going to sit here and let you treat me like this. No. No. No. So accept this as my resignation. I'm officially out of your life." I gave him the meanest glare I could muster before I headed to the door. But I stopped and turned back to him. "You haven't acknowledged my birthday in ten years even though I get you a gift every year. You've never spent Christmas with me, forcing me to spend it with Harper. You've never made me smile. You've never made me laugh. And there are days, like today, when I wish you would just die."

I walked out and shut the door behind me.

John stared at me, concern in his eyes. "Aspen—"

I slapped him as hard as I could. The hit came out of nowhere. My actions were uncontrollable. "Go back to Isabella. You two are perfect for one another." I didn't look at him again as I marched to my desk.

Jane watched me with sad eyes. "Aspen, are you okay?"

I grabbed a box and quickly stuffed anything important inside. "I just quit." I sniffed then wiped my tears away. "He'll hire someone to replace me by tomorrow." I grabbed my box and purse and approached her desk. "It's been a pleasure, Jane." I quickly shook her hand then walked out, grateful I would never have to step inside of that prison again.

***

I called Rhett the moment I got inside my apartment.

"Hey, Battleship."

It was so nice to hear his voice. It sounded so upbeat, so warm. My horrible day almost melted away just at the tone of his voice. "Can you come over?" My voice was full of tears.

His voice turned serious. "Are you okay, Aspen?"

"Can you just come over?"

"I'm on my way," he said. "I'll be there as soon as I can, okay?"

"Okay," I whispered. I hung up then stood in the kitchen, unsure what to do with myself.

Two minutes later, he burst through the door. His blue eyes were wide with panic, and he immediately came to me and cupped my face. The pads of his thumbs brushed my tears away. "Aspen, I'm here. It's okay. I'm here."

I wrapped my arms around him and held him close. My head rested on his shoulder and I closed my eyes, enjoying the feel of him in my arms. It was hard to stay angry when I felt something this incredible. I had a love all women wished for. I had a man who loved me for who I was. He was my best friend as well as my lover.

"Talk to me," he whispered.

I finally stopped crying then leaned back and faced him. "My dad told me he would only give me the company if I married John."

Anger burned in his eyes. Now they were gray, smoldering, and threatening.

"So I quit. I got so angry that I exploded and told him off for everything he's done to me...I told him I wish he were dead."

"Good," he said. "You had every right to say that."

"I just couldn't do it anymore. How could he want me to marry a man who hurt me so much?"

"You don't deserve that, Aspen. I'm glad you quit. You made the best decision."

"I wanted the company but..."

"It's okay," he said. "There are other ways you can pursue your passion. There are other ways you can help the environment. This isn't the end, Aspen. It's never the end."

I nodded and my breathing returned to normal.

"You're going to be so much happier now," he said. "And don't stress about money. You can live with me until you find a new job—or live with me permanently." He smiled slightly.

"Are you asking me to move in with you?" I asked with a light laugh. "Right now? Really?"

He shrugged. "If your answer is yes, then yeah, I'm asking. If your answer is no, then I'm just an insensitive jerk." He rubbed his nose against mine. "Do you have an answer?"

"I'd love to live with you."

He beamed. "I knew that's what your answer would be."

"God, you're cocky."

He chuckled. "I just know how much my girl loves me. I knew how much you wanted the company...marrying John would have been a simple solution." His eyes filled with emotion.

"You're the only man I would ever consider."

"I know." He stared into my face, affection in his eyes. "This actually worked out for me as well."

"Meaning?"

He sighed. "About a week ago, Isabella threatened to destroy my company if I didn't tell your father I was an escort. I said no, obviously. And she just served me today."

My jaw dropped. "What...why didn't you tell me?"

"Because I knew you would have told your father and lost everything you were working for." His thumb moved down my cheek then rested on my neck. His eyes glowed like a thousand stars in the night sky. "I couldn't let that happen. I knew how important it was to you."

"But not more important than you." That bitch really had no limit to the terror she would cause. She would do anything to make someone miserable. "That's not even fair. She's my problem, not yours."

"We're family," I said. "What's mine is yours."

E.L. Todd

Rhett was a treasure I never expected to find. He came in such a pretty package but I never expected him to be so pretty on the inside as well.

"I'd never betray you, Aspen. You know that."

"I do," I said quietly.

"And I knew you would never marry John to get what you wanted."

I shook my head dramatically. "I would never marry him. Period. He came to me last week and tried to get me back. I kicked him out of my office. The sad part, he's still with Isabella. Is that the most messed up thing you've ever heard?"

"No," he said simply. "It sounds like John and Isabella are the opposite sides of the same coin. They should get married."

"They really should," I said. "And that's just sad."

His hands moved to my shoulders and he looked down into my face. "It looks like our lives just got a million times better. Chase is my brother again, going to ball games and the movies, and you're finally free of that tyrant you call a father. I think we need to celebrate."

"That I don't have a job?" I teased.

"I can get you a job if you really need one."

"Oh yeah?" I asked.

"Well, there are a few." He had a twinkle in his eyes, a look of mischief. "You can be my private escort..."

"And when you say escort..."

"I mean, my own woman who pleases me when I want."

"As opposed to what I'm doing now?" I kept a straight face and tried not to smile.

"Well, exactly what you do now. But you'll get paid for it."

I turned away, a hint of a smile on my lips. "Classy."

"It's just for me, so it is classy."

"I have a master's and years of work experience for one of the most profitable companies in the country. I'll find something."

"Yeah, probably," he said. "But the offer is always on the table." He gave me a playful look.

"How about you take me on this table right now?"

He froze, and his breathing stopped for several seconds. "You went from crying after quitting your job to asking for sex?"

"Yep."

Affection glowed in his eyes. "I'm glad I made you feel better."

"You're right, Rhett. Now our lives are perfect. I should have quit a long time ago. If I'd known I'd be this happy, I would have. Now, let's not let some jerks ruin the remainder of our day. It's time to make love, not war."

He slowly guided me to the table and lifted me onto the surface. "That's the best speech I've heard since the State of the Union address."

"That's not much of a compliment," I said. "Politicians don't know their head from their face."

"Well, it was a damn good speech. Hit me right at home." He guided my hand to the area over his heart and looked down at me. He suddenly became serious. "You came into my life and made it a bright and beautiful place. It was unexpected and I wasn't ready for it. But it was the best thing that ever happened to me."

I felt his heartbeat through his shirt, quick and powerful. "I'm really glad I sunk your battleships."

A slight smile glowed in his eyes. "If I told you I let you win, would you believe me?"

"No."

"One of these days, you should let me win—boost my ego."

I got his jeans loose and pulled them down. His cock sprang out, happy to see me. "I don't think you need an ego boost."

***

"Let's play a different game," Rhett said. "One you've never played before so it will be fair."

"You're really a sore loser, huh?" I sipped my wine on the couch and gave him a teasing look.

"I am a sore loser," he said. "When my opponent cheats."

"Just admit you suck."

"You suck—literally." He looked at me and chuckled.

I swatted him playfully. "Pervert…"

He moved beside me on the couch. "Tell me a game you haven't played."

I shrugged. "Monopoly."

"You've never played Monopoly?" he asked incredulously.

"Everyone says it's really long and boring," I said. "So I've never bothered."

"Let's play that," he said.

I smirked. "So, we'll play a game you've done but I haven't?"

"Hey, throw me a bone here," he said. "I need to beat you at something."

"Why can't you just admit I'm better than you at board games?" I asked. "You're a better cook than I am."

"Baby, all of Manhattan is a better cook than you are."

I smacked him again. "I'm not going to suck anymore if you keep that up."

He immediately turned apologetic. "Sorry, I take it back."

"That's what I thought."

A knock on the door interrupted our conversation.

"Expecting company?" he asked.

"No. Maybe it's a pizza."

"Why would it be a pizza?" he asked.

"I order them so often that they just assume I want one," I said with a shrug.

He chuckled then walked with me to the door.

I peered through the peephole and almost dropped my wine. "It's my dad," I mouthed.

Both of his eyebrows shot up. "Really?" he mouthed back.

I nodded.

He eyed the door then looked back at me. "Do you want me to answer it?" he mouthed.

I didn't know what I wanted to do.

Dad knocked again. "I heard voices a moment ago."

Why did people always sneak up on me when I was being loud? I put down my wine then cracked the door open. The second I saw his face, my anger came back. I hadn't thought about him in a week. Not going to the office every morning was odd at first, but after the initial change, I didn't think twice about it. I didn't miss being treated like pigeon vomit on the bottom of a shoe. "Yes?" What did he want? To sue me? The idea was so ridiculous, but since we were talking about my father, it was believable.

He glanced at Rhett then looked at me again. "Can I have a moment of your time?"

"I won't work for you again," I said coldly. "Only when the company starts to fall apart and you realize what an asset

I am that you notice my absence. Forget it." I started to close the door.

"Aspen." His authoritative voice stilled me. "That's not why I'm here."

I opened the door again. "I don't care why you're here. All I care about is you going away. Now."

"Please," he said calmly. "Can we take a walk?"

"I'm not going anywhere with you." He'd never come to my apartment before. I didn't think he even knew where I lived.

"Then can I come in?"

"No," I snapped. "Rhett and I are busy right now."

"Then can I come by at a different time?" he asked.

"Don't come back at all." I shut the door in his face. Once he was hidden from view, my blood pressure went down slightly.

Rhett stood there quietly, his thoughts unknown to me.

Then Dad knocked again. "Aspen, I just want to talk."

I opened the door again. "I've wanted to talk every day but you've never listened. Why should I listen to you?"

He shifted his weight then put his hands in the pockets of his suit. "Because you're a much better person than I am. You have compassion and I don't. I'm hoping I can take advantage of that one last time."

Did he just pay me a compliment? Or did he consider compassion a weakness? "What's so important?" I asked with a sigh. "Did something happen at work? Can you not locate a file? What?"

"No," he said. "This has nothing to do with work. I just want to speak to my daughter." His voice came out quiet and weak.

He never referred to me as his daughter before. It was only by name.

"Can I come in?" he asked. "Just hear me out. You don't have to talk to me again if you don't want to. But please listen to me."

I turned to Rhett, silently asking him what I should do.

He kissed my cheek. "I'll go home and give you guys some privacy. Call me when you're done."

I didn't want him to leave but I knew it wouldn't be appropriate for him to stay. "Okay."

He turned to Dad, nodded, and then walked out.

I cleared my throat. "Well, come in."

He stepped inside and looked around at my small apartment. It was pitiful in comparison to his house in Connecticut and the apartment he had in the city. In his eyes, I was just a poor beggar. "Nice place."

"Thanks," I said even though I knew he was lying. I crossed my arms over my chest while I stood there.

He looked around for another moment before he turned to me. His hands were in his pockets and he seemed out of place. His suit cost more than everything in my apartment.

"Dad?" I prompted. There were a million other things I'd rather be doing than staring at a man I despised. Rhett and I were having a wonderful night until Dad decided to ruin it. I wanted to get back to the man I loved as quickly as possible.

"This isn't easy for me to say...I was never very good with words." He didn't make eye contact. "Your mother was always better at this sort of thing."

"Just say what's on your mind." I wasn't trying to comfort him or offer help. I just wanted to rush him.

"I feel like I owe you an explanation," he said quietly. "I didn't visit your mom in the hospital because...it was too hard.

You don't know what it's like to watch the one woman you love lose her mind. When I went to see her and she didn't recognize me, I couldn't do it anymore. That's why I didn't go."

That was the worst explanation I've ever heard. "Love isn't supposed to be easy. You put your pain before hers. How do you think she felt? Having no idea who anyone was? In sickness and in health, remember? You should have been there, spending the entire time telling her who you were and holding her hand before she fell asleep. Just because things got tough doesn't give you the right to turn your back on her. All you explained was the fact you're a coward. A fucking coward." I hardly cussed and I never did it at my father, but I was too angry to censor myself.

He stared at the floor. "I'm not saying what I did was right. I'm just explaining myself."

"Well, congratulations. You made me despise you more than I already did."

He looked at me, his eyes full of hurt.

I shook my head. "You should just go..."

"No," he said immediately. "I'm not done."

I sighed loudly, not masking the fact I was extremely irritated.

"The reason why...I'm so distant with you is because you look just like your mother. You have her eyes. They're identical."

I stared at him blankly.

"You remind me so much of her and it just hurts. I feel guilty for not being there for her. I feel guilty for not being a better husband."

"And being a shitty father," I said. "So I get punished because of your issues? How is that fair?"

"I..." His words trailed away.

"You've been the biggest tormentor I've known. Don't come in here and try to justify your behavior. I have better things to do than listen to a bunch of meaningless words and lies."

"I'm not justifying my behavior," he said with a stronger voice. "After you said those words to me, I realized just how...much I hurt you. I realized how much I destroyed your spirit. I realized...how much you hated me."

He didn't already know that?

"The truth of who I was as a person and parent hit me hard. I realized every horrible thing I said to you. All the jabs I made, all the hurtful things I said, and every time I ignored you when you clearly needed me...echoed in my mind. Instead of taking your side when I should have, I put myself first. I only cared about myself, not my daughter, who's beautiful, smart, and wonderful. How you put up with me for so long is beyond my understanding."

That was the last thing I expected him to say. Not only did he admit his faults but he seemed contrite. He actually admitted his behavior was wrong. That was the first time such a thing has ever happened.

"When you said you wished I were dead—" He paused for a long time. "I realized just how much I messed up. And when I realized I didn't blame you for feeling that way...I knew I was not only a terrible father but a terrible person."

I didn't agree with or deny his statement.

"I realize it's probably too late to salvage anything between us, and you have every right not to want to speak to me again, but...I'd really like another chance to be a real father to you. It's unfortunate that I only understood your worth once you were gone, but I do understand it, and I appreciate it. If there's any way you can give me another chance, I would like to prove I can make this right."

His words echoed in my mind long after he said them. "You're asking for a lot. This abuse hasn't just occurred when I worked with you. It's been going on my whole life. You can't just erase that."

"I'm not trying to erase it," he said quickly. "I want to start over and build a new relationship. I don't expect you to trust me or even like me. But maybe you will—someday."

I didn't realize how hard it would be to give someone another chance. I was tired of being hurt and stabbed in the back. It was time for a change. I would only accept people who genuinely cared about me.

"I can tell that's not an easy request," he said quietly.

I met his look and didn't speak.

"I also came here to give you something. I hope you'll take it."

Flowers and candy won't fix this.

"I've been at the company for far too long, and I do a piss poor job running it. Everything you said about me was true. I'm a selfish man who cares more about his personal interests than other people. You, on the other hand, are nothing like that. So, I'm offering you the CEO position—if you still want it."

I froze at his words, unable to believe he just said them. I'd been working for this for years, and now he just offered it to me. I hadn't married a respectable man and I hadn't accomplished anything noteworthy.

"I'll retire and play golf—pretty much what I was doing anyway. It's time for me to step down. Honestly, I don't really care about that company anymore, as you've probably figured out."

I gave him a suspicious look, wondering if there was a catch to his offer. "I'm not married and I don't plan to be anytime soon."

"Your personal life is irrelevant to your job. Do what you want, Aspen."

"You don't care about your image anymore?" I questioned, not believing it.

"No. I just want you to be happy."

I wondered how sincere he was being. People often said one thing then took it back when the circumstances changed. "Rhett and I are madly in love but that's not how we started. He's an escort that I hired to pose as my boyfriend so you would give me the company. Somewhere down the road, people are going to figure it out, and that will ruin your image."

Dad looked at the floor, clearly caught off guard by what I said. "You hired someone to pretend to be your boyfriend?"

"I was desperate," I admitted. "I was sick of you making me feel terrible about John."

He nodded. "My afflictions run far below the surface, don't they?"

The question sounded rhetorical so I didn't speak.

"Aspen, that doesn't matter. If the truth gets out, it gets out. Do what you want and be happy. The opinions of people you don't even know are irrelevant."

I couldn't hide my surprise. Once I admitted the truth about Rhett, I assumed it would change everything. "Really?"

"Really," he said. "You need to be in that office, Aspen. Not me. I hope you'll accept my offer."

"Is it conditional?"

"No. I'm not asking for anything in return—except a chance."

I considered his offer for a long time in silence.

"Please take it, Aspen. You deserve it."

"If I take it, it doesn't mean that I'll ever forgive you."

"I understand that. These things take time."

Taking over the company was exactly what I wanted. I was passionate about it and I cared about it. It mattered to me. It wasn't just a job. It was more than that. "Then I accept."

A hint of a smile crept into his lips. "That's wonderful. I'm glad."

I looked at the ground, unsure what to do.

"So...if you aren't busy, do you want to get some ice cream?" His voice sounded hesitant.

My eyes found his and I stared at him in shock. I told him I was hurt he never spent any time with me, never took me out for ice cream. And he remembered. Just that alone was a good start. "Sure."

"And invite Rhett," he said. "I'd like to get to know him better."

I smiled at him for the first time in my life. "Okay."

***

Dad stared at my monster sundae with a hint of amusement. "You're going to eat that all by yourself?"

"And she'll eat hers faster than I'll eat mine." Rhett nudged me in the side playfully.

I speared my spoon into his bowl then shoved the ice cream into my mouth.

Rhett turned to Dad and shook his head. "She's a bit of a thief and a cheater."

"A cheater?" Dad asked.

"Every time we play Battlefield, she creams me," Rhett said. "I think she has something up her sleeve."

"Did you ever consider the possibility that you might just suck?" I asked.

He nudged me in the side again. "You're lucky you're cute."

"You're lucky I love you."

I stole another bite of ice cream.

He growled at me.

Dad watched our interaction. "This is serious, isn't it?" There wasn't disappointment in his voice.

"Very," Rhett said as he looked at me. "I asked her to move in with me, actually."

"I agreed but now I'm not so sure." I gave him a teasing look.

"The only reason why I offered is so I'll learn your secrets," Rhett said. "I'll get to the bottom of your unusual game-playing talents."

"Good luck with that," I said sarcastically.

"So Rhett," Dad said. "You're an escort?"

I suspected this would come up eventually.

"Yes," Rhett said with confidence. "I founded the company years ago. I escort men and women—"

"Men?" I asked.

"Yeah," he said simply. "So?"

"I just didn't know that," I said with a shrug.

Rhett turned back to my father. "I pose as a boyfriend and only allow handholding and waist touching. There's no kissing or anything more intimate involved. I like my job and Aspen doesn't mind it."

"I don't," I said. "But if any girls get the wrong idea, I'll take them out."

"I'd like to see that," Rhett said with a smile.

I acted like I was clawing someone.

Dad stared at us blankly. "As long as you're happy, then I'm happy."

He was really trying.

"The fact you started your own company is impressive," he said.

"Thanks," Rhett said. "I like being my own boss."

"Is this lucrative?" Dad asked.

"Dad." I gave him a pissed look.

"Sorry." Dad held up his hands in surrender. "My apologies. I didn't mean to be rude."

"It's okay," Rhett said. "Every father wants to know his daughter is well taken care of. To answer your question, I do very well and made smart investments so Aspen will want for nothing. I'm not loaded by any means, but I'm more than happy with that salary."

Dad nodded. "That's very impressive. Congratulations."

"Thank you," Rhett said.

"You make way more than I do," I said with a laugh.

"Not anymore," Dad said. "Now you're a very wealthy woman."

"Ooh..." Rhett leaned toward me. "You're my sugar mama now."

"I am, aren't I?" I snatched his cherry then ate it.

"But you can always have my cherries," he said.

Dad continued to watch us. "You two remind me of me and my late wife. We were very playful together. The moment we met, we just knew it would last forever."

Dad never talked about Mom, even when she was alive.

Rhett nodded. "I think I can speak for Aspen when I say we feel the same way."

"We do?" I asked with a smile.

"Would I have asked you to move in if I thought otherwise?"

"No, probably not."

"You're my future wife," he said. "I just know it."

My heart melted when I looked at him. When I first saw him in that coffee shop, I never expected an intense love affair to happen. I assumed a gorgeous man like him could never want an average woman like me. And I never expected our souls to connect in such a profound way. It seemed like I'd known Rhett my whole life, that the past had always included him even if I couldn't recall it.

Dad looked down. "Aspen, I'm sorry I forced John on you. Now I feel even worse."

I turned to him and saw the remorse in his eyes. "It's okay, Dad. I forgive you."

His lips upturned in a smile. "You do?"

"Yeah."

Rhett put his arms around my shoulders and held me close. "To new beginnings." He held up his cup of ice cream then clanked it against mine. Then he tapped his against my dad's.

I held mine and pressed it against my father's. "To new beginnings."

E.L. Todd

book two of the beautiful entourage series

Troy & Harper

Gorgeous CONSORT

AVAILABLE NOW

Show Your Support

Like E. L. Todd on Facebook:

https://www.facebook.com/ELTodd42?ref=hl

Follow E. L. Todd on Twitter:

@E_L_Todd

Subscribe to E. L. Todd's Newsletter:

www.eltoddbooks.com

E.L. Todd

Other Books by
E. L. TODD

Alpha Series

Sadie
Elisa
Layla
Janet
Cassie

Hawaiian Crush Series

Connected By The Sea
Breaking Through The Waves
Connected By The Tide
Taking The Plunge
Riding The Surf
Laying in the Sand

Forever and Always Series

Only For You
Forever and Always
Edge of Love
Force of Love
Fight For Love
Lover's Roulette
Happily Ever After
The Wandering Caravan
Come What May
Again and Again
Lover's Road
Meant To Be
Here and Now
Until Forever
New Beginnings
Love Conquers All

Beautiful Entourage

Love Hurts
The Last Time
Sweet Sins
Lost in Time
Closing Time

Southern Love

Then Came Alexandra
Then Came Indecision
Then Came Absolution
Then Came Abby
Abby's Plight

Printed in Great Britain
by Amazon

22515067R00174